The Guaranteed Society

By Leonard Baker

THE JOHNSON ECLIPSE
A President's Vice Presidency

BACK TO BACK
The Duel Between FDR and the Supreme Court

THE GUARANTEED SOCIETY

The Guaranteed Society

BY LEONARD BAKER

The Macmillan Company
New York

FOR DAVID AND SARA

CONTENTS

The Guaranteed Society

SST: 1
The Billion-Dollar
Ticket

One

ON JUNE 5, 1963, President John F. Kennedy inaugurated the
guaranteed society.

He stood bareheaded, his shoulders warmed by the late-spring
sun, before the graduating class of the Air Force Academy at Colorado Springs as he announced that "the United States will
commit itself to an important new program in civilian aviation."

The federal government, he said, "should immediately com-
mence a new program in partnership with private industry to
develop at the earliest practical date the prototype of a commer-

cially successful supersonic transport superior to that being built in any other country of the world."

"Spurred by competition from across the Atlantic and by the productivity of our companies," the President said, "the federal government must pledge funds to supplement the risk capital to be contributed by private companies."

For every one dollar of "risk capital" put up by private companies to develop this supersonic transport, SST—an airplane that will fly for private airlines and earn them a profit—the federal government is putting up $6.50.

But this is only one aspect, perhaps the most minor one, of the pledge made that June day. That pledge means the beginning of a new society for the United States, a new arrangement between the government and private capital. When Dr. Jerome B. Wiesner was President Kennedy's science adviser, he told a Senate subcommittee that it should not regard the SST as "an isolated instance." Dr. Wiesner continued: "It is a new experience for the federal government, but I don't think it will be the last occasion when we will have a necessity of this sort. . . . I don't think you should regard this only as a supersonic transport, but really as another step in the understanding and development of a very complicated economic and social problem in this country."

The impact of that "new experience" was not understood back in 1963. It has come more sharply into focus since, however. The area of concern is not money. Whether it be in the form of a subsidy to business or a welfare payment to the poor, such expenditures are within the American tradition. This new arrangement goes beyond that. It reaches toward a point where the government takes all the risks and private capital reaps all the rewards. It reaches toward a point where the individual will see the United States not as a land of opportunity but as a land of certainty.

Although this guaranteed society appears to offer a glowing promise, actually it threatens to exact a high price. For the guaranteed society to succeed, the federal government must enter the private economy with a force greater than it ever has shown before in peacetime. The government must dictate prices private industry charges, establish the profits private industry earns and supervise the wages the working man receives. And as the guaranteed society succeeds, problems of the United States—problems that threaten the quality of American life—will remain unsolved. For the guaranteed society is a ruthless society in which might prevails. And only to the most cynical does might make right.

The SST is the beginning of this new society—and still its most brilliant example.

"The federal government is guaranteeing everything," shouted Senator William Proxmire, Democrat of Wisconsin, on the Senate floor in 1966 as he damned the supersonic transport. "Would not a businessman fight for this kind of opportunity?" he continued. "What would he have to lose? . . . And the taxpayer is the pigeon, the fall guy—as Texas Guinan or P. T. Barnum would put it, the sucker."

The SST is a multi-billion-dollar machine. Development costs alone—that is, building two prototypes and flying them a total of one hundred hours—had reached by 1968 an estimated total of $1.455 billion. Of that cost, the government has promised to pay $1.264 billion. Private industry will pay $191 million. Between the ending of this development phase of the airplane and the actual delivery of the first SST to an airline for commercial service, a minimum of an additional three billion dollars will be required. How much of this the government will put up has not yet been determined, except that the government will be responsible for some of it.

True, the SST will be a remarkable plane, a phenomenal aircraft, when flying in the 1970s. Capable of cruising speeds of eighteen hundred miles an hour, it will carry three hundred and fifty passengers a range of up to four thousand miles. The airplane will be encased in titanium to protect it from the searing temperatures a body meets when it travels at almost three times the speed of sound. Developing that metal for use as the airplane's outer skin will be a technological revolution. Longer than a football field, the SST will require more than two hundred miles of air space to turn around. The pilot will need a closed-circuit television system to monitor his own landing. If airports can be developed to receive the airplane, the SST will cut long-distance traveling time for commercial travelers in half. The supersonic transport will tie the ends of the world closer together.

Undoubtedly there is glamour in its challenge. "Today the challenging new frontier in commercial aviation and in military aviation," said President Kennedy that June day in 1963, "is a frontier already crossed by the military—supersonic flight."

The principle of the federal government giving a subsidy to private industry is very much a part of American life, but the word *subsidy* may not be used. Only one federal program of assistance to industry uses that word, the program of aid to the merchant marine. To the businessman the word *subsidy* has a connotation of "handout," and the businessman does not like to be known as the recipient of a handout from the federal government. So he cloaks the benefits he receives from Washington in complicated and often difficult-to-understand devices such as tax concessions, depletion allowances, monopolies and the like. Still, the businessman gets the money. According to figures in the federal budget, American businessmen receive twice as much federal assistance in dollars as do American working men and almost one hundred times the dollar assistance given by the federal government to middle-class home-owners and renters.

Those are modest estimates because they account for only those items listed in the budget as specific aids to business. There are many other items in the budget that benefit the business community directly, without being identified as handouts to business. One such item, for example, is the more than $100 million subsidy for corporate aircraft. Private airplanes parking at federally operated airports are charged ridiculously low fees, between $2 and $12 for landing. At Washington National Airport it is cheaper for a businessman to park his airplane than it is for him to park his car. These parking fees for airplanes do not meet costs. The taxpayers make up the difference—and the difference is easily $100 million—between what large corporations like United States Steel and General Motors are charged and what they should pay to meet the costs of handling their aircraft.

In addition to such bonuses in the federal budget, large corporations also are masters at manipulating the income-tax laws. The internal-revenue code makes concessions to small businesses, a means of encouraging them to grow into big businesses. Large corporations take advantage of these concessions by splintering themselves into subsidiaries rather than into divisions of one corporation. Such tactics, charged Treasury Secretary Henry H. Fowler in a 1967 speech, do not "rationally entitle the enterprise to be the recipient of a host of tax exemptions." The fact that the enterprise does enjoy a host of tax exemptions by such a tactic, the Secretary said, is a "special preference" which is "clearly inequitable."

This assistance to industry, whether gained by direct handouts or by subterfuge, whether it is specifically spelled out in legislation or whether it is a product of manipulating tax laws, is not a twentieth-century trademark. Assistance to industry dates to the origin of the United States. If the subsidy of the SST were only another step in what has been a steady path of financial subsidies to American industry, it would not be a "new experience" at all and probably not a dangerous one either.

The very first Congress in 1789 enacted legislation reserving trade along the American coast, from American seaport to American seaport, to ships built in the United States and owned and operated by United States lines. That same Congress gave a tariff break, amounting to a 10 percent reduction in custom duties, on imports to America carried on United States vessels. That legislation established the first standard against which future assistance would be measured. The federal government would create situations in which opportunities for an industry would be multiplied. It gave American ships an edge in competing against ships of foreign countries. This was a general practice at the time. Other nations discriminated against American ships.

The American government would not, however, guarantee the success of any particular member of that industry or of the industry itself. Competition between American shiplines for coastal trade and competition between American lines and foreign ships continued. The government was willing to be industry's helper, not its custodian.

Even the building of the transcontinental railroads in the nineteenth century—the greatest "giveaway" to American industry until the launching of the interstate highway system in the 1950s and the planning of the SST in the 1960s—followed that standard of enlarging opportunity rather than guaranteeing success.

The subsidy to the railroads was in the form of land grants. Some seventy different railroad lines received grants totaling 183 million acres and valued then at more than $400 million. In addition, federal and state governments supplied $853 million in assistance of other kinds to the railroads. Obviously the railroads benefitted from this aid, but not so much as is sometimes thought. Nine out of ten railroads receiving assistance eventually passed out of corporate existence; the large helping hand the government had offered was not enough to guarantee success—nor had it been intended to so guarantee.

The object of the federal assistance had not been the railroads. The object, instead, had been the creation of a transportation system across the nation, from the East to the West and from the North to the South. There was no way that the trapper in the Northwest or the farmer in the Midwest, the cattle rancher in Texas or the shoe manufacturer in Massachusetts could reach his markets without a transcontinental rail system. That aid to the railroads, abused as much as it was by the railroads, was designed to create opportunities for hundreds of American industries, for millions of American workers.

In the twentieth century the new subsidies went to aviation. The first subsidy for airmail service was $7 million in 1929. This subsidy is a cash grant over and above the cost of delivering the mail. It currently totals $63 million and goes to all lines engaged in short hops. "Although the carriers receive the subsidy, it is, in effect, the smaller communities that are its direct beneficiaries through the operations of carriers such as the local service air-lines," the Civil Aeronautics Board, which administers the subsidy program, has explained. What the CAB is saying is that the subsidy is not meant primarily to guarantee the airlines economic success. Instead, it is to make certain that mail is delivered by air to small communities that otherwise could not support airmail service. There is justification in believing that the CAB's statement is not mere rhetoric. The carriers must demonstrate a need for the subsidy, and when the demonstration fails to convince, the subsidy ends. Early in the 1950s, for example, the CAB was paying large subsidies to American airlines engaged primarily in international traffic and domestic trunkline service. By 1960 those subsidies had completely ended and have not been revived. The same rationale—of helping a community rather than guaranteeing success to an airline—is behind the government's picking up the bill for an air-traffic control system.

Also in the twentieth century federal assistance to agriculture broadened. The history of federal aid to the farmer begins with the Homestead Act of 1862, which made Western land available for settlement. That same year the Land Grant College Act donated free land for agricultural schools. It was not until sixty-seven years later, in 1929, that the federal government seriously began to involve itself in the problem of crops. It then enacted the Agricultural Marketing Act. When price-depressing surpluses appeared on the market, loans from a $500 million fund were available to farmers to encourage them to keep their crops off the market until the surplus condition ended.

With the coming of the New Deal in 1933, assistance to the farmers broadened and a second standard emerged against which subsidy programs should be measured. With the New Deal, the federal government began its concern with farm prices, soil conservation, a "fair return" or "parity" for the farmer. Farmers are millions of individuals who buy their equipment and raw goods from a few suppliers and sell their products to a few retailers. Because there are so many farmers scattered over so much of the United States, they are basically incapable of national organization. There are several "national" farm organizations, but each organization speaks for a group of farmers; none speaks for the "farmer." But the farmer must deal with a market that is easily rigged against him. The industries from which the farmer buys are few in number and can set the prices the farmer pays at an artificially high level. At the same time, the outlets through which the farmer sells his products are likewise few in number, and they can peg the prices they pay for the farmer's products at an artificially low level.

An equalizer was needed. The government assumed that role. It offers to buy farmers' products at a price high enough to assure parity, meaning that the farmer no longer must deal with a market rigged against him. The federal program succeeded in assisting the farmer to survive, and it also succeeded in feeding America and much of the rest of the world. The federal program was needed to sustain and widen opportunity. Those farmers wise enough or able enough to mechanize and enlarge their holdings did very well with that widened opportunity. But the federal government did not guarantee the future of the farmers; that continues to be their problem.

This second standard to go along with the first one of widening opportunity—was that of filling a need, a need that otherwise could not be filled.

Adhering to those two standards, widening opportunity and filling a need, the federal government in the 1930s also began programs of subsidy to individuals. These programs were spectacularly successful in fulfilling their intentions: widening and sustaining opportunity for persons basically anxious to work, capable of working and experienced at working but unable to work because of economic conditions beyond their control. This federal emphasis on helping the individual caused one of the great political fights of history—the haves against the have-nots. President Franklin D. Roosevelt was not economist enough to grasp the theory that the economic pie could be expanded to provide assistance for all. His New Deal was built on the Robin Hood principle, taking from the rich to give to the poor. That the rich, through federal assistance to industry, had received so much from the federal government in the past and still were, even in the 1930s and later, did not deter them from criticizing the poor for accepting assistance from the federal government.

During the 1930s and then in the 1940s two new standards for federal assistance were developed. The first was the standard of humanitarianism. The federal government did have an obligation to help those individuals who had passed beyond the time when opportunity was meaningful to them. This was direct subsidy, then—welfare—for the aged, the sick, the blind, the mothers who could not work because they must care for young children.

The second new standard developed in this period was that the federal government should subsidize some industries for defense purposes. There has been much civilian benefit and much benefit to specific industries because of the need to subsidize or assist in some manner certain defense industries. Most of the postwar growth of aviation is attributed to developments pioneered for military use. A radar system that can bring a bomber back to its home base can also bring a passenger airliner into an airport safely—and there is no reason why it should not be so used. There were abuses also. When the United States began the interstate highway system in the 1950s and upped its share of the highway construction money from 50 percent to 90, it did so in the name of national defense.

"Our roads ought to be avenues of escape for persons living in big cities threatened by aerial attack or natural disaster," former President Eisenhower wrote in his memoirs to justify his support of the highway program. "But I knew," he continued, "that if such a crisis ever occurred, our obsolescent highways, too small for the flood of traffic of an entire city's people going one way, would turn into traps of death and destruction."

The interstate highway system was launched, of course, as a stimulant to the automobile industry. Once construction began—and the road builders who earned their incomes from constructing the highways, the suburbanites who drove to work on the highways, and the housing developers who built where the highways reached all joined with the automobile manufacturers to support the program and give it an unstoppable political momentum—then the argument that the roads were built for defense was dropped. Evacuation of large cities as a civil-defense measure has been an out-of-date policy since the late 1950s. Actually no one ever seriously considered the interstate highways as "avenues of escape." In the mid-1950s, for example, New York City and other large cities had elaborate plans supposedly showing how the city could be evacuated in a relatively brief period. But there were no plans to do anything with the people once they were evacuated; no one considered that New York's eight million residents would need shelter, food, medical attention and other necessities. Evacuation of large cities as a civil-defense measure was a tasteless joke; it was conceived to cloak an industrial subsidy in a national purpose.

Still, the argument that government assistance was indeed to assist rather than to guarantee retained value. When in the early 1950s the Eisenhower Administration, curiously in the name of countering "creeping socialism," tried forcing the Tennessee Valley Authority to give a guaranteed market to some private utility companies (this was the Dixon-Yates contract), members of Congress were able to block the move.

Another occasion when that argument of government aid being to assist rather than to guarantee proved useful involved the stockpiling of metals considered "strategic" to the nation's defense. The United States spent a total of $3 billion purchasing metals that might be in short supply if another war came. Eventually the stockpiles became boondoggles, means of subsidizing the mining industry. The government was not buying what metals it wanted to store against the coming of another war. Instead, the government was buying what the mining industry wanted to sell. In effect, the government was guaranteeing the future of the mining industry. When this became obvious a Congressional investigation, called at the command of President Kennedy and headed by Senator Stuart Symington, Democrat of Missouri, put a stop to the worst abuses. That the abuses could be ended demonstrated the value of using the premise of national interest rather than the interest of a specific industry in developing a policy.

The premise that the government should not seek to preserve any specific industry had been so much a part of the American economic system that in September 1964 Gardner Ackley, a member (and later chairman) of the President's Council of Economic Advisers, could tell a gathering of businessmen: "It is probably correct to say that our national goals do not include nor even imply the preservation of particular companies."

But Mr. Ackley was incorrect. Fifteen months earlier the

United States had made such a pledge. With its commitment to the SST, the government had pledged to preserve the aircraft manufacturing industry. And this is why the SST is such a sharp break with the past. It does not increase competition. It is not necessary. It is not a humanitarian expenditure. It is not needed for defense. The purpose of the SST is to guarantee the future of the aircraft industry.

The supersonic transport first began emerging within the Federal Aviation Agency* as a specific program in 1959. Two years later Congress appropriated the first money earmarked for the SST program. This was $11 million for research. Few in Congress took serious notice of it. The only discussion on the House or Senate floors came when Senator Symington (a former Secretary of the Air Force) objected to the funds being spent on a commercial supersonic airplane at the same time that the Administration was saying "no" to a new Air Force supersonic bomber. In the same way another $20 million was later appropriated, also without serious discussion or examination.

The two appropriations—the original $11 million and the follow-up $20 million—were clearly labeled in the budget as being for preliminary research on a supersonic transport. No subterfuge was involved. But the money also was clearly not a significant amount. The first appropriation represented approximately one hundredth of one percent of federal expenditures; the second, two hundredths of one percent. Nor was it unusual for the federal government to spend some "seed" money on early research with plans to turn the fruits of that research over to private industry at a later date. No one in Congress at that time could visualize the extent or the nature of the ultimate commitment to the SST.

Although those initial amounts were small, they did spark interest within the airplane manufacturing industry. That industry saw itself facing the possibility of going out of the mass-production business as the Pentagon, its chief customer, shifted from bombers and fighters to missiles. An SST could reverse that possibility.

*When the Federal Aviation Agency later was absorbed into the Department of Transportation, it became the Federal Aviation Administration. To avoid confusion, I am using the original name throughout. There has been no change in the agency's operations.

This interest was quickly reflected in the attention shown the SST by the friends of aviation in Washington.

During a Senate subcommittee's hearings on the SST in 1963 there was the following dialogue between two men who were among aviation's most zealous advocates in Washington, Senator A. S. Mike Monroney, Democrat of Oklahoma, the chairman of the subcommittee, and Najeeb E. Halaby, then head of the FAA:

SENATOR MONRONEY: There is no big package business beyond the present subsonic jets unless we also are in the ball game on the supersonics.

MR. HALABY: That is absolutely true.

A little later Alan S. Boyd, then chairman of the Civil Aeronautics Board and later Secretary of Transportation in President Johnson's Cabinet, appeared before the same subcommittee. He laid the SST's "make work" aspect on the line even more clearly. "What," he asked, "is our aircraft manufacturing industry going to manufacture?" He continued: "In other words, what happens to our own aircraft manufacturing industry? Is this something of value to us as a national resource? I feel very strongly that it is."

In America's history many industries "of value to us as a national resource" have died or are dying. The canals built in the early 1800s as arteries for commerce were replaced by the intercontinental railroads, and the long-distance railroads in turn are being replaced by the airplane. The coal miner has been thrown out of work by the coming of natural gas, fuel oil and electricity. Eventually the workers in these industries will, in turn, be bumped from their jobs by the coming of atomic power for residential use. The harness maker lost out to the automobile. And the gas-station attendant may eventually be out of work because of the electric automobile. The elevator operator has been automated out of work, and the trolley-car conductor has been replaced by the bus driver. The federal government has felt a responsibility to help those geographical areas that become economically depressed to find new industries. It has felt a responsibility to help those persons thrown out of work for a variety of reasons to learn new skills and find new jobs. In the 1930s, with the WPA, the federal government provided temporary work while the economy pulled itself out of a depression. But the federal government never before has felt a responsibility to guarantee that an industry and the jobs of the workers in that industry will be preserved, as it is doing with the SST and the aviation industry.

The reason that the government has taken this turn with the aviation industry is that it is more national than any other industry. Coal mining is limited pretty much to the Appalachian region. The elevator operators cannot make their voices heard in the bureaucracy of organized labor. Railroading was not a national industry, even though its tracks crossed the country; its leadership was centered in the financial capital in New York City. In contrast, the aviation industry stretches across the United States. And so does its political support.

In 1963, when the SST still was in its "maybe" stage, Representative Bob Wilson, Republican of California, made this statement to his colleagues in the House:

> From personal observation in my own district and in the larger southern California aerospace industry complex, and from reliable reports from other areas with like industries, I know that our aerospace companies have declined to a fraction of the employment level of two or three years ago. Even where they have made the transition from aircraft to missiles or spacecraft successfully, these companies no longer provide the volume of employment they once did. This is particularly true in my own district, where unemployment has been high and several plants have substantial overcapacity.

For those reasons, he explained to the House, he supported the SST. "It is imperative," he stressed, "that our country embark immediately upon a program leading to the first flight of a superior supersonic commercial transport."

His statement was echoed the next year from the other side of the continent. Long Island had been a large aircraft manufacturing center, but it was losing defense contracts and unemployment was increasing. "One of the promising air frame contracts of the future is the proposed supersonic transport," said Representative John W. Wydler, Republican of Long Island, in a letter to his constituents. "Long Island industry should play an important part in its development and production."

As it crosses the nation, the aircraft industry stretches its sub-contracts into hundreds of communities. Robert J. Serling, when he was United Press International's aviation editor, estimated that one result of the SST project is that "companies scattered throughout forty-six states will share in subcontracts to the tune of $30 billion." If anything, that is a conservative estimate. At the beginning of 1967 the FAA announced that the Boeing Company had won the principal contract for the SST's air frame and that General Electric had won the engine contract. Boeing immediately held a news conference to announce the larger subcontractors. Boeing is located in Seattle, Washington, in the northwestern part of the United States. It announced large subcontracts to companies located in half a dozen states, but, according to a company official, a major share of the subcontracting work would go to the Republic Aviation Division of the Fairchild Hiller Company. The Republic plant is located on Long Island, clear across the continent from Boeing, almost as far as it was possible for Boeing to go.

Boeing estimated that Republic's own subcontracts would go to "as many as a couple of hundred" smaller companies. These contracts would fan out from Long Island to the northeastern part of the United States. What happened with Republic will happen to the other major subcontractors. Each becomes the hub of a wheel dispensing money and work connected with the SST to the geographical area in which it is centered.

There was no restraining the local reaction to the announcement by Boeing. A couple of days later *Newsday*, the major newspaper on Long Island, carried a long editorial endorsing the SST for the most righteous of reasons. "As the men of foresight in Moscow and Paris and London already realize," said the editorial, "the development of supersonic passenger planes will not merely save a few hours flying time; it will usher in a new era in transportation. The airlines of the world already see the shape of this coming era." There was one point the editorial did not mention, which was covered in an adjacent cartoon. The cartoon showed an airplane marked "supersonic transport" flying over Long Island and a roll of paper marked "contracts" being parachuted down.

"Look What's Landing Here!" proclaimed the cartoon's caption. The cartoon was just in case some people on Long Island did not realize the make-work impact of the SST on their community.

With its long experience of dealing with the government, usually with the Pentagon, the aviation industry well understands the value of having Congressmen appreciate the job impact of a contract on their constituency. A member of Congress is visited by labor-union leaders, presidents of local companies; he is constantly reminded by newspaper editorials and, on occasion, even by the government agency involved. As a result, enthusiasm bounces from the local communities to the halls of Congress.

Not all Congressmen concede that their support of the SST is based on local interest. In 1967, for example, Representative Lloyd Meeds, Democrat of Washington, insisted that "I speak not partisanly for the Boeing Aircraft Company which is home-based in my state of Washington but rather wholeheartedly in behalf of the United States of America. For I am convinced that the nation will lose jobs, suffer by an increasing imbalance of payments, and forfeit its leadership in aircraft technology if the SST is not built."

Another West Coast Democrat, Lionel Van Deerlin of California, was not quite so insistent. "One of the many beneficiaries of the appropriation for two prototype supersonic transport aircraft would be the Rohr Corporation of Chula Vista, California, in my own Congressional district . . ." he said. "At Rohr, at least five hundred and as many as two thousand new jobs would ultimately be created. This fact alone would be very persuasive in soliciting my support for the [SST] appropriations." Then Representative Van Deerlin added, "There are numerous other reasons supporting the passage of this bill."

But another Democrat from Washington, Boeing's home base, was blunt. Representative Brock Adams urged his fellow House members to support the SST and share the wealth. "The SST appropriation," he said, "is an appropriation which will have an impact on every state in the union. The contracts and subcontracts reach into thousands of communities."

This make-work aspect has been well packaged, wrapped in some rather glittering statistics. Repeated over and over again in testimony before Congressional committees, in speeches by friends of the SST project and in articles by journalists friendly toward aviation, the figures take on a glowing certainty. They were best expressed by Stuart G. Tipton, president of the Air Transport Association, in a speech early in 1967.

"Development and long-term production of the SST will create an average level of 50,000 jobs for the prime contractors. Another 100,000 jobs will be created for subcontractors. It is estimated that these 150,000 jobs will create another 100,000 nonmanufacturing jobs in such industries as wholesale and retail trade, professional services; business services; finance, insurance and real estate; transportation; communication, and other public utilities; and agriculture. That's 250,000 new jobs and an estimated annual payroll of two and one-half billion dollars."

Mr. Tipton went on: "The total employed civilian labor force has been forecast to reach 87 million by 1975 compared to 74 million in 1966. Two hundred and fifty thousand jobs created by the SST would amount to about two percent of thirteen million additional civilian jobs created by 1975, or one of every fifty new jobs."

There is no arguing with Mr. Tipton's statistics, which cannot yet be proven but which probably will turn out to be accurate. And no member of Congress wants to be accused of voting against one out of the fifty new jobs expected to be created in the next decade, particularly when some will be in his own Congressional district.

The significance of Mr. Tipton's statistics, however, can be questioned. There has long been a rule of thumb, used primarily by the Pentagon in estimating the job impact of a defense contract, that a $10,000 investment creates one primary job with the main contractor and three to four secondary jobs with subcontractors and in related industries. The rule developed at the Pentagon as a result of the Pentagon's long experience in dealing with the job impact of the contracts it dispenses. Mr. Tipton's statistics are in line with this rule of thumb. The total cost of the SST, when he made his speech, was estimated at between $4.5 billion and $5 billion. That is approximately 50,000 jobs with the prime contractor, as Mr. Tipton said, with the other jobs following also according to the rule of thumb.

The difficulty with this estimate is that the same rule of thumb says that any investment of $5 billion in the economy will create the same number of jobs. There may be an argument for the government and industry spending another $5 billion it is not now spending and creating 250,000 jobs, but that argument is not necessarily an argument for the SST. A case can be made that other make-work projects would be of greater value to the economy. Employees in the aircraft industry generally are skilled workers with more than adequate educations. If their plant closes, they face many problems (and should be assisted), but their skills and their education should be able eventually to lead them to other decent jobs. Perhaps it would be better to spend the $5 billion on projects that would employ primarily slum dwellers, people without job skills or decent educations. Or perhaps it would be better to spend the $5 billion in areas of obvious concern, such as eliminating air and water pollution.

This is a question of priorities, but the question rarely has been raised in the government about the SST. Early in the Senate hearings one Senator, Philip A. Hart, Democrat of Michigan, did come close to raising the point. He wondered aloud at the hearings whether, from the financing system being developed for the airplane, "there might evolve a pattern which would insure that we do mesh the gears better between industry, private business, and government, enabling society to respond to some of the needs, the cost tag on which makes it prohibitive for private industry, initially at least, to move." However, the question was not again raised.

The way the backers of the SST managed to side-step this question of priorities is actually what enabled them to rise above the other special interests all clamoring for a bite of the federal dollar, to fly toward the guaranteed society with the American people along as passengers. The question of priorities is not usually raised by committees in Congress. Congressional committees are filled with friends of the areas in which the committee is concerned

The committees try to get the most funds for their areas. When Senator Monroney began—not ended—his hearings on the SST, he described the SST as "a challenge that we cannot afford to ignore." Perhaps a wealth of documentation challenging the validity of the SST concept might have persuaded him that the challenge could or should be ignored. The tone of his remarks suggests not.

Senator Monroney's subcommittee is part of the Senate Commerce Committee, which is chaired by Senator Warren Magnuson, Democrat of Washington. Senator Magnuson has long been an advocate of a larger role in aviation for the federal government. It probably would be unfair to say that his interest in the SST stems from a company based in his home state, Boeing, receiving the major air-frame contract or that Boeing received the contract because of Senator Magnuson's chairmanship. But as *Fortune* magazine pointed out in December of 1967, "When Boeing booms, the [Northwest] region booms—and never before like now." Boeing has received the SST contract, and thousands of residents in Senator Magnuson's state will have booming incomes because of the SST. Can anyone expect Senator Magnuson to fight for a cancellation, a slow-down or even a review of the SST project?

The full Congress usually acts as a check on its committees. But this did not happen with the SST, because too many members of Congress saw some of those 250,000 jobs Mr. Tipton talked about in their Congressional districts. When Congress fails to check its own spending tendencies, the Administration can do the job. But this also did not happen with the SST.

The FAA, which is supervising the SST's development, is a mixed breed. Because it sets safety standards for the nation's airways, it is part regulatory agency. But it also operates the air-traffic control system and is charged with promoting the growth of aviation. Founded in the late 1950s, the FAA in the first ten years of its existence has emerged as a greater advocate of aviation than any group of enthusiasts on Capitol Hill. This mixed situation creates a built-in conflict of interest. To compare it with another federal agency, while the Securities and Exchange Commission is charged with keeping the sale of stocks honest, it is not in the stock market itself. The SEC looks in from the viewpoint of an outsider. The FAA looks in from the viewpoint of an insider.* Beyond the FAA is the White House. But President Kennedy did not wish to fight business on this issue. He fought business on principles but not on specifics, giving industry billions of dollars in tax deductions through an accelerated depreciation schedule and going along with such projects as the SST. Also he was advised to support the SST. That advice came principally from his Vice President, Lyndon B. Johnson, who chaired a committee in 1963 to weigh the pros and cons of the SST. Mr. Johnson's support of the SST carried over when he became President. Dating from his days as a Texas Senator, Lyndon Johnson always has been an advocate of the "big" project—for understandable reasons. He was one of those government officials chiefly responsible in the late 1950s for the United States entering the space race. The careful placing of space installations has helped begin a transformation of the South into an industrialized and more open region. He too was not interested in stopping the SST's flight. And once the President makes known his commitment on a project, lesser government officials believe they make known their oppositions only at great risk to their positions.

It was this make-work aspect of the SST that persuaded the government to enter the guaranteed society—to eliminate risk for

---

*This built-in conflict of interest goes beyond the economics of the airplane. A number of knowledgeable and respectable persons, including many aviation enthusiasts, have raised serious questions about whether a safe SST can be built and flown. These questions have been answered by the FAA, but not all of them, I believe, satisfactorily. The FAA claims that the SST will be a safe aircraft, perhaps the safest ever built. In the past, when a new airplane went into commercial service, a series of accidents was necessary to pinpoint its troubles. This was not because the plane was not well tested by the FAA but because, apparently, each new development in aviation produces problems which cannot be anticipated. The SST can be expected to have more problems than past aircraft because it is such a far advance in aviation.

The FAA is responsible for the development of this airplane—and the SST is the first aircraft for which the agency has been assigned such a responsibility—and also for the certification of the SST as a safe flying instrument. The FAA must judge the quality of its own product. No government agency should be put in the position of having to say that a project on which it urged the nation to spend billions of dollars, as well as the energies and talents of thousands of persons, should be junked. That is what a certifying agency always must be prepared to say.

the private entrepreneur and to assure profits and wages. But this aspect was not used to sell the SST to the public. Although it was mentioned and pointed out, government officials hoped to find what the public would consider a better—perhaps even a more moral—rationale for the building of the SST. Their search is interesting because it gives some glimpse of their determination to enter the guaranteed society.

Two

At the beginning of the SST's development it was hoped that the SST could be passed off not as a "new experience" but, rather, as another old experience—that is, have the Pentagon pick up the bill. If the SST's development had begun in the 1950s rather than in the 1960s, the Pentagon might have gone along. During that period the Defense Department was most responsive to the needs of the industries with which it had a close relationship. This situation gave rise to the charge of the "warfare state" and led President Eisenhower, who had presided over this development, to warn against it as he left the White House.

"We must guard against the acquisition of unwarranted influence, whether sought or unsought, by the military-industrial complex," President Eisenhower said to the American people in a farewell address the evening of January 17, 1961. "The potential for the disastrous rise of misplaced power exists and will persist," he continued. "We must never let the weight of this combination endanger our liberties or democratic processes."

In 1961 Robert Strange McNamara took over the Pentagon and also seemed to take President Eisenhower's advice as his guide. In his tenure as Defense Secretary, Mr. McNamara made many mistakes. However, they are all overshadowed by his one great accomplishment. He established—and for the first time—civilian control at the Pentagon. The emphasis for spending funds shifted from the needs of the defense industries to the defense needs of the nation. In time Secretary McNamara became a personal advocate of the SST, heading one of the many committees endorsing its construction;* but he saw no reason why its cost should be charged to the Pentagon, which already was subject to much criticism for a fantastically high budget. The decision to keep the costs of the SST off the nation's defense budget was not an arbitrary one.

Since the late 1940s the Pentagon has had considerable experience with airplanes flying faster than sound. Fighter bombers had chalked up more than one hundred thousand hours of supersonic flight by the time the FAA was first promoting the SST. These airplanes, however, were small craft, able to carry one or two persons, and traveling not nearly so fast as the speeds envisioned for the commercial transport. The Pentagon had done some experimenting with a supersonic bomber, the B-70. But there is considerable difference between the fuselage and the engine needed for a military plane and those needed for a passenger plane; basically the passenger plane must be much quieter and more comfortable for the rider. Although there would obviously be some exchange of information in the military and civilian research, the proposal for a commercial SST was like nothing the Pentagon was then considering.

Nor did the SST seem worth adding to the Pentagon's roster of airplanes. Speed is essential at times in moving men and military equipment, but the factor of air time is a relatively minor point. More significant in consuming time are such things as getting the men and supplies ready to load onto a plane, transporting them to the airplane, loading them—and, at the landing, the reverse of these procedures. In those few instances where air time can make a difference, the Pentagon planners do not anticipate having the first-class airports available to them that the SST will require.

*A Pentagon official who read this book in manuscript form disputes me. "I know of no statement by Secretary McNamara," the official told me, "which would justify saying that he is a 'personal advocate' of the SST. He chairs a committee of advocates."

When Mr. McNamara, before retiring as Defense Secretary, appeared before a Congressional committee in 1968, he promised that "in the future, even our largest transport, the C-5A, will be able to deliver its cargo to 'primitive' airfields well forward in the theater of operations. And where formerly only relatively light land force equipment could be airlifted, our C-5As and C-141s will be capable of carrying virtually all types of equipment organic to Army divisions." The ability to land at primitive fields is essential because facilities like Dulles International Airport near Washington and John F. Kennedy International Airport in New York are not available in such areas as Vietnam. In contrast to the C-5A, the SST's requirement for first-class airports was considered "inflexible" by the Pentagon planners.

This Pentagon decision was a stiff blow to the supporters of the supersonic transport. Most people involved with aviation concede that the commercial fleet of subsonic jets dominating the American skies in the 1960s could not have been built without government contracts. These planes, or the experience necessary for the development of these planes, came originally from contracts to build the bombers and the supporting aircraft for the Air Force. Without a military justification, the supporters of the SST—the officials in the Federal Aviation Agency, the members of Congress and the aircraft manufacturers—had to seek other justifications.

The first offered was "balance of payments." In the early 1960's particularly, the Kennedy Administration and the members of Congress were concerned by an apparent dollar drain. In adding up American foreign aid, United States purchases abroad and spending by Americans in foreign lands, it appeared that more money was leaving the United States than was coming in. The drain seemed to be reaching serious proportions, and then in June 1963 Pan American World Airways made an announcement that indicated the drain would become worse. England and France had joined together in a combine to build a supersonic transport, called the Concorde. Although the Concorde would not be as large nor as fast as the American SST then under consideration, it would come out on the market first. Obviously, if it were the only supersonic transport available, it would garner whatever sales potential existed, perhaps pull dollars from American airlines to Europe. BOAC and Air France, the English- and French-government-owned airlines, had ordered Concordes, but no American airlines had yet placed an order for one. Then on June 4, 1963, Pan American announced that it had ordered six Concordes. The very next day President Kennedy declared that the United States government would proceed with the building of an American SST.

The figures appear persuasive. If, during a fifteen- or twenty-year period, American airlines order one hundred Concordes at $20 million each, its expected price, that seems to be a total of $2 billion dollars leaving this country's borders. This may not be enough to transform the dollar drain into a flood, but it is adequate to make it a stream, perhaps. Conversely, if European and Asian airlines purchased one hundred American SSTs at $40 million each, the mid-figure between the top and bottom of the projected price range for the American airplane, that seems to be a total of $4 billion entering this country's borders.

Those figures have a solid ring to them—particularly when they are presented to the Congress with appropriate charts, graphs and projections. The figures seemed to say that if America did not build an SST, it would lose $2 billion by American airlines purchasing the Concorde. While if America did build an SST, it would gain $4 billion by foreign airlines buying the American supersonic transport. Late in 1966 Defense Secretary McNamara had some of his Pentagon "whiz kids" examine that thesis, using the computer and cost-analysis techniques which enabled him to assume his mastery over the Defense Department.

The resulting report seriously challenged whether an American SST would appreciably increase the money flow into the United States, as the Federal Aviation Agency consistently has claimed. First, it pointed out that approximately one out of two purchases of American-built airplanes by foreign airlines traditionally are financed by American lending agencies. Such purchases do not add to the plus side of America's balance of payments, the Pentagon report said. Second, the report argued that the sale of each American SST abroad might mean the loss in sales of at least one

American subsonic airplane. Any dollar flow from the sale of the supersonic then should be decreased by the cost of the subsonic, the report maintained. Finally, the report asserted that the sale of SSTs to foreign airlines would mean the loss of American passengers to those airlines, and that also would mean a deduction from any figure entered on the plus side of the balance-of-payments ledger due to the sale abroad of an American SST. The conclusion was that, at best, the sale abroad of an American SST, rather than meaning a plus to the balance of payments equal to its full sale price, would mean a plus of only 5 to 10 percent of its sale price during the course of the airplane's life.

This conclusion by the Pentagon study group, although supported by logic as well as by computerized studies, may be wrong. Likewise, the Federal Aviation Agency's claims in the other direction may be wrong, as the Pentagon study suggests. There has been no attempt by the government, neither in the Administration nor in Congress, to cut through the conflict and ascertain the truth. The FAA, to which the Pentagon report was referred, hesitated to make the study available to the public until after so much of it had been leaked to various news media that sitting on the report served no purpose.

Still, balance of payments is offered as a justification for the SST.

Another justification offered is "prestige." According to this argument, the leading nations of the world are in a prestige race, the winner being the one building the biggest and fastest supersonic transport. "The combined British and French supersonic development program [to build the Concorde] threatens the position of leadership which the U.S. air industry now holds," Senator Monroney said when his subcommittee kicked off its 1963 hearings on the American SST.

And *Fortune* magazine, in its February 1967 issue, asked, to buttress the prestige argument: "What is the dollar value, for example, of the fact that even President de Gaulle is obliged to fly on an American-made plane when he travels abroad to agitate against U.S. political objectives? Assuming anyone is aware he is flying on an American-built airplane—probably not very much. A good case can be made that a simple item like the Singer sewing machine, which can be used by millions of people all over the globe, is a better prestige builder than, for example, the luxurious S.S. *United States*, built and operated with a federal subsidy.

Actually the discussion over prestige is really not an argument. Either one believes that the "big" project is a way to gain respect or one does not. To those who go along with the big-project side, however, there is a danger worth pointing out. Senator Hart first raised it in some early hearings.

"So long as we accept this [the SST] as a symbol of prestige," he said, "we are saying that every time ... [another nation] takes the new step, hereafter—I am sure it won't be cheaper next time—we will go through this. Clearly, this is a precedent that is not just a precedent for precedent's sake. We know from history, we will come up to bat every twelve years."

The Senator's point is a valid one. If the SST becomes the symbol of the nation's prestige, as the missile became the symbol of its defense, then the United States will have jumped on a tread-mill. Every time another nation proposes an airplane faster than the American SST, the pressure will be on Congress to finance a larger and faster American plane.

In its December 31, 1966, issue *The New Yorker* commented on this possibility:

> As nearly as we can make out, this supposed inevitability [of America building an SST] is based on the fact that the British and the French and the Russians are working on supersonic airliners, this country therefore being obliged to build a yet faster one to preserve its "leadership" in aviation—success that, in turn, will doubtless drive the Russians back to their wind tunnels for something faster still. And so aviation will progress from speed to speed, from boom to boom. Fortunately, this advance, in the very nature of things, cannot long continue. Once the designers have produced an airplane capable of twenty-five thousand miles per hour, the race will be over, because such a plane will depart this world altogether, having achieved what is called "escape velocity."

In addition to the justifications of balance of payments and prestige, there is a third justification offered: The government, it is insisted, eventually will have all of its investment in the SST returned to it through a surcharge collected when the SST is sold by its manufacturer to the airlines. This justification is the most difficult to examine because it weaves a tortuous path through the financial intricacies of the SST; few are able to follow that path. But it is also the most important because it challenges the validity of the SST itself.

First, something about the airplane.

The supersonic transport prototypes are scheduled to fly in the early 1970s. The plane, mass-produced, is expected to be ready to carry passengers on commercial flights by the late 1970s. Those dates are tentative; no one can predict exactly what technical "bugs" will develop in the design of the airplane or how long it will take to smooth them out. Actually, the target date for commercial flights is years behind the original schedule announced immediately after President Kennedy committed the United States to building the SST.

Although the airplane, when it flies, will have a cruising speed approximately three times that of the subsonic jetliners of the mid-1960s, it will not travel from airport to airport three times as fast. A flight from New York to London, now about six hours, will take three hours. An around-the-world flight would take approximately thirty hours or slightly less, compared to twice that of the jets of the 1960s.

Why can an airplane able to fly three times as fast as the jets of the 1960s travel only twice as fast? There are two reasons.

The first is that an airplane spends considerable time in the air at less than its cruising speed. This will be particularly true with the SST, which will not be able to reach its maximum speed until it hits about 65,000 feet. Taking off from New York, the SST will need approximately forty minutes to reach that altitude, level off and zoom at its 1,800-mile-an-hour level. When the airplane nears England, it must begin to decelerate about thirty or forty minutes before entering a landing pattern. Another possible slowdown may come from waiting in a holding pattern for the opportunity to land. Waits now are so lengthy—and the prospects for the future are that they will become longer—as to wipe out any gain in air time made by the SST. On a Friday afternoon in 1968, for example, it is not unusual for more than twenty airplanes to be backed up in holding patterns for a chance to land at Kennedy Airport in New York.*

The second factor slowing down the SST is the sonic boom. Certainly a nuisance, very likely a health problem, perhaps a real threat to the safety of Americans, the sonic boom is the biggest technical obstacle the SST faces. If the sonic boom could be eliminated, or if the complaints of the sonic boom could be ignored, the SST very probably would be a commercially successful plane. But the sonic boom can neither be eliminated nor ignored.

When an object moves through the air at speeds greater than the speed of sound—760 miles an hour at sea level and 660 miles an hour at the cruising altitude of the SST—it sends air rippling away from it, much like water ripples away from a moving boat. This is the sonic boom. To the person on the ground standing in the path of this rippling air, the experience is like that of hearing thunder—but worse. In addition to the nuisance value of being in the path of constantly rumbling thunder, the victim of a sonic boom may find his house falling down about him. Tests made by the Federal Aviation Agency show sonic booms shaking houses, knocking glasses over, cracking windows. One unpublished government study of the sonic boom's impact questioned what would

*If the SST enthusiasts really wanted to encourage the growth of aviation rather than merely build a bigger and more expensive airplane, there is no mystery about how it can be done. The first step would be to ban commercial flights on short hops, such as those between New York and Washington and New York and Boston. This would not represent a hardship to the traveler. Because of automobile traffic tie-ups going to and from airports, the traveler actually makes better time when traveling between New York and Washington using the train. When train speeds between these two points are increased, the advantage of the train will be even more marked.

The second step, at New York, would be to use La Guardia Field for all domestic flights. Having eliminated the very short hops, La Guardia would be able to absorb the domestic flights that had been using Kennedy Airport. The third step is to limit Kennedy to international flights. These steps would so relieve the clutter in the sky over New York that flying would be much faster—airplanes would not have to hold while waiting for the chance to land—and also much safer.

The final step is to build a fast mass-transit system from the center of the city to the airport. Within several years jumbo jets will be landing five hundred passengers at a time. Unless there is a mass-transit system available to the passengers of these airplanes—and the planes will be landing at the rate of one every few minutes—the airplane passenger may find his trip from Kennedy Airport to Manhattan more time-consuming than flying from London to New York.

happen to the structural integrity of the skyscrapers in Manhattan if an SST suddenly went supersonic while over the city. This is not an improbability. It would not take much for an SST to go from 600 to 660 miles an hour while cruising over Manhattan.

Also the sonic boom's impact would be widespread. An SST flying across the United States at supersonic speeds and at an altitude of approximately sixty thousand feet would leave a sonic-boom trail behind it all the way across the country and more than fifty miles wide.

For these reasons it is generally presumed that the SST will not fly at supersonic speeds over land. The FAA, however, has never made a firm policy decision against flying the airplane at supersonic speeds over the United States. And there is a growing suspicion that, when the airplane is flying commercially, the FAA will expect the public to assume the nuisance and the danger of the sonic boom in the name of progress. This suspicion was best enunciated by Senator William Proxmire of Wisconsin, speaking in 1967 to the Senate. "The FAA has apparently concluded either, first, that the task of muffling the boom is impossible," said the Senator, "or, second, that it is content to build a plane that would be limited to ocean flights, which drastically reduces chances that the plane would be a commercial success ... or, third, that the public is just going to have to learn to live with the boom no matter how destructive or disturbing it may be. I have a feeling, judging from past FAA pronouncements, that it is probably the latter."

The airplane would be much more valuable if it could fly at supersonic speeds over land. (Flying at subsonic speeds over land, as present jets do, gives the SST no competitive edge over subsonic airplanes. And it is more expensive to fly an SST at those relatively low speeds than it is to fly a subsonic jet.) If the sonic boom could be ignored, an SST could pick up passengers in Los Angeles, fly on to Chicago, where it would pick up more passengers, continue to New York, where it would pick up its last load, and then zoom on to London, where it would discharge all its passengers. If it cannot fly over land at supersonic speeds, those Los Angeles and Chicago passengers will fly to New York on regular airplanes and board the SST there. The effect on the SST's economics of ignoring the sonic boom is to broaden the airplane's appeal beyond the relatively few travelers who fly long distances over water. Such travelers account for less than half of all air travelers.

That is the airplane that supposedly will return the federal government's investment. The story of the extent of that investment begins in June 1963 with President Kennedy's pledge to assist the aviation industry in building the SST.

The announced cost of developing the SST then was $1 billion. This was to pay for the building of the two prototypes and for their flying one hundred hours. By 1966 the development cost had escalated 30 percent, to $1.3 billion. Escalation happened before any construction took place; only specifications had been drawn up. By 1968, after contracts had been let but before major construction had begun, the estimate for development costs had jumped again, to the $1.455 billion figure. Even this figure is not a great deal more than a guess.

This becomes clear after talking with government officials, members of Congress and other persons knowledgeable about aviation. Once development of a project begins, its costs have a way of escalating out of proportion and expectation. One former Pentagon official, anticipating a further increase in the development cost of the SST, has pointed out that "development costs of aircraft have often been underestimated by a factor of two—especially where the necessary state of the art has yet to be attained."

In Washington there is not much argument with that assertion. The TFX fighter-bomber airplane was intended by Defense Secretary McNamara to be the most carefully budgeted airplane ever built by the Defense Department, carefully budgeted so that its development costs would not balloon out of expectation. Still, its costs jumped so high that Secretary McNamara declined to give the cost either publicly or to members of Congress. The unit cost of that airplane had increased between two and three times. It was not that Secretary McNamara's computers turned up wrong answers like a slot machine refusing to pay off; it was that there are too many unexpected problems in designing a new airplane to predict accurately its cost in advance.

Outside of Washington also there is little argument with the claim that development costs of aircraft jump. England and France have been working for years on their supersonic airplane, the Concorde. The two nations have limited their objectives to cut costs. The Concorde will fly twice the speed of sound, not the near three times the SST is supposed to hit. The Concorde will be encased in aluminum, a metal already available, not titanium, which is still largely an expensive mystery. For these reasons the Concorde should not be so difficult a plane to build, nor so expensive. Still, the Concorde's development costs soared more than 50 percent beyond original estimates, eventually hitting $1.4 billion, just about the same figure as the estimate for developing the technically more difficult American airplane.

Senator Magnuson insists that great efforts are being made to insure that the development costs of the American plane will not escalate far beyond the early estimates. But in a 1966 question-and-answer session on the Senate floor he conceded: "No one can guarantee that a development program of the size and complexity of the SST will not cost more than the estimates at its beginning. This is inherent in the development process." That is the only thing about the SST that is not guaranteed—that its cost will not soar above the estimates.

Originally the government and industry were to split the development cost on a 75-25 basis. Translated into dollars: When the development cost was first estimated at $1 billion back in 1963, the federal government committed itself to $750 million and private industry was obligated for $250 million. That was a ratio of three federal dollars for every one private dollar. Immediately, however, the manufacturers began lobbying for the government to pick up a larger share of the tab. The greater the taxpayers' investment, the less risk to the companies.

"I doubt," said a Boeing vice-president in 1964, "if many people appreciate the fact that if a company such as Boeing were to undertake a supersonic production program it would be necessary to commit one-fourth of our facilities and one-fourth of our manpower for at least a decade before $1 of profit would be earned, and again this does not take into consideration interest on the investment which could easily aggregate several hundreds of millions of dollars. And this all assumes a successful program." The official, John O. Yeasting, continued: "Again, let me say that risk is not a stranger to the Boeing Company nor to the aerospace industry and when all the facts are understood I believe it will be recognized that the industry is simply endeavoring to exercise 'prudent judgment' in assessing the risks of the supersonic program."

So "prudent judgment" transferred the risks to the taxpayer.

Also, the greater the taxpayers' investment, the less chance of the government pulling out of the project if it turns sour in later years. Government officials tend to spend more money to save a program rather than admit they are in error. The Navy was building a radio telescope; top cost was $20 million, or so the estimate said. Before the project was junked, the federal government had invested $64 million in it, much of that in an attempt to save the original $20 million investment. A billion dollars was poured into the building of an atomic-powered airplane that never flew, the money continuing to go into the project long after it became obvious the airplane was a bust. Similar momentum built up for the SST. In 1966 one of the members of the appropriations subcommittee of the House of Representatives having jurisdiction over the Federal Aviation Agency made this comment:

> In the budget for the FAA we made cuts in every area except the supersonic transport. We should not go up the hill and down the hill on this matter. We have contracts at the present time for research on a supersonic aircraft—and the program should be funded. We must not violate our contracts. We need to go forward. The funds should be provided.

In addition to presiding over the building of the supersonic transport, the Federal Aviation Agency has the responsibility for the safety of the nation's airways. This is one of the most complicated jobs in modern complicated America. At any time, for example, there are between eight thousand and ten thousand airplanes in the air, some four thousand of them crowding the skies in the triangle formed by Washington, Boston and New York. Keeping these craft in their respective air lanes, preventing collisions, financing the improvements to keep airports up to date—all this is an enormously expensive job. But funds for this work were cut back. This cut came when the men who work in the FAA's control towers at the airports were charging that the towers were "seriously underequipped, undermanned." Even *Time* magazine, in an article intended as a strong boost for the FAA, conceded that while America's airways "are the most extensive and best-controlled in the world, they are far from foolproof."

The SST, however, flew on through the appropriation process in 1966 untouched.

The argument that the SST is sacred, that its funds should be left intact, carried over to the Senate side of the Capitol. By the summer of 1966 the federal government had committed $231 million to the SST. Before the Senate was an appropriation for an additional $280 million for the SST. Senator Proxmire then moved to cut out $200 million, leaving $80 million for the airplane. The cut was not so serious as it appeared; the $80 million remaining would have been sufficient to carry the program to the end of 1966, and more money could have been allotted then. The move would have endangered the SST somewhat but not ended the program. Senator Leverett Saltonstall, Republican of Massachusetts, urged the Senate to appropriate the full $280 million, however, saying the $280 million should be spent to protect the $231 million already allotted.

"If we only appropriate $80 million, the program stops at that time [the end of 1966]," said Senator Saltonstall, "and the $80 million plus $231 million has gone down the drain." The Proxmire move failed by a vote of fifty-five to thirty-one, and the full $280 million was appropriated.

Senator Saltonstall's use of the phrase "down the drain" suggests another well-used phrase: "throwing good money after bad."

This kind of momentum—the argument that because an initial investment has been made, more funds must be poured on—is what the aircraft industry was trying to build up, and it succeeded. The federal government announced that it would increase its share of the development cost from 75 percent to 90 percent. The increase produced no opposition from the business community, which has become more and more dependent on government assistance and more friendly to the concept of federal handouts. Eugene R. Black and Stanley De J. Osborne, two experienced businessmen, compiled a report for the White House on the SST. Released in 1964, the report was highly favorable to the concept of the SST and recommended that the federal government increase its share of the cost from 75 to 90 percent. Said the two men in their report:

> An American supersonic transport is in our national interest, and . . . help directly from Government, instead of aid covered by military budgets, such as has been the case for the vast majority of previous aircraft, should not be viewed as a subsidy, but as a necessary element in our overall national economic panorama.

That is how the government's obligation grew to $1.264 billion. There is still more.

When government officials first talked of the SST early in the 1960s, they neglected to mention that once the prototypes are developed and test-flown there will be another expenditure. This will total $800 million to turn the prototype into a production model, to build the assembly lines, tool up and gather in all the paraphernalia such a major undertaking requires.

"The source of these funds has not been determined," Senator Magnuson has said, "but private financing will be sought."

Both the industry and the Federal Aviation Agency, however, anticipate that the federal government will put up a large chunk of this money, probably at the same 90-10 ratio as for the development costs. This means another $700 million-plus on the taxpayers' bill.

The third and last section of funds to be raised is between $2 billion and $2.5 billion for actually producing the airplane. Senator Magnuson has stated that for this money, "financing is expected to be from private sources."

This prediction could come true. By the time the money is needed, it should be known whether the SST will fly, whether there is a market for it, how much it will cost and whether it will make money. If these answers have a positive cast to them, then there should be no trouble raising private funds.

Conversely, if the answers have a negative cast, the government will have to put up the money—to protect its investment. The problem will not be faced until after the scheduled flight testing of the prototypes in the early 1970s.*

Despite the vagueness of the cost estimates, the only certainty seeming to be that they go up, the federal government and the aviation industry claim that the taxpayers' investment in the supersonic transport will be repaid. When Najeeb Halaby was first pushing the program on Congress, he insisted: "We do not intend and in fact it is one of the ground rules of the program that this not be a subsidy inducing airplane." But at another point he conceded the possibility of a limited subsidy, saying: "Unless manufacturers demonstrate faith in the program by undertaking to share substantially, there will be doubt of the justification for funding by the government. This is an important point and should be emphasized, because it indicates very clearly that this is not to be an *unrestricted subsidy*, a giveaway program or a handout in any respect." (Italics added.)

Other officials spoke more freely of the possibility of the SST becoming a subsidized airplane. If the airplane does require an operating subsidy (in addition to the funds poured into its building) when it is flying commercially, that operating subsidy would be administered by the Civil Aeronautics Board. Alan Boyd, when he was chairman of the CAB, discussed this possibility before Senator Monroney's subcommittee. "I think the supersonic transport may very well generate a requirement for subsidy," Mr. Boyd said. A few moments later he emphasized that point again. "I think it boils down to this," he said. "If there are supersonics flying and they are attracting business, we are going to have to subsidize our carriers unless they have them. And if the supersonic is not an economical machine, we subsidize them for operating them. If they

---

*In using the figures $800 million and between $2 billion and $2.5 billion, I am giving the FAA the benefit of the doubt. There is no reason to believe that those two figures will not escalate almost 50 percent, as the development costs already have done.

don't get the machines, then we subsidize to keep them from going broke with their subsonics, because the foreign carriers will be taking the bulk of the business."

What Mr. Boyd was saying was that the United States must guarantee the existence of the American-owned international air carriers. If these carriers operate without supersonic transports, then a profit must be guaranteed them from federal funds to make up for any loss in business to European lines flying supersonics. If the American lines do use the supersonics, but those supersonics prove too expensive to operate at a profit, then the United States government must guarantee to pick up the extra costs of those supersonics. Mr. Boyd had added the airlines to the aircraft manufacturers as an industry that should have a profitable future guaranteed by the United States government.

Still, it is insisted that the SST will be a self-supporting program. The government will receive its investment back by collecting a royalty on each airplane sold. Stuart Tipton, the president of the Air Transport Association, explained the plan this way:

> The government investment is to be paid back with the three hundredth delivery. The manufacturer will thus pay royalties of 4.3 to 6.7 million dollars for each aircraft delivered. There is some flexibility in these arrangements for the manufacturers to meet cash flow problems. In any event the government investment is to be repaid from the first three hundred sales.

Giving Mr. Tipton the benefit of the doubt and using his higher figure, $6.7 million, when that royalty is multiplied by three hundred sales, the result is $2.01 billion. Rather than being enough to pay the government back its investment, that is barely enough to pay the government interest on its investment. Interest must be charged. The government borrows the money it uses and pays interest on that money. If it does not collect interest on money it lends, then the government is definitely offering a subsidy—in addition to competing unfairly with commercial banks.

If private lending agencies had advanced the money, they would want about a 15 percent return on their investment. The government will not seek that much of a return. The February

1967 *Fortune* article estimated the dollars involved in the government's collecting interest on its investment. After reporting that the Federal Aviation Agency was unhelpful in figuring the impact of interest rates on the cost of the SST, the article then said:

> A rough estimate of simple interest at five percent on only the $1.1 billion investment now planned by 1971 comes out at about $600 million on a straight line repayment program beginning after the first plane is delivered in 1974. At fifteen percent, the interest would come to about $1.8 billion. If the government's investment eventually rises to $4 billion [a figure which *Fortune* believed the industry was hoping to receive from the government] a charge as high as fifteen percent would boost interest costs to about $6 billion, making the manufacturers' bill astronomically higher than anything discussed publicly to date. Since the manufacturers plan to amortize the government investment, building the financing costs into the price of the plane, the cost to the airlines of the SST would radically increase and a vicious circle of damaging economic effect would occur to limit the size of the market.

That analysis by *Fortune,* appearing in an article intended as a boost for the SST,* leads to the conclusion that a sale of perhaps six hundred planes may be needed for the government to break even, royalties on the sale of the first three hundred to cover the investment itself and royalties on the sale of the second three hundred to cover interest charges. The power of the press being what it is, the first time government officials met with newsmen for a not-for-attribution discussion about the SST after the *Fortune* article appeared, they conceded the government would have to regain its interest. They said then—this was the spring of 1967—that royalties from the sale of three hundred planes would repay the federal government its investment, and royalties from the sale of the next two hundred planes would give the government a 6 percent return—the interest payment—on its money. This means, according to the government, five hundred SSTs must be sold as a minimum.

Even Mr. Tipton has indicated that he accepts the correctness of this, saying that since royalty payments "are to continue for a fifteen-year period, they will go well beyond the 300th delivery,

*By the end of the year, however, *Fortune* was suggesting that the SST was one item the government could cut back on somewhat.

and this phase of royalty payments will produce a return on the government investment comparable to levels normally received by industry." Of course, unless the government receives interest it will have tendered private industry a handout of hundreds of millions of dollars, perhaps an amount equal to the cost of building the SST.

But the question of whether the federal government regains its investment hinges on whether five hundred SSTs will be sold.

The market for the SST is dependent on three factors, at least. One is the cost of producing the airplane at the point that it is turned over to the airlines. The second is its operating cost, once it is flying commercially. The third is the interest on the part of the public in flying at supersonic speeds.

Estimates vary on how great this market will be through the twentieth century. Mr. Tipton estimated a market for five hundred airplanes. If the sonic-boom problems could be eliminated, he added, permitting the SST to fly over land, the market could grow to twelve hundred planes. The Lockheed company, which lost the contract to build the SST's air frame to the Boeing company, has estimated a market of five hundred planes. Boeing had estimated the market to be twice that. The more realistic estimates run between one hundred and fifty planes to six hundred planes. Actually, no one knows.

In the report by Eugene Black and Stanley Osborne, the one recommending that the nation proceed with the building of the SST, its authors acknowledged:

> We are convinced that no one will have an actual gauge of the true market for these aircraft until a prototype has flown, until the sonic boom problem has been satisfactorily put aside, and until the plane's fundamental economics have been proven.
> A mistaken estimate of the market could be a fatal error for industry and government. One must be able to see real orders from the airlines, and we do not believe these will be firmly underwritten until the airlines can see what they will buy.

That report was published in 1964. But its essential point about market estimates continues valid. When the Appropriations Committee of the House of Representatives reported out its Transportation Department bill for the fiscal year of 1968, it enthusiastically endorsed the SST. But it also conceded: "The market for the aircraft cannot be actually determined today. Studies and debates cannot answer these questions."

The conclusion that estimates of the SST's market potential must remain vague until after the prototype is flown also was part of the report made on the supersonic transport by the Defense Department. Because the market is so vague it is difficult—impossible actually—to determine the cost of building the SST on an unit-cost basis. The government's figure is a total of $4.5 billion in private and government funds to get the SST to a point where the airlines are flying it.

Should that $4.5 billion be divided by one hundred and fifty planes sold, by three hundred planes sold, or by six hundred planes or more sold? Until there is a reasonable estimate as to what that answer should be, the unit cost of building the SST cannot be determined. And that unit cost is the first item needed in calculating the sale price of the SST to the airlines.

This leads to the "vicious circle" mentioned in the *Fortune* article. If the SST market is small, the cost of each airplane must be higher in an effort to recoup that $4.5 billion and the interest charges. The higher the cost, the fewer the airlines buy. The market shrinks even more. The price continues to go up—unless the government writes off its announced plan of collecting its investment.

The operating costs of the SST will run high also. The supersonic transport is a violation of the historic rule of transportation: A transportation advance is expected to be cheaper to operate than its predecessors as well as faster, more comfortable and sleeker. In aviation, operating costs are figured on a basis of seat-mile costs, how much it costs to fly one passenger seat one mile. Again the estimates differ as to how much more expensive the SST will be to operate than its predecessors, but there is little disagreement that it will be more expensive. This will be particularly true when the seat-mile costs of the SST are ranked against the seat-mile costs of the jumbo 500-seat subsonic jetliners expected to be in service by the late 1960s.

The problem with the SST is that of fuel; it gulps fuel like a baby drinks milk. At takeoff, about half the SST's weight will be fuel, compared to less than 10 percent representing a payload. If a supersonic transport waits in line to take off or flies a holding pattern before landing, or if it must fly off course because its regular destination is closed by weather, the seat-mile cost of the SST will jump faster than the airplane zooms up to its cruising altitude. These problems are not remote improbabilities. They already are realities. In April 1967, for example, Dr. William J. Ronan, a New York State transportation official, said, "You now are experiencing on just ordinary days twenty-minute delays in departure from Kennedy Airport. In bad weather you have even more serious delays." He continued: "There actually have been jet aircraft that have had to return to the dock for refueling after standing in line so long that their fuel supply was lower than it should be for the flights they were about to make."

And the more expensive the plane is to buy and the more expensive it is to operate, the more expensive a ride on it must be. And the more expensive that ride, the fewer the number of passengers will to buy tickets. Although air traffic is increasing and is expected to continue increasing, the increase is coming not from first-class travelers but from persons interested in cheaper fares. The big surge in business is with family plans, packaged tours and off-season trips. This discount business produced two-thirds of the airlines' passenger revenues in the early 1960s. It now accounts for three-fourths of such revenues. When the jumbo jets, capable of carrying five hundred passengers each, start flying, the surge probably will become even greater.

Against this trend toward the cheaper flight, the SST will be a more expensive flight. The Pentagon study of the SST's economics concluded that the airlines will buy few SSTs, giving the passenger determined to go supersonic less chance to choose a convenient flight. The jets of the 1960s earn a profit when, on the average, 55 percent of their seats are filled. By buying fewer SSTs, the airlines would be aiming at a break-even point of 75 percent. The Pentagon study said, in addition, the airlines would have to charge SST passengers a surcharge of between 10 and 20 percent over what first-class passengers on subsonics pay.*

The Pentagon study was not alone in concluding that the SST will be a more expensive airplane for passengers. Most persons outside of the government and the industry agree with that conclusion. Kurt H. Hohenemser, professor of aerospace engineering at Washington University in St. Louis, has asserted that "the SST market is obviously limited to the first-class traveler" because of the airplane's higher operating costs. Professor Hohenemser then went on to point out that these first-class travelers "at present [1966] account for eight percent of the transatlantic traffic or 230,000 yearly passenger trips on all transatlantic airlines combined." He continued: "A single U.S. SST could offer 180,000 yearly passenger trips. If the British and French were to operate one Concorde, and TWA and Pan American one U.S. SST each, they would produce 540,000 seats per year, or two and a half times the present first-class traffic volume."

Even if Professor Hohenemser has underestimated the market for an SST by fifty times—probably an impossible error—the potential sales still do not loom very large.

The Concorde will be flying commercially several years before the American SST. It will not be as fast—twice the speed of sound compared to almost three times the speed of sound for the American plane—but it will cost about half as much. Current estimates of the sale price of the two planes are $20 million for the Concorde and $40 million for the American SST. The Concorde price is likely to stay static because the plane is far enough along in its development to permit reasonably accurate cost predictions. The American SST is not far enough along for such predictions, and its price is likely to go above the $40 million figure. Cost estimates never go down. Even with the American plane's greater speed, the time saved between takeoff and landing will not be very great. Will the airlines pay $40 million for an airplane that flies

*Perhaps even the Pentagon report, as critical as it was, pulled some of its punches. One member of the Pentagon team that authored the report and who read this book in manuscript form insisted the surcharge would be 30 percent.

from New York to London in three hours, or will they choose the airplane costing $20 million that flies from New York to London in three hours and twenty minutes?

Stephen Enke, the former Deputy Assistant Secretary of Defense for economics who led the Pentagon task force studying the economics of the SST, finally concluded about the airplane: "The simple truth, however, is that such a complex and technically advanced aircraft must be an investment gamble in its first generation." But the aircraft industry is not doing any gambling. It has a guarantee. The taxpayer is the gambler.

One reason the taxpayer is unaware of that gamble is the gimmicks used by the Johnson Administration. On two occasions the President's budget message did not list any funds for the SST; the money was added later in largely unnoticed supplemental appropriations. Another time President Johnson got good publicity value out of the airlines having to pay a small deposit for the SST.

The airlines had been asked to put up $100,000 if they wished to reserve a place on the SST's delivery schedule. Once construction of the prototype started they would be expected to produce a second $100,000. This $200,000 deposit would be part of the purchase price, whatever the final price tab settled on. In 1967 the Administration proposed that the airlines increase this deposit from a total of $200,000 to $1 million for each position reserved on the SST's delivery schedule. Since the airlines involved had ordered approximately fifty airplanes, this had the impact of increasing the airlines' total deposit from $10 million to $50 million.

Whether the deposits the airlines put up for the SST will actually cost the airlines any money is an intriguing question. One member of the Civil Aeronautics Board, which watches over airline rates, warned the airlines not to expect to write off that $1-million deposit as current operating expenses and then use it as an excuse to raise fares—in effect, to pass the $1-million cost on to the airlines' customers.

"The United States carriers who are involved in the SST delivery positions are all subsidy free and in a sufficiently healthy earnings position that there should be no fear of the current write-offs triggering rates or fare increases," said board member John G. Adams. Then he added: "At least I hope not."

This extra $40 million from the airlines' increased deposits is not a significant amount. The individual airline is putting up $1 million toward an airplane that may cost $40 million, and then the airline may collect that $1 million back through increased fares. The federal government is getting an increased advance equal to less than 4 percent of its investment in the development of the SST prototype. But the extra funds did relieve some of the immediate pressure on the Johnson Administration. The move also created good publicity for the program. Proclaimed *The New York Times* in a front-page headline: "U.S. TO GO AHEAD WITH SUPERJETS—BUT AIRLINES WILL BE ASKED TO SHARE BUILDING COST—CARRIERS SAID TO AGREE."

But the Administration's gimmicks are no worse than those used by Congress. When the 1968 fiscal-year budget was presented to Congress, the actual figure requested for the SST was $198 million for that specific year. It was also during that year that Congress appeared to go on its budget-cutting spree, and it even appeared that the funds for the SST had been cut by a significant amount—$55 million.

As both the House and Senate appropriations committees made clear, however, the cut was not a real one. The SST funds included $54 million in a "payback reserve." In the event the contracts with Boeing and General Electric are canceled, the government would use the reserve to pay penalties. The House committee pointed out that it is not likely "the government will be required to terminate the program" and directed the FAA to spend the reserve on the SST, bringing the spending figure back to the Administration request.

"Almost all of the reduction recommended," the House committee pointed out, "is based on a difference as to the source of the funds for the program, not in the amount of funds provided for the program." Then the committee directed that the SST program "be conducted at the level recommended in the budget." The Senate committee and the Congress concurred. With the exception of money with which to wage the war in Vietnam, money for 1968 expenditures on the SST may be the only funds in that year's budget to survive the Congress' and the Administration's economies.

This attitude of the SST-at-any-cost carries through in the 1969 budget. Because of the Vietnam war, expenditures for civilian purposes were chopped back ruthlessly in the budget President Johnson presented to the Congress. As much as possible, every federal agency, every recipient of federal funds, every program carried on with some federal dollars was expected to take a dollar cut—except, that is, the SST. The President wanted Congress to appropriate $223 million for the supersonic transport. That is about a 50 percent increase over the amount appropriated the previous year.

About two months after the budget was first presented to Congress, the FAA announced there would be a substantial reduction in that $223 million figure. The cutback was made necessary not because of any rethinking of the value of the airplane in relation to the nation's other needs but because the SST had to go back to the drawing boards.

The arithmetic of the SST financing is complicated and tortuous. But the figures add up to an unfortunate conclusion. The plane is going to cost many billions of dollars to build, will be extremely expensive to fly, will appeal to a very narrow market and will produce a limited gain—all meaning that the taxpayers cannot reasonably expect to get their money back.

But the only important thing with the SST is the aircraft industry—that it have something to build and that it earn money. The validity of the SST as an aeronautical concept, as an economic development and as a part of the American tradition is secondary, perhaps even insignificant, to that primary point: building a guaranteed society for the aircraft industry. This almost was acknowledged on the House floor during the debate on the 1968 appropriation. Holding the floor was Representative Edward P. Boland, Democrat of Massachusetts. Representative Boland is chairman of the subcommittee that appropriated the funds for the SST, and he was making a strong case for the airplane. But he had to concede that the airplane faced many problems: the sonic boom, the "technical feasibility of the project itself," the amount of money eventually to be spent and the government's share of the cost.

Are those problems being solved? Without solutions in the offing, the taxpayers are buying a pig in a poke. It is a super-sleek, titanium pig, but still a pig in a poke.

Representative Boland said of these problems: "This represents a bridge which we shall cross when we come to it."

As expensive as is the SST in dollars, the money may turn out to be, in the end, the least costly item listed on the debit side of the SST ledger. There is a story, perhaps apocryphal, about the president of General Motors and a young man sitting together at a dinner party. At one point the president of General Motors said to the young man, "What business do you think General Motors is in?"

Somewhat taken back, the young man answered that General Motors was, of course, in the business of manufacturing automobiles.

The president of the company answered, "No." He continued: "The business of General Motors is to make money for its stockholders. If it makes money by manufacturing cars, fine. But if some day it must turn to a new product to continue making money, it will."

Traditionally, American industries follow that rule. They search for a need that must be fulfilled, design and manufacture a product to fulfill that need, then sell that product at a profit. In the mid-1960s, for example, it became apparent that some of America's biggest needs were cleaning up its polluted waters and dirty air. Immediately, commercial companies began experimenting in this field, and those companies that did experiment in the 1960s will be the money-makers of the 1970s.

The aviation industry, however, does not have to bother about needs to be fulfilled or about research and development in new products. It has the SST. The airplane's funding and ultimately its profit are guaranteed by the government. As a result, several serious needs are going unfulfilled in America.

America's merchant fleet is in a state of decline. New production techniques are needed to design new ships that can carry more goods, travel faster than present ships, use fewer crew members and cost less to build and operate. This kind of project would be ideally suited to the airplane manufacturers. Their expertise could be transferred quickly and effectively to the problem of shipping large quantities of goods by water. But this opportunity is being largely ignored. It does not promise the guarantee of the federal government picking up most of the costs as does the SST.

Another transportation problem is that of moving commuters and short-distance travelers fast, comfortably and cheaply. In the 1960s the United States paid for its emphasis during the 1950s on highway and aviation. Both the roads and the airways were clogged, creating dangers and time-consuming tieups. One answer, perhaps the only answer: mass-transit facilities to carry the commuter into the city faster and cheaper than he can come in by car, and high-speed trains to carry passengers short distances, such as between Washington and New York, in less time than a traveler believes he can make the trip by airplane. The problem is a technological one. And while some industries, with federal assistance, are taking steps to solve this particular problem, none can bring the massive technology to its solution as can the aviation industry.

Desperately in need of a technological revolution is the housing industry. Millions of American homes are substandard or are rapidly deteriorating to that point. Conventional construction methods have not been able to stem this tide toward turning the cities of America into vast slums. Could the aviation industry, using all its knowledge of new materials and its ability to develop fuel systems, devise a new, cheaper, more efficient way of building houses? Could it solve the problem of inadequate housing? It has the knowledge. It has the manpower. It has all the other resources. But it also has the SST, so it does not concern itself with housing.

For the aviation industry to enter any commercial enterprise means breaking with its traditional way of doing business. The airplane manufacturers have dealt almost exclusively in the past with the government; 75 to more than 90 percent of these companies' business has been with the Pentagon. They did not have to compete; generally, the Pentagon decided what kind of a weapons system it needed, and usually only one company had the capacity to build it. The manufacturers did not have to worry about costs. The contracts with the government called for the federal government to pay costs plus a fixed fee that is the manufacturers' profit.

The manufacturers expect the SST to be a similar type arrangement, and it is. They prefer this kind of arrangement. In the early 1960s the Lockheed aircraft corporation made clear its preference for government work over private contracts when it submitted a statement to a Senate subcommittee studying the problems of converting defense industries to nondefense uses.

"With nearly 96 percent of our current sales going to the U.S. and foreign military customers," the statement said, "we cannot yet claim any great success in diversifying into nongovernmental areas. We believe this is not the result of inadequate foresight or lack of planning but rather reflects the great difficulties that we, in common with other aerospace companies, have in entering the commercial fields in spite of our desire to do so and our constant exploration of promising possibilities."

The statement explained that "the aerospace industry has little experience in competing for markets in most commercial fields and suffers not only from this inexperience but also from the lack of the kind of organization it needs to compete—extensive dealership organizations, for example, or other commercial outlets for its products."

What that statement really does is outline the problems in reorienting an industry from government business to a free-enterprise direction. Such a reorientation is difficult but not impossible. Even in the 1950s and 1960s companies were broadening their sales outlets, creating the kind of experience that Lockheed said the aerospace industry lacked. The Xerox corporation is the most outstanding example, with its development of dry copying machines. When the Eastman Kodak camera company decided to compete with Xerox in the dry copying business, it faced the same problem of building up a sales force. The problem, however, was not insurmountable. Solving it, in fact, turned out to be quite profitable. But in contrast to these kinds of examples, the aircraft industry is the best example of what the historian Samuel Eliot Morison meant when he wrote, "Nobody in big industry really wants free competition nowadays. . . . [Businessmen want to produce] predictable goods at a predictable cost, to be sold at a predictable price." To paraphrase Professor Morison, big business wants the guaranteed society.

But that question of priorities, like the question of the amounts of money invested in the SST, is not the most significant question about the SST. Neither question is the one around which the most serious dangers of the guaranteed society revolve.

With so much money invested in the SST, the United States government obviously will have to watch over the airplane's development. What happens if the SST is faced with a costly delay because a union goes on strike? The time lost in the development of the airplane and the increased costs due to an unanticipated wage hike will add dollars to the price of the airplane, too many dollars to an already too costly airplane. The United States government does not permit such strikes in defense industries. Could it allow such a strike to harm the SST?

The United States government must watch the price of the raw goods sold to the manufacturers. Any unexpected increase in their costs also will send the cost of building the SST soaring. It must be as careful with subcontractors. Exorbitant profits cannot be allowed. They too would increase the final cost of the SST and threaten the government's investment.

Because it has more money invested in the SST than does Boeing or General Electric, the government must determine the airplane's final selling price. It is the government's investment to be returned. And when the airlines are presented with the price, however high it may turn out to be, they must be careful before saying "no." The American airlines need government business, government approval of the routes they fly and the rates they charge. The airlines may determine that buying an SST, even if it means a loss, might be the wisest business course. Keeping friendly with the government is an old aviation practice. When the Federal Aviation Agency opened Dulles International Airport near Washington in the early 1960s, a number of airlines transferred flights from the more appealing Friendship Airport at nearby Baltimore to Dulles because they did not choose to make enemies at the FAA.

The government also will have to rethink its motivations in setting rates. In the past the cost of an airline ticket has been based on economics, usually the result of a hassle between what the airlines must charge to earn a profit and what the traffic will bear. But setting fares for the SST will have more of a political cast. To encourage supersonic travel and stand a better chance of recouping its investment, the United States will want to keep SST fares low. But a number of smaller nations, unable to afford supersonics and with airlines flying subsonics, will want SST fares kept high to discourage supersonic travel. The result is a price war between nations.

The government has given the SST air-frame contract to one company, Boeing, and in so doing has elevated the Boeing company into a monopoly situation. Boeing will have the experience, the talent and the ability to control all supersonic aircraft construction in the closing decades of the twentieth century. Other companies will turn to it for subcontracts, will follow its lead, will be unable to challenge it. Is it wise federal policy to use taxpayers' dollars to give a single company such strength? The only way the government can protect the rest of the aviation industry against any potential misuse of this monopoly power is to keep a tight fist on all of the company's operations.

These questions mean that the government must enter the aviation industry with more strength than it ever has before shown in the private economy outside of wartime. Nothing about the SST can be guaranteed unless everything about the SST is guaranteed. No longer is the federal government providing aid to private industry; now it is the custodian of private industry. No longer is the federal government being a stimulant to private industry; now it is the dictator of private industry.

In 1967 when the debate in the House of Representatives on the supersonic transport was coming to a close, Representative William Fitts Ryan of New York opposed the government financing of the airplane and criticized the Congressional action approving the spending of the federal funds. "This reflects," said the Manhattan Democrat, "on the wisdom of Congress and suggests to the public that there may be a point to claims of 'pure pork barrel' which surround the issue of the SST."

In politics "pork barrel" is a euphemism for make-work projects. Never before has "pork" cost America so much—in money and energies, in needs ignored and most importantly, in the quality of American life.

MERCHANT MARINE: 2
The Subsidized Sailor

One

IN EARLY OCTOBER 1966 a former Wall Street lawyer named Robert H. B. Baldwin told an audience of maritime officials, "I must confess that I believe that the United States merchant marine has inadvertently created an extremely unfavorable public image."

Mr. Baldwin spoke after having served for the previous year as Under Secretary of the Navy in the Defense Department; one of his chief responsibilities was dealing with maritime officials to make certain that needed supplies reached American troops in Vietnam. It was a heavy responsibility, and his words this October 5 were blunt.

"To the general public," he said, "the U.S. merchant marine is in a state of near collapse; its very existence hangs on nothing but a government subsidy and no new idea has been generated since the days of the Clipper Ship."

That is not only the image. That is the reality.

Secretary Baldwin's statement was a plea to one of the least known industries in the United States to break away from its subsidized past. As if in answer to that plea, the comments from the industry's leaders began a few weeks later.

The federal subsidy to the merchant marine, said Joseph Curran, the president of the National Maritime Union, must be increased or there will be a "continued decline of the United States merchant marine, putting us still farther behind the rest of the world in this field." A new idea? A break with the past? No, simply more of the same.

The Committee of American Steamship Lines, a trade group representing most of the subsidized merchant lines, came next. The plans to subsidize construction of thirteen new merchant ships in fiscal year 1967—at a cost to the taxpayers of $143 million—is "far below the annual number of ships needed for the subsidized lines to carry out an orderly vessel replacement program."

Perhaps the final response to Secretary Baldwin's plea for a turning away from the old approach of subsidy, subsidy and still more subsidy came from Edwin M. Hood, president of the Shipbuilders Council of America. "To replace a fleet growing obsolete in block and to expand it to a size suitable to both our economic dependency on international trade and our free world commitments," he said, "will require a considerable amount of federal government support for both ship construction and ship operations." A new idea? Again, no—just a call for greater subsidies.

The American merchant marine is a phrase referring to an industry that builds ships, sails and mans them. The industry is represented by shipyard owners, the heads of ship lines and union leaders. It is not a uniformed service like the Army or Navy but a private, commercial operation. It does, however, exist on federal subsidies. The annual amount of subsidy averages $400 million with occasional variations. The ship-construction subsidy, for example, is about $50 million less in fiscal year 1969 than it was in fiscal year 1968. Since 1936, when the present law governing maritime subsidy was enacted, the total of federal funds bolstering the industry has totaled near $4 billion. For this money that they pay, the American taxpayers have a very leaky ship.

To carry goods in international commerce, the merchant marine has ships that are antiquated and inefficient, also expensive to operate. Each year American ships carry less of the world's commerce. In October 1967 the Foreign Trade Division of the Bureau of the Census released figures on the American merchant marine's share of the nation's waterborne foreign trade for the previous year. The figure was 7.3 percent. This was the lowest percentage since 1921, which was the first year such statistics were kept. The previous year the figure had been 8 percent. In 1960 it had been 11.1 percent; in 1945, 68.4 percent; and in 1921, 48.7 percent.

The size of the fleet dwindles also, by more than one fourth in the number of boats since the early 1950s. This decrease in the American fleet has not been matched elsewhere. While the American fleet decreases in size, world trade has increased and so has the world fleet, by almost two thirds.

And not only is the federal subsidy a bad bargain; it is also a very bad policy. Nicholas Johnson, who served as Maritime Administrator for twenty-eight months and tried to reverse the tide of ever more subsidies, best explained why the policy was a harmful one.

"The issue," Mr. Johnson said to a Congressional committee, "resides in the fact that we must appropriate tax revenues to subsidize an industry that is not economically competitive. As a result we must ask not 'How much shipping would we like to have?' but 'How much shipping are we willing to subsidize?'; minimally, 'How much shipping must we subsidize in order to meet national needs?' The need for subsidy also means the shipping industry must annually undergo the federal government's budget process—not just for some useful financial support for research and development, not just for some remunerative government procurement, but for its very existence."

His point is not in dispute; the industry does depend almost solely on the largess of the federal government for its continued existence, for a federal guarantee. But the industry does not object to this. It welcomes it. As long as the industry is poltically powerful enough, it is assumed a guaranteed income from the federal subsidies. The SST inaugurated the guaranteed society. The merchant marine is that society's newest recruit.

The merchant marine has taken a dying tradition, a defense need which it otherwise ignores, a political muscle which is far out of proportion to the industry's real strength, a flair for political lobbying; it has stirred them all together to produce a system of interlocking subsidies so complicated that few even within the government understand them. But the subsidies add up to a guarantee for the men who manufacture the merchant ships, the men who operate them and the men who sail them.

Traditionally a strong merchant marine was a necessity for a nation that wanted to be a world power. In the seventeenth and eighteenth centuries, for example, England thrived on the mercantile system. All her colonies were required to consider the mother country the hub of their commerce; they sold to and bought from England. England enforced that system not only because she had military might, an army and a navy, but also because she had a great merchant fleet. But the mercantile system was also a stranglehold. The American colonies objected to being so limited by England, and that objection was the spark that caused the American Revolution and the birth of the United States of America.

It was against this background that the first Congress passed legislation encouraging the building of an American merchant fleet. The members of that Congress well understood from personal experiences the value of the United States having its own merchant fleet and not being dependent on the ships of another nation to carry its goods to foreign markets. The Congress then did not act arbitrarily. All nations at the time encouraged the growth of their own merchant fleets by penalizing the merchant fleets of other nations that touched their shores. The classic example remains the tariff concession enacted by the First Congress for goods carried on American ships. This meant it was cheaper to ship goods bound for American ports on American vessels; the tariff paid at the American port was less.

During the nineteenth century, however, nations began opening up their ports to all ships engaged in international trade on an equal-treatment basis. By the time of the Civil War, a British ship or a French ship could do as well carrying goods to an American port as could an American ship. The need for a national merchant fleet appeared to be lessening.

Congress began subsidizing the merchant fleet in 1845. These subsidies were in the form of contracts to carry the mail; the first was for $200,000 a year. An argument can be made, as the Civil Aeronautics Board makes now for its grants to local airlines, that the assistance was not to the shipping lines but to the communities touched by the lines. Otherwise, it is argued, those communities would not have had any mail service. Theoretically that is true. Actually it was not always so true. The contracts often were for amounts far above the cost of carrying the mail. That excess was a direct subsidy. And the "mail" sometimes turned out to be empty letter sacks, placed aboard the merchant ships as a flimsy justification for receipt of the subsidies.

The situation was ripe for scandal. In the nineteenth century, particularly, many members of Congress looked on their offices as a means to obtain a larger financial reward. Industries considered payoffs a standard operating technique. With men willing to receive and men willing to give, money was passed. This graft eventually was exposed and the ensuing scandals ended the mail contracts—for a time. When the heat passed, Congress enacted another set of laws authorizing a mail subsidy. This continued into the twentieth century. In the late 1930s a Senate committee, headed by Senator Hugo L. Black, Democrat of Alabama, investigated the mail contracts given by the federal government to the merchant marine. The results of the investigation revealed that the merchant marine was in a sorry moral state.

"It was found extremely difficult to bring to light the essential facts regarding the companies which have been receiving from the Government millions of dollars each year under so-called 'mail contracts,'" said the Black committee report. "Most of them have made such effective use of the corporate fiction that their holding companies, subsidiaries, affiliates, and associates present a vast financial puzzle which yields true facts only to the most persistent investigation and painstaking analysis."

The committee was not yet finished. "Private ownership and operation of merchant and aerial transportation with Government subsidy has resulted in a saturnalia of waste, inefficiency, unearned exorbitant salaries, and bonuses and other forms of so-called 'compensation,' corrupting expense accounts, exploitation of the public by the sale and manipulation of stocks, the 'values' of which are largely based on the hope of profit from robbing the taxpayer, and a general transfer of energy and labor from operating businesses to 'operating on' the taxpayer," the committee report said. It continued: "Measured by results, the subsidy system, as operated, has been a sad, miserable and corrupting failure. Many of its apologists have been shown to be those who have directly received financial profit, or those who for various reasons have been influenced by those who did directly profit from it."

The Black committee report then showed how far the merchant-marine industry was willing to go in keeping its "corrupting" subsidy and how far other segments of American life were willing to be corrupted. "Not the least of these influences," said the report, "has been the millions of Government dollars flowing through the hands of the immediate recipients, their associates, affiliates, subsidiaries, holding companies, and allies into the treasuries of newspapers, magazines, and publicity agencies. Evidence before this committee has illustrated the existence and effect of these evil influences."

Because of Senator Black's work,* Congress and the Roosevelt Administration were compelled to think anew about the merchant marine and how best to subsidize it. The fleet could not just be jettisoned. There was an apparent need for merchant ships for defense.

When the First World War began, the United States had been

*Senator Black in 1937 was appointed to the Supreme Court by President Roosevelt.

relying on ships of foreign nations to carry its cargo; suddenly these ships were withdrawn and the United States was without carriers for its products. The situation became worse in 1917 when the United States entered the war and had trouble finding ships to transport its army to Europe. A massive shipbuilding program was begun. The Emergency Fleet Corporation built more than two thousand ships, but most were delivered after the war had ended. The United States had been caught short and was seriously hampered in its war effort because it did not have a shipbuilding capacity that could be expanded immediately to meet the demands of the war.

In the years following the First World War the merchant ships in world trade expanded enough to suggest that problem would not reoccur if another war came. But members of Congress and public officials in 1936, when the present law was written, just two decades after the United States had been caught short by an inadequate merchant marine, did not wish to take that chance. A merchant marine and shipbuilding capacity must be maintained, they believed.

And that is the principal justification for the multimillion-dollar subsidy to the merchant marine. It was written into the 1936 law that the merchant marine act "as a Naval and military auxiliary in time of war or national emergency." It is the justification most often cited by members of the industry and Congressmen friendly to the industry. It is, in fact, the only justification for the subsidy. Of the four standards for government assistance developed throughout America's history, the subsidy to the merchant marine can come under only that of national defense.

The first standard was that of increasing competition. The present merchant-marine program does not increase competition in any way; actually it stifles competition within the industry, discourages its growth and ups the price American producers must pay to ship their goods on American boats.

The second standard was that of filling a need that otherwise would go unfulfilled. The only need the present subsidy fills is

that of keeping money in the pockets of the members of the merchant-marine industry. In the past this standard has applied to
national needs, not to such cynical desires by pressure groups.

The third standard was that of humanitarianism. This does not
fit either. Members of the merchant marine—the sailors, the
builders and the owners—are not crippled, blind, elderly or in any
other way unable to earn a living.

The fourth standard is that of national defense. If the present
subsidy program can be defended as a necessary defense item,
then the merchant marine is not a member of the guaranteed
society. But the subsidy cannot be so defended, as the Vietnamese
war demonstrates.

If the United States enters a full-scale war, the entire merchant-marine fleet would be at the disposal of the United States
government—as it was in World War II and as every other segment
of the economy would be also. But the problem is not one of full-
scale war. By the late 1960s the prospect was for wars such as the
one fought in Vietnam, neither a minor police action nor a full-
scale conflict, serious enough to require some imposition on the
civilian economy but not serious enough to require that the economy be mobilized for war as it was between 1941 and 1945. This is
the new kind of national emergency the country and the merchant
marine faces. And it is in responding to this kind of emergency
that the merchant marine fails.

When the military buildup in Vietnam began in the middle of
1965, the Military Sea Transportation Service—MSTS, the Pentagon agency concerned with transporting soldiers and military
supplies—was faced with finding hundreds of ships to travel an
eight-thousand-mile supply line. At the beginning of the buildup
about 90 percent of all supplies going to Vietnam went on ships.
Two years later the percentage had increased to 98 percent. At
first the MSTS recommissioned some forty ships from its reserve
fleet. These are ships not used except when a military need compels them to be hauled out of their mothball state. Most of these
ships were built during the Second World War, were used again
during the Korean War and had not been used since. They are out-

dated, inefficient, expensive to operate and cost between $400,000 and $500,000 to recommission.

This, of course, was not enough ships. The merchant marine had to be called on. MSTS and the country were in luck. Atlantic and Gulf Coast operators of merchant ships had been hit by a strike, making it impossible for them to use their ships to ply their regular routes. As a result, the shipowners happily chartered their boats to the government. By September 3, 1965, the subsidized shipping companies had chartered fifty-two ships to the federal government for service to Vietnam. In the same period MSTS also chartered forty-three ships from nonsubsidized operators.

After September, however, the MSTS needed even more ships for its ever-increasing supply problem. Not only was there reluctance on the part of the subsidized ship operators to produce more ships; they even began pulling off some of the ships they had chartered to MSTS. What had happened was that the strike had ended and the ship operators wanted to return to their more lucrative regular routes.

"Many of the subsidized operators desperately needed some of the chartered ships in order to re-establish service on their normal trade routes to regain or hold their regular customers," explained the Maritime Administration in a formal statement. The statement continued: "For these reasons, on November 2 [1965], MSTS made an industry-wide solicitation for the charter of additional ships and the renewal of existing charters."

Although MSTS was appealing to ship operators who had received subsidies in the past with the understanding they would be responsive in times of national emergency, the response was poor when the national emergency actually came. By March of 1966 MSTS had thirty-two subsidized ships and eighty-nine nonsubsidized ships in its service. That is twenty fewer subsidized ships than it had in service the previous September and slightly above double the number of nonsubsidized ships. That decrease in the number of subsidized ships available to MSTS came at a time when shipping needs to Vietnam were increasing, not decreasing. Although they had accepted the subsidies in the past in the name of national defense, the subsidized operators showed themselves more responsive to the lure of personal profit than to national defense needs. They were corporate draft dodgers.

With the merchant marine refusing to respond to its nation's call, MSTS had to rely more and more on recommissioning ships from its reserve fleet. Within one year, from July 1965 to July 1966, 101 ships had been recommissioned. It was a remarkable feat. The ships were more than twenty years old and had been laid up for ten years. They were reactivated in an average time period of twenty-one days. They went immediately from reactivation to sailing across the Pacific Ocean. The ocean crossings served as their "shakedown" cruises. Any difficulties—and some always showed up during the first several weeks at sea—were fixed en route. These reserve ships—familiar in World War II as "Victory" ships—served creditably.

The need for an adequate sealift will always be part of America's military needs. The cost of shipping to Vietnam demonstrates why. To sealift a ton of goods to Vietnam costs $30. To airlift a ton of goods to Vietnam costs $400 if the airplane is the most modern and efficient. New and larger cargo planes scheduled for production in the late 1960s will lower the disparity in shipping costs but still will not equalize costs. Airlift is faster, three days compared to almost three weeks for the boat trip. But this is not a crucial factor once a regular shipping schedule has been established. Despite this need, however, there is no indication that the subsidized fleet will change its position in the future and be available for defense purposes in brushfire wars.

The merchant marine does not accept that it is at fault or derelict. Early in the Vietnam buildup, when criticism of the merchant marine's role was first being voiced, the industry took the offensive, attempting to shift the blame to Defense Secretary McNamara and his aides. Representative Edward A. Garmatz, Democrat of Maryland, then acting chairman of the House Merchant Marine Committee, stated the industry's position in a letter to Secretary McNamara. The letter, which the Congressman made available to the press, criticized the Pentagon for not having "a concise maritime logistics plan to support armed forces." To the argument that the merchant marine was not responding to the Pentagon's call for ships, Representative Garmatz countered that the Pentagon was not making full use of those ships available and that there were lengthy delays at Saigon in unloading the ships.

When the buildup began in Saigon there were problems and delays. These are always inherent in any sudden step-up of military activity. But they were not all due to the military or to the congestion at Saigon. Some of them were due to the merchant marine. When Robert Baldwin became Under Secretary of the Navy, one of his first jobs was to see if he could untie the logistics knots in the supplies going to Saigon. "After a trip to Southeast Asia in December of 1965," he has said, "I was convinced that one of the most forward steps we could take to alleviate our port congestion problems was to engage the service of fully self-sustained container ships." He is speaking here of the concept known as "containerization."

Containerization means simply packing goods in quantity before shipping. The product is packed at its point of manufacture into freight or truck cars. These cars are shipped to the boat, loaded, then unloaded at the port of destination, and then finally the cars are sent to their final stop, either by truck or by railroad. It differs from the traditional means of shipping goods in which the product is loaded onto a truck at the factory, taken off the truck at the dock, placed on the ship, taken off the ship, then loaded into another truck, then finally carried to its destination. By eliminating a few steps, considerable amounts of money and time can be saved.

The Matson Lines, operating out of Hawaii, was the first of the large shipping lines to develop containerization as a serious policy. The company never has released its savings figures, considering such information proprietary. But in late 1965, W. R. Starr, a vice-president of the company, gave a talk in which he used some statistics that suggest the tremendous savings involved. First he defined containerization as "a trucking service from the Pacific Coast to Honolulu and back, using the ocean exactly as a highway is used." He then explained that the average round-trip voyage time of a conventional ship is twenty-eight to thirty-five days. For a container ship, the average is fourteen to sixteen days. The savings in time is because of the savings in loading and unloading the ship. "To discharge this tonnage for a conventional ship would require about eleven thousand longshore man hours and five days of port time for the vessel," said Mr. Starr. "The *Monarch* [a ship equipped for containerization] can be discharged with 355 man hours and only eleven hours of port time." Matson does not receive a federal subsidy. It had to develop containerization if it wanted to survive economically. It has survived—and very handsomely too.

Such savings in time and money are always important in commercial shipping. Such savings, particularly the time saved, in the early days of the Vietnam war were crucial. But what happened when Under Secretary Baldwin suggested that containerization be adapted for use in Vietnam?

"When the Navy proceeded to accomplish this goal," he said, "it brought violent opposition. Not only were maritime groups vocal in their objections, but their opposition took the form of vitriolic letters and telegrams."

Despite this opposition, the Navy continued examining the concept. "The more we studied the potentials of the container service, the more attractive its use became, and even those who were skeptical in the military eventually became my staunchest supporters," said Mr. Baldwin. "The initial service to Okinawa has been an outstanding success and subsequent voyages have improved beyond our initial goals and have complemented our other cargo operations. We are now engaged in extending this service to additional ports and are encouraging operators to obtain additional container vessels. . . . Now I recognize that container vessels are not a panacea for all port problems. . . . The point I want to make with this example is simple. The Navy did not invent containerized service. The maritime industry did and its usefulness in this war is great. But rather than grasping the opportunity to use this innovation to present the image of a forward-looking industry by pressing for its immediate use, a defensive stand was taken."

There is not much mystery to why the industry opposed

containerization. The system is more efficient. That means it requires fewer men on the docks and on the ships to load and unload goods. That appears to mean fewer jobs. Of course, if prices of loading those goods could be reduced to bring American ships more in competition with foreign ships, there would be a greater demand for American ships and more, not fewer, jobs. Also, not all merchant ships are equipped to handle containerization, meaning that some shiplines might have been inconvenienced. The merchant marine had then received a total of more than $3 billion in subsidies from the American government, had been kept afloat only by the taxpayers. But at the time of the Vietnam war it was concerned as much as possible—perhaps only—with making the most profit it could.

This was emphasized by Defense Secretary McNamara when he appeared before a Congressional committee early in 1967. He was speaking then with eighteen months experience in shipping large quantities of supplies and men to Vietnam. "There is," said the Secretary, "a firm requirement for reliable, responsive sealift augmentation for a wide range of limited war situations, a requirement which the present subsidized U.S. liner fleet, for various reasons, has not met."

The Secretary re-emphasized the statistics of the merchant marine's poor showing in the Vietnam war. In July, August and September of 1966, military shipping had increased by 165 percent over the same three months in the previous year. "However," Secretary McNamara said, "only about a third of the increase was obtained from the U.S. liner fleet, both subsidized and unsubsidized." And even those merchant-marine ships that were made available for defense shipments, he continued, belonged to "the ship operators who had been given preference in carrying peacetime defense cargoes." Not only had they been given preference but, until a short time before the Secretary spoke, those ship operators had negotiated freight rates with the Pentagon rather than compete for contracts. Competition can lower prices. Negotiation guarantees a high price.

"When the heavy demands for sealift to Southeast Asia began to develop," continued the Secretary, "most of the liner operators chose to continue to ply their normal commercial trade routes, and in the July–September 1966 period only 8 percent of the subsidized fleet and something less than 10 percent of the nonsubsidized liner fleet were under charter to MSTS."

To obtain the needed sealift in the Vietnamese war the Defense Department relied on the unsubsidized tramp* fleet (seventy-three tramps, about 70 percent of the United States tramp fleet, by January 1, 1967) and on recommissioning ships from the reserve fleet (153 ships by the beginning of 1967).

Actually, shipping for the Vietnamese war was not the major worry at the Pentagon. "While these resources have successfully met the needs of the present emergency," said Secretary McNamara of the tramp fleet and the ships pulled from the reserve fleet, "they may not all be available in another emergency a decade hence. By 1975 most of the ships in the NDRF [the reserve fleet] will be thirty to thirty-five years old and will require larger expenditures for conversion to assure satisfactory reliability. Moreover, the unsubsidized tramp/irregular fleet will probably have disappeared because its aging World War II vessels cannot be replaced at an economical price."

His statement means that in the future the United States must rely more on the subsidized fleet than it has in the Vietnamese war. But this, the Secretary asserted, "is disturbing not only because of the problem of responsiveness but also because of the cost implications involved. We know from past experience, and we cannot realistically expect it to be otherwise, that unless the operators are assured a good profit, at prices established in a tight market, their ships will not be forthcoming voluntarily in an emergency. This makes the subsidized liner fleet a very costly form of sealift for the Defense Department to hire, just when it needs it most."

The Secretary then reminded the Congressional committee that the merchant marine is subsidized by the taxpayer "on the premise that this shipping is required for potential national security needs. Yet," he continued, "despite this large annual subsidy, virtually all our sealift needs since World War II have been met

*A tramp ship is one that does not sail a regular route but goes, instead, where its cargo dictates.

without requisitioning merchant ships. Moreover, it seems clear that the most likely requirements for sealift augmentation in the future will be associated with limited war situations like Vietnam."

After making those statements, Mr. McNamara began meeting with officials of those merchant-marine lines receiving federal subsidies. The purpose of the meetings was to develop a more assured means of having the merchant marine turn out in times of limited warfare. A plan, dubbed RESPOND, was developed. If it comes into operation as scheduled in fiscal year 1970, it will work this way: Those merchant-marine lines agreeing to provide a certain number of ships during times of national need will be the ones to receive the lucrative Pentagon shipping contracts in peacetime. The interesting point about the plan is that the subsidy question is skipped entirely. The industry still receives the subsidy, and the fiction that the subsidy is necessary to maintain the nation's defense shipping lines continues to be honored by politicians. But with RESPOND the Pentagon has acknowledged that if it wants ships it must find some other way of securing them. It must offer its own peacetime shipping business as bait.

The merchant marine takes money with the understanding that it will come to the nation's assistance when it is needed. But when it is needed, it does not come forth. And the expectation for the future is that it will not come forth.

The industry has been told it cannot have it both ways. In words unusually blunt for a government bureaucrat, James W. Gulick, then acting Maritime Administrator, told a meeting of the industry in October 1966:

> It is all very well to demand a great investment by the government of dollars—and dollars indeed would be very welcome. However, I for one could not in good conscience explain to the rest of the world our abandonment of the fight for freedom, or to our nation's poverty-stricken areas our lack of interest in their plight, nor could I face a G.I. in Vietnam who has just given the best he has to offer and say that our own special interest in this industry requires dollars and we don't care what had to be given up to get them.

But that of course is exactly how the industry does respond. It wants greater subsidies to guarantee its income all around. It objects strenuously when the Defense Department hires foreign-flag ships to carry goods to Vietnam. It objects to having to compete for Pentagon contracts rather than negotiating them with an assured high profit. It objects when the Pentagon seeks other ways to supply its military forces.

As long as the merchant-marine industry can claim it is receiving a subsidy for defense purposes, it is not a member of the guaranteed society. It is, instead, a defense industry. And the nation must and does expect to pay for its defenses. But once that defense justification has been destroyed, as the merchant marine destroyed that justification by its failure to respond in the Vietnamese war, then there is no justification for the subsidy. The merchant marine is a guaranteed industry. It is a member of the guaranteed society.

Two

The aviation industry which pushed the SST is a national industry. The merchant marine is much more localized. One is an elephant; the other a mouse. Yet both succeeded in entering the guaranteed society. Where the aviation industry used a wide-ranging approach, the merchant marine used a much more selective, but no less powerful, approach.

An example of the merchant marine's political power came in 1963 when the Kennedy Administration reached a decision to sell American wheat to the Soviet Union. That decision-making had been an agonizing process. There were political considerations primarily. What would be the public reaction to the federal government blessing and arranging a large business transaction between the United States and its Cold War enemy? Once the decision had been made, however, the political problems disappeared—almost.

Conservative and isolationist sentiment was located primarily in the Midwest, but this was a great wheat-producing area. Any isolationist or anti-Russian sentiment there largely disappeared before the possibility of unloading some wheat and earning a profit. Even the businessmen's organizations, not at all friendly to John F. Kennedy, came out in favor of free enterprise and backed the wheat sale.

The only remaining problem was organized labor. The shipping of the wheat to the Soviet Union would be a big business venture itself, and the maritime unions wanted to be sure they got a share. Other factions in the industry backed the unions; they wanted their share also. As a result the President agreed to the deal only if half of the wheat sold to Russia was shipped on American merchant vessels. These ships are much more expensive to operate than are foreign merchant vessels. Russia balked at paying this higher price. It bought most of its wheat elsewhere and shipped it on lower-cost, non-American vessels. The maritime industry's action in this case is a classic example of how an industry operates in the guaranteed society. Rather than attempt to reduce costs to become competitive, the industry demands that the government guarantee it a profitable business.

Another example of the political muscle of the merchant marine came in 1966. The Johnson Administration determined that the nation's transportation system was in a mess. The highways were choked. Air lanes were crowded. Only the sea lanes were empty. The first step to end the hodgepodge, said the Administration, was to create a Department of Transportation. "Vital as it is, mammoth and complex as it has become, the American transportation system," said President Johnson, "is not good enough." He continued: "I urge the creation of such a [Transportation] Department to serve the growing demands of this great nation, to satisfy the needs of our expanding industry and to fulfill the right of our taxpayers to maximum efficiency and frugality in government operations."

The proposed department would oversee every federal transportation agency. It would employ 100,000 persons and spend $6 billion a year. It would watch over aviation, highway construction, railroad safety, the regulation of barge lines and the merchant marine—every means of commercial transportation. But when the legislation authorizing the establishment of the department passed Congress, the merchant marine was excluded from its authority. Every other means of transportation was pulled into the new department. But not the merchant marine.

The industry had worked very hard to have itself exempted from the new department. Why?

The merchant marine was one of the first industries to develop what has since become a standard device for industries dealing with Washington—a subgovernment. Congress is too big an organization and its work too complex and diversified for every member to understand every bill that comes before it. Because of this, committees study matters, formulate legislation and watch over its enforcement. When members of Congress friendly to a particular industry achieve a position in Congress where they can have an impact on that industry, then that industry's future is secured. When the aviation industry followed this path to come to the SST, it was only using a technique developed earlier by the merchant marine.

Although Senator Black, for example, had investigated the industry and exposed the corruption within it during the 1930s, his was not the pertinent committee for the drafting of remedial legislation. This was done by the Senate Commerce Committee and the House Merchant Marine and Fisheries Committee. Over the years members of Congress from Congressional districts or states with considerable shipbuilding assets and with the ports where the merchant ships docked joined these committees—and still do, of course. The result: The committees were stacked with friends of the merchant marine.

The most essential ingredient in the 1936 maritime law was its labyrinthine quality. This is the second essential feature of a subgovernment—developing a complicated law that only an experienced bureaucracy is able to administer. This is a protection against interference from the top. At any time if someone is appointed to head the Maritime Administration with hopes of reforming the system, his problem will be grasping hold of the

MERCHANT MARINE: THE SUBSIDIZED SAILOR 69

system first. This is almost impossible. Only the experienced civil servants who have been dealing with the law for years really understand it, really appreciate its faults, sense its weaknesses, know where it should be changed. They do not tell if they can help it. In the mid-1960s, when the maritime law was thirty years old, one federal official from outside the bureaucracy called an official within the bureaucracy to ask his opinion of a policy. The second man answered by offering what he believed the Congressional opinion of the policy was, the union attitude, management's ideas. "But no," insisted the first man, "I want to know what you think about it." But the second man had been involved in the bureaucracy too long to have opinions or, at least, to express opinions. He was a member not of the United States government, which is responsive to all the taxpayers, but to the subgovernment of the merchant marine, which is responsive to the industry.

Protection of this subgovernment was the reason behind the merchant marine's fight to have itself exempted from the new Transportation Department. The Maritime Administration had been a member agency of the Commerce Department, but it operated relatively independently. Commerce rarely bothered to exert authority over it. This was fine for the merchant marine. It could continue operating through the subgovernment—a friendly Congressional committee and an obscure and complicated bureaucracy that no outsider could penetrate. But if the Maritime Administration became, instead, an integral part of a large department devoted to solving the problems of transportation, the friendly Congressmen would not have quite as much impact. They would be only one of several groups of Congressmen demanding special favors from the Transportation Department. They would be only one of several groups of Congressmen attempting to dictate to the Transportation Department. The bureaucracy also would be affected. No longer would it be part of a department that did not care what it did. It would be part of a department watching closely everything it did.

"I think the reason for this fear [of the industry being brought under the Transportation Department] is that they know the federal government," said Representative Clarence J. Brown, Jr.,

Republican of Ohio, "just like the grace of the good Lord—what it giveth, it can take away." And then at another point Representative Brown also told the House: "The committee on Merchant Marine and Fisheries, of course, has hit the ceiling on this move because [the committee] would have the Maritime Administration moved away from the executive branch and closer to Congress."

The Congressman had described the situation perfectly. The maritime industry and its representatives in Congress wanted to keep control of the federal subsidies to the merchant marine in the Congress because this would guarantee the continuation of that subsidy. To give greater control of the industry to an executive-branch agency, particularly an agency with power and drive still undetermined, could mean the eventual diminishing of that subsidy, of that guarantee.

To hold onto that guarantee the maritime industry—particularly its labor leaders—engaged in one of the rawest displays of political power Washington had seen in many years.

"In my twenty-four years in Congress," said Representative Chet Holifield, Democrat of California, "I have never before encountered the atmosphere of pressure from lobbyists, such a barrage of distortion of the truth, as has occurred during consideration of the Department of Transportation legislation."

Representative Holifield had been instrumental in writing the legislation to include the merchant marine in the new department. He singled out for criticism Paul Hall, president of the Seafarers Union of North America. Mr. Hall had reportedly charged, Representative Holifield told the House of Representatives, that "this Administration is no good. They don't do what they say they will. Lyndon B. Johnson's word is not worth two cents as far as the maritime end is concerned. I don't think they can be trusted."

Representative Carl Albert of Oklahoma, the Democratic leader in the House and usually sympathetic to the feelings of labor leaders, shook his head sadly. "I could hardly believe my eyes when I read the statement," he said. "It is difficult for me to believe that any person in a responsible position in organized labor would do or say some of the things that have been attributed to Mr. Hall."

Mr. Hall's statements by themselves were not the determining factor in persuading the House of Representatives to exclude the merchant marine from the new department. There were several pressures. The shipbuilders and the shipline operators, working at the subgovernment level, were able to influence some members of the House. But this still was not the key. The proposal to create a Transportation Department including the merchant marine was a proposal by a Democratic Administration to the Democratic-controlled Congress. This meant that one of the usual sources of Democratic political strength would have to get after the House members and urge them to vote "right." The standard sources of political strength for the Democratic Party are minority groups, city political machines, Southerners and organized labor.

The minority groups were not interested either way. The city politicians had more interest. A city like New York, for example, is a major port. Representative John J. Rooney, Democrat of Brooklyn, has many dock workers in his Congressional district. From the chairmanship of the appropriations subcommittee that dispenses money to the merchant marine, he watches over the industry's best interests. He is an important member of the merchant-marine subgovernment. Because of the camaraderie in the House, particularly between members who may need a federal appropriation for a favorite project and a senior member of the Appropriations Committee like Representative Rooney who can vote "aye" for the project, the position of members such as Mr. Rooney on issues like the merchant marine is influential. Southerners also were prone to support the maritime industry; several shipyards are located in the South.

But the most important element was the position taken by organized labor, not just a few maritime unions such as Mr. Hall's but the main body of American labor unions. This is the American Federation of Labor and the Congress of Industrial Organizations—the AFL-CIO—under the leadership of George

Meany. Because of its own internal political problems, it backed the merchant marine in the 1966 fight over whether the merchant marine should be included in the Transportation Department.

Almost since the AFL and the CIO merged in the mid-1950s the federation has been beset by troubles. Mr. Meany, its president, has been under almost continuous attack from within, his position as head of American labor becoming more and more precarious.

The first public crisis came in the late 1950s over charges of union corruption. The result was the expulsion of James R. Hoffa's Teamsters Union from the merged labor federation, at the insistence of the younger union leaders and with Mr. Meany's grudging consent. The next issue was discrimination against Negroes by labor unions. Again Mr. Meany sided with the older union leaders who look upon their unions as the first Henry Ford looked upon his automobile manufacturing business; they run them any damn way they please. The third internal crisis in the merged labor movement came in the mid-1960s when a group of labor leaders, rallying around Walter Reuther of the United Automobile Workers, argued that organized labor should lead in cleaning up the slums, training the culturally deprived and in ending the Cold War. Again Mr. Meany was on the other side, the side that insisted union leaders should do no more than keep their members well paid and their own salaries comfortably high.

To survive politically in these kinds of disputes George Meany needs all the support he can muster within the AFL-CIO. The maritime unions, old hands at this kind of political infighting, give George Meany the backing they can, and that is a great deal. The Maritime Trades Department of the AFL-CIO represents more than five million union members, which is a number greater than one third of the entire membership of the AFL-CIO. All of these members do not actually do work connected with the maritime industry. Only about 500,000 do, and of these, only about 50,000 actually sail on ships. But the other union members have aligned themselves with the maritime unions to promote their unions into a powerful political bloc within the merged labor federation.

In the high councils of the AFL-CIO the maritime unions and

their followers are with George Meany, always have been, probably will be for many years. They shun the other labor leaders who sound as if they want to transform the labor-union movement into an outfit of social workers; they speak against them; they vote against them. And the payoff for them is the formal support of the AFL-CIO for the maritime union members' entry into the guaranteed society. At the time of the proposed Russian wheat sale in 1963 it was George Meany who insisted to the White House that half the wheat sold go on American ships. And when formation of the Transportation Department was before Congress it was the merged labor federation, not only the maritime unions, that lobbied among Democratic members of the House to exempt the merchant marine. One House member from the Midwest, where a ship larger than a rowboat seldom is seen, tells of a head of a bricklayers' local coming to see him. "Vote to exempt the Maritime Administration from the Transportation Department," said the bricklayer. "Okay," replied the Congressman, who did not consider the issue one worth making a fight over. "But, tell me," the Congressman, his curiosity aroused, asked, "why?" The union leader shot back: "Don't worry about 'why,' just vote to exempt." And if there were any questions among the Democratic members as to where the AFL-CIO stood, on the day of the vote George Meany sent each House member a telegram asking him to vote to exempt.

The vote came on August 30, 1966. Representative Edward Garmatz formally offered a motion to exclude the merchant marine from the Transportation Department then under consideration. Mr. Garmatz's Congressional district is Baltimore, both a port and a shipbuilding city. By this time he also was chairman of the House Merchant Marine Committee. He is a significant member of the subgovernment. His successful move was supported by 150 Democrats and opposed by only 106. Enough Democrats had reneged on their President to exempt the merchant marine from the Transportation Department.

In fairness to those Democrats, it should be pointed out that the Administration did not appear greatly interested in the issue. The Johnson Administration had asked that the merchant marine be included in the new Transportation Department. But as soon as the maritime industry made known its opposition, the Administration made no serious effort to push its request through to law. The Johnson Administration apparently felt, as other Administrations before it have felt, that the merchant marine is not worth making a fight over. The Presidency is a political power, and the President must be careful of the causes in which he expends his political power. Should he use up some of that power on the merchant marine? Less than one half of one percent of the federal budget is involved. The call for reform has no public support; the public is unaware of the issue. So reform of the merchant marine was dropped by default.

The industry knew it would be. Back in 1965 when an Administration committee had produced some proposals for changing the maritime subsidies—proposals that might have eased the industry out of the guaranteed society—the Administration quickly assured the merchant marine there was no cause to worry. Vice President Hubert H. Humphrey appeared before a conference organized by the International Brotherhood of Boilermakers, Iron Ship Builders, Blacksmiths, Forgers and Helpers. The intent of the conference had been to build up pressure for increased federal subsidies to American shipyards. The first thing the Vice President did was tell his audience not to worry about any Administration proposals the industry did not like.

"In my legislative experience," said the Vice President, "I learned that there are always adjustments and compromises." Then he proceeded to make clear that it will be the Administration "adjusting" and "compromising." He said that "when we get through with a bill up on the Hill [in Congress], sometimes we are just happy to have our name left on it." In case any doubts remained, the Vice President assured the conference he was in favor of more ships, not fewer. "I don't see any reason," he said, "why every port in the world should not get a view of an American ship. This is the real voice of America." To his audience, his words had only one meaning, the correct one: more subsidies.

With this background it is not surprising that the maritime unions felt powerful when the issue did reach the House floor the next year. In their display of power then the merchant-marine unions were little concerned with the fate of organized labor. Any record a member of Congress had made prior to the fight on the Transportation Department was ignored. The labor movement's friends of long standing were browbeaten as well as labor's enemies. One member of the House threatened by the maritime unions with political extinction was Thomas L. Ashley, Democrat of Ohio. When he heard during the House debate that Paul Hall had so threatened him, Representative Ashley commented, "If this were not so patently arrogant, I would be constrained to laugh." For Representative Ashley there was an amusing touch because, as he told the House, "It was only two years ago that my Republican opponent made the point, day in and day out during the campaign, that I was one of the few members of Congress to have a 100 percent right-for-labor voting record."

It was in 1966, then, that the merchant marine sailed into the guaranteed society. Its only justification for a subsidy—that the merchant marine would come to the defense of its country—was proving a fraud. The subsidized fleet was not responding to its nation's call. And in that year an attempt to bring some order to the industry by incorporating it into the Transportation Department failed because of a raw display of political power.

For the American public the entry of the merchant marine into the guaranteed society may be worse than the entry of the SST. The SST at least will go faster than the airplanes of the 1960s. But the guarantees to the merchant marine buy only vessels that go as slow as the ships of the 1950s and before.

Three

The merchant marine claims it cannot exist as a free-enterprise industry. The best argument from the industry on this point comes from Edwin Hood of the Shipbuilders Council. Speaking in

1967 on the subject of "Putting the Maritime Problem in Clear Perspective," he said:

> Practically all of our industries which are successful in world markets owe their success to one of two reasons, both of which relate to superior technology.
>
> In the first category are industries which have a technology superiority paid for by the federal government through massive research efforts. This has been particularly relevant to the progress of the aerospace and electronic industries. The anticipated federal fiscal 1968 appropriation for design of the commercial supersonic transport aircraft is $200 million to $250 million and this amount is merely the first increment of a multibillion-dollar research and development project.
>
> The second category includes those industries which owe their technological advantage to the tremendous consumer purchasing power of our citizenry, such as the automotive and chemical industries. Nearly the same number of automobiles are stolen each year in the United States as exist in Russia; annual production here equals the total number of automobiles in all of England.

It is true, as Mr. Hood says, that the maritime industry enjoys neither the advantage of massive federal financing of technology nor the attraction of a mass market. But it is not true that the industry must exist on federal handouts as a member of the guaranteed society.

The merchant marine receives three different kinds of subsidies. They are the operating, the ship construction and the cargo preference subsidies. The first two are written into the 1936 law. The third subsidy, cargo preference, developed in the post-World War years. It is these subsidies that total approximately $400 million a year.

When the first two subsidies were written into the law, two justifications were offered. One was defense, the responsibility that the subsidized merchant marine avoided when the Vietnamese war came. The second was known as the essential-route doctrine. For a ship to be eligible for subsidy it must, among other things, ply a regular route among the international ports, and the Maritime Administration must have some jurisdiction over the choice of those routes.

The purpose behind this doctrine is to assure that means exist to transport American goods to all the markets of the world where they might be sold. In the past the doctrine has been extremely valuable; a manufacturer would not lose a foreign sale because there was no means of transporting his goods. In more recent years the essential-route doctrine has proven less valuable. There are few, if any, ports that are not routinely touched by cargo ships. The number of "flags of convenience" have multiplied so rapidly that a manufacturer does not have to worry about finding a ship to carry his goods. These flags-of-convenience lines usually are shiplines owned by Americans but chartered in other countries to avoid the high costs of operating under a United States charter. Most American manufacturers, in fact, choose to ship their goods on foreign lines because of the cheaper costs.

As a result, the Maritime Administration does not enforce that essential-route doctrine stringently. Either the lines touch all required ports voluntarily or the Administration permits the requirement to lapse. Whichever—and it has been argued without any final determination—the essential-route doctrine does not place an undue hardship on the American merchant marine. The merchant marine, however, continues to receive the operating and ship-construction subsidies.

The operating subsidy runs about $200 million annually. About $40 million of this goes to keep a dozen luxury passenger lines afloat. A passenger on the S.S. *United States,* for example, is paying only approximately half the cost of his transportation. The taxpayers pay the other half. The rationale for this kind of handout is the same used when the prestige argument is raised for the SST—that America's position in the world is somehow enhanced by large and ornate vehicles touching foreign lands. Whether the nation's prestige is so served by such an ostentatious display of wealth, particularly among the economically underdeveloped nations, is an unproven point. "Showing the flag" is a phrase representing a practice that has some value when military ships are involved. It has no value when civilian ships are involved.

The remainder of the operating subsidy goes to keep afloat the three hundred general-cargo merchant ships, which are owned by only fifteen companies and which ply regular routes. These American shiplines are part of international conferences. These conferences, in turn, set the rates charged by all their members in shipping goods by boat between nations. They are little different from cartels. The Joint Economic Committee of the Congress looked into these conferences in 1966 and found that shipping rates were arbitrarily set high. "Cost of service as a measure of the lowest price that could be accorded does not enter the case at all," said the committee's report. "Value of service as a measure of the highest price that can be exacted is the sole relevant criterion." In effect, the federal government is subsidizing the merchant ships so they may be competitive with foreign lines, then the government permits the subsidized American lines to belong to conferences that rule out any competition.

In figuring out the operating subsidy, the United States determines what it costs a foreign line to carry goods between two ports. Then it determines what it costs an American line to carry the same goods between the same two ports. The cost to the American line is greater. The United States government then pays the American line the difference between its cost and the estimated cost for the foreign line. That is the operating subsidy. The impact of the subsidy is that there is no incentive for the American line to become more competitive. Because of the operating subsidy, it does as well financially as the cheaper foreign lines.

The operating subsidy is designed to insure that American ships continue to sail. It is not designed to insure that America's transportation system improves. The subsidy, for example, does not subsidize the cost of fuel. For a ship to go faster, additional fuel is required. But the shipowner must pay for that additional fuel himself; the government will not share the cost. The result: There is no incentive to build or operate faster ships. The industry is guaranteed an income by going slowly. The clipper ships of a century ago went almost as fast—and sometimes even faster— than today's merchant ships. Twenty knots an hour was top speed in the 1860s. It still is. Few industries have had such limited progress.

The operating subsidy pays the salaries of American seamen chiefly. About seventy-two cents of every dollar a seaman earns on an American-subsidized ship is paid by the taxpayers. And of every dollar these seamen pay in dues to their unions, therefore, seventy-two cents is paid by the taxpayers. This money goes to the coffers of the seafaring unions, some of whose officers are among the highest paid union officials in the nation. Joseph Curran of the National Maritime Union, for example, receives more than $80,000 a year.

Subsidizing salaries of seamen so grandly means there is no incentive to mechanize the ships. If the government presses for mechanization to reduce both the cost of transportation and the size of its operating subsidy, the unions resent it and fight the move—as Robert Baldwin found out when he tried introducing containerization in the port of Saigon. The owners of the subsidized shiplines do not care about mechanization. With the taxpayers guaranteeing most of the salaries the owners pay, there is no reason for them to concern themselves with reducing crew size. The shipbuilders do not care either. They are building for a subsidized market. They receive no additional funds for building a better ship, a more efficient ship, a ship less costly to operate. So they do not build such a ship. They are subsidized also, and they have no desire to rock the boat—a boat well guaranteed and subsidized. Never has inefficiency paid off so grandly.

Salaries of merchant seamen sailing American ships, as well as their living conditions, were among the worst in the world—but that was in the 1930s and before. A series of strikes then—hard, bitter, sometimes violent strikes—produced changes. Both the salaries and the living conditions improved. In the mid-1930s a merchant seaman earned slightly less than another American working in industry ashore. The American seaman did earn slightly more in the 1930s than did his European counterpart. Thirty years later the American seaman earned double the salary of an American working in an industry ashore. He earned triple what his European counterpart earned in the mid-1960s.

But the unions are controlled by men who experienced the bitter days of the 1930s and before. They remember them well. These union leaders are kept in power by complicated voting rules which give more voting power to the experienced seaman. And the experienced seaman is the one whose memory also goes back to the turbulent Thirties and the decades before. Other unions also have stormy histories. The coal miners, led by John L. Lewis, fought desperate and dangerous battles for every advance they made. Conditions for them in the 1930s were worse than the conditions experienced by the seamen. The automobile workers in the 1930s waged pitched battles with company police to earn their right to a decent income and safe working conditions. For other unions the story is similar. Yet these unions did not use their experience as arguments against modernization. The coal miners under John L. Lewis adopted a conscious policy of encouraging mechanization—knowing full well it would eventually put them out of work. The automobile workers have not fought mechanization either; they have insisted on the various companies taking measures to soften the economic blow on the worker, an understandable position. But they have not fought progress as the maritime unions have.

To continue receiving this subsidy for cargo ships the merchant-marine industry must—in addition to plying regular trade routes—buy ships built in American shipyards, staff them with American citizens only, supply them with goods of American origin, as well as keep their books by accounting procedures set down by the Maritime Administration. The accounting procedures are a technique of the subgovernment. The procedures are so involved, so much a traditional part of the way the merchant marine operates that no outsider can penetrate their mysteries. The outsider cannot determine if the subsidy system, which hinges on the merchant-marine accountancy procedures, is helping or hurting the industry. Occasionally a student of the merchant marine finds one of the simpler items, such as the government not subsidizing fuel and thus encouraging the merchant marine to go slow. But such discoveries are rare.

The insistence on "buy America" is bad economics. It was written into the 1936 law at a time when the government felt it had to take action to encourage a flagging industry. It has stayed around to a point where it is no longer necessary. The provision of hiring only Americans, for example, might have been a justifiable protective device when there was an overabundance of American seamen, as was true in the 1930s. It has not made economic sense for a long time. The seamen's market has been dwindling, meaning that the prices the ship operators must pay for crews is bid up as the ships compete for American seamen. Of course, this is not a problem for the ship operators. The taxpayers pay most of those salaries, no matter how high they go. What is happening is that every pressure on the ship operator pushes up the cost of shipping on the American merchant marine.

Of all the "buy America" provisions the one that is the most expensive to the industry—most expensive in that it restricts the growth of the industry, encourages it not to modernize—is the provision that requires all merchant ships which receive operating subsidies to be built in American shipyards. A ship built in an American shipyard costs twice as much as a ship built in a foreign shipyard. Also, the recipient of an operating subsidy must—if he is to continue receiving the subsidy—replace his ships as new ones become available.

This could result in a squeeze play on the operators. If they don't use an American-built ship, they lose their operating subsidies. But the purchase price of an American ship would be double that of a foreign ship. Again the taxpayers come to the rescue. They pay slightly over half the cost of building these ships in American yards—the exact amount is 55 percent. This is the ship-construction subsidy. It enables the operators of the subsidized lines to buy American-built ships at the same prices foreign-built ships sell for. It had been running about $100 million a year, enough to subsidize the building of approximately fifteen ships a year. Fifteen new ships a year means that the subsidized fleet of three hundred merchant ships will be replaced every twenty years. But those figures also restrict the size of the subsidized American merchant fleet to only three hundred ships. The construction subsidy is placing a lid on the size of the merchant fleet. This far you can grow, it says, and no farther. This is what Nicholas Johnson meant when he said, "As a result we must ask not 'How much shipping would we like to have?' but 'How much shipping are we willing to subsidize?' "

In the last several years the construction subsidy has risen—

close to $150 million. This increased sum, however, is buying fewer ships, thirteen instead of fifteen. This is because of higher ship-construction costs but more because of the ships being larger and more modern. Still, with only thirteen ships being built each year instead of fifteen, the American merchant fleet will be replaced with new ships every twenty-three years rather than every twenty years. Replacing the fleet means that larger, more modern and faster ships come into use. And this means that goods can be carried on American ships with greater speed and at less cost the faster the fleet is replaced. Building only thirteen ships a year and replacing the entire fleet every twenty-three years means the advancement of the industry is being held back even more.

The industry itself is not terribly concerned. The operators of the shiplines charge the same prices as do the foreign members of the international conferences. Then the federal government pays the difference in the cost between the more expensive American ship and the cheaper foreign ship. The ship-construction industry is not terribly concerned either. The government guarantees that it will have a market for its expensive product. Actually the work done on cargo ships in American shipyards represents less than 10 percent of their total business. Most of their work is done for the Navy. Their worry is not that they may lose an important financial segment of their work but that the federal government may spend more funds on ship construction and this money will not go to the traditional shipyards.

Defense Secretary McNamara, faced in the Vietnamese war with a merchant-marine industry reluctant to produce for the nation's defense as expected, proposed to bypass the ship-construction subsidy. He advocated the building of $40 million floating warehouses that could be stationed in various parts of the world. If a brushfire war broke out, American troops could be immediately flown to the scene of action; their supplies could be pulled from the floating warehouses. The merchant marine has launched a strong campaign against this proposal in Congress. The building of these floating warehouses would not be done by the conventional shipyards. Once they were on station, there would be less demand for merchant seamen and the subsidized ships. This means that one of the justifications for the operating subsidy and the construction subsidy—that the merchant marine is needed in cases of national emergency—would be lessened, endangering the entire subsidy structure. The lobbying effort against the warehouses was successful in the battles of the 1967 and 1968 budgets. The proposals for floating warehouses were again part of the budget in the 1969 document. But there were a couple of changes designed to win acceptance for the concept. The floating warehouses themselves were changed enough in design to make them more likely to be constructed at the subsidized shipyards. Also, the Administration contemplated proposing a massive shipbuilding program—subsidized, of course—in the 1970 budget and beyond. The figure mentioned was a subsidy of $300 million a year. Not only was that increased subsidy supposed to buy industry agreement for the floating warehouses, but it also was to buy consent from the industry for a temporary cutback. To relieve inflationary pressures in 1969, the ship-construction subsidy had been sharply cut, by more than $50 million.

The Administration believed it needed the floating warehouses for national defense. And it believed that it had to take temporary action to relieve inflation. It believed in those two things so strongly that it was willing to buy the industry's support with promises of large subsidies in the future. Nicholas Johnson said the present subsidy program asks, "How much shipping are we willing to subsidize?" The answer seems to be enough to quiet political discontent.

Another worry the ship-construction industry has goes back to the time when Nicholas Johnson was Maritime Administrator. He began making strange noises, noises that also threatened the shipyards. Prior to his tenure, most heads of that agency had been content to oversee its operations, to see that they ran smoothly. But most chose not to rock the subsidized boat. The agency itself was virtually unknown to the public. When Nicholas Johnson was sworn in as Maritime Administrator, in March 1964, most Americans—even most Americans in Washington—were unaware the agency had been without a head for months.

Mr. Johnson, then only twenty-nine years old, had no maritime experience. He joked that among his qualifications for the post was that "I had seen a ship before." His lack of experience, rather than being a drawback, was an asset. He was not committed to any particular aspect of the industry, nor to any particular formula for dealing with it. He had fresh ideas, and those ideas upset the industry.

"Everything has improved [in speed] except ships," he said when he was Maritime Administrator. "Why is this?" he continued. "There is no technological reason why you can't go across water faster than twenty miles an hour. Since the clipper ship, most of the improvements have been relatively slight. . . . Some sailing ships, for sustained periods, could go faster than today's ships."

There has been no fundamental change in the basic design of ships in thousands of years. They have been made larger, sleeker, given new and more powerful means of locomotion—from the oar to the sail to the engine. But ship design itself has remained static. Mr. Johnson asked this question: "In its most basic fundamentals, what is the end result you are trying to achieve?" He answered: "There is a fundamental difference in thinking between those who try to improve ships' hulls and those trying to move ocean cargo competitively."

Nicholas Johnson's interest in moving ocean cargo competitively turned him away from the traditional ship design and the ship-construction subsidy toward the surface-effect ship. Such a ship travels over the water rather than through the water as does the traditional ship. And because it does not need power to displace water, it can move at much greater speed than does the ocean-displacing boat, perhaps five times as fast. Mr. Johnson described the surface-effect ship as a "fantastic achievement that could perhaps make general cargo displacement ships obsolete."

This is exactly what worried the shipyards of America—that the general cargo ships they built would be made obsolete. They were not interested in change. They knew how to build ships, not whatever it was that Nicholas Johnson was talking about. Actually, the kind of expertise required for the research and construction leading to a successful surface-effect ship is a possession not of the shipbuilding industry but of the aircraft and space industry—and continues as an opportunity for that industry, a means for that industry to break out of the guaranteed society if it ever chooses.

Rather than accept Nicholas Johnson's attitude as challenge to do better, the industry accepted his attitude as a reason to have him bounced from his job. Joseph Curran of the National Maritime Union asked President Johnson to fire Nicholas Johnson from his position as Maritime Administrator because the young Johnson had, said Mr. Curran, "a negative approach" to his job. John Rooney of the House Appropriations Committee and the representative of the Brooklyn dock workers commented, "Some of the proposals now being advanced seem to be directed toward the demise of the merchant marine rather than to its promotion."

Early in 1966 there was even a move on in the House to abolish the post of Maritime Administrator, one way of removing Nicholas Johnson when the President refused to oust him.*

The third subsidy the merchant marine receives, after the operating and construction subsidies, is the cargo-preference subsidy. It is a latecomer, but it is still blooming, currently at about $100 million a year. During the Korean war much of America's tramp fleet was occupied carrying goods to Korea. When the war ended there was a sharp drop in the need for tramp ships. President Eisenhower talked of legislation that would directly subsidize the defense nature of the American merchant marine—and that was all. The implication of his words was that the government would subsidize enough of the merchant marine to keep it alive so it could be expanded in case of war or national emergency but that the government would not be concerned with keeping the merchant marine afloat in peacetime.

The industry's friends in Congress reacted quickly. Legislation was introduced requiring almost anything ever made in America to be carried on American ships. The compromise achieved was twofold. First, the old subsidies dating back to 1936—those were the operating and ship-construction subsidies—were left intact. In addition the cargo-preference subsidy was created. This requires

---

*Nicholas Johnson eventually left the Maritime Administration at a time of his own choosing to become a member of the Federal Communications Commission. He and President Johnson are not related.

that one half of all nonmilitary government shipments go on
American tramp ships not otherwise eligible for subsidy. The
announced object of the cargo preference subsidy was to increase
the tramp fleet. Because this guaranteed market existed, so went
the argument, shiplines would contract for and operate the
tramps. A subsidy was necessary because the American tramps cost
more to operate than do the foreign-owned ships. The subsidy in
this case is paid by the agency shipping the goods, such as the
Agriculture Department when it sends Food for Peace shipments
abroad, rather than being administered by the Maritime Administration as are the two other subsidies. The taxpayers, of course,
pay the bill in all three cases.

The merchant marine continues to ride high. After knocking
the Maritime Administration out of the new Transportation
Department in 1966, the industry began a drive to have the
agency separated from the Commerce Department and become an
independent agency, responsible almost entirely to Congress. This
would have removed what little supervision over the agency that
remained. This move was a little too blatant a grasp for power, so
the industry tried another course—and reached its destination.

In the past the executive branch had set spending limits for the
merchant marine, the maximums the subsidies could reach. The
White House then sent these figures to the appropriations committees of the House and Senate, which approved these figures. The
appropriations committees could appropriate less money than the
White House recommended but not more.

Under a proposal approved by the Congress in 1967
the Administration has lost this power. The friendly Senate
Commerce Committee and the even friendlier House Merchant
Marine Committee now set spending maximums. They say how
high the subsidies can go. They present the appropriations committees with a set of figures. This change was approved by both
the House and the Senate with very little discussion. The general
public was barely aware of the change. If it had been, few members of the public would have appreciated the significance. Few
members of Congress cared; they had their own favorite industries

to watch out for. And so the bill became law and the merchant marine slipped even further into the guaranteed society.

There seems to be unanimity among objective observers that the merchant marine cannot continue on its present course. Shortly after becoming Transportation Secretary Alan Boyd told a Congressional committee, "The maritime industry must not be allowed to die and it must not be nationalized. To do nothing would assure the former and to meet everyone's demands would require the latter." Nationalization is, of course, the direct result of the guaranteed society.

When Robert Baldwin spoke to the merchant marine about its image in early October of 1966 he also insisted to the members of the industry: "You cannot be satisfied with a status quo position, for a merchant fleet worthy of this country's support cannot stand on its ability to service a captive market—it must stand on its ability to compete in the markets of the world."

Nicholas Johnson, after his tenure as Maritime Administrator, was not hopeful that changes would be forthcoming. "The program attracts almost no public attention," wrote Mr. Johnson. "The details of governmental maritime aid, and the interrelationship between the numerous government agencies involved, are complex and difficult for outsiders to understand. Turnover among policy personnel has been high; from 1950 to 1965 there were eight Maritime Administrators, seven Secretaries of Commerce and nine Under Secretaries of Commerce for Transportation. And the industry has created and nurtured one of Washington's most powerful subgovernments—lobbyists and friends in and out of Congress and the executive branch."

One person extremely familiar with the merchant-marine industry commented: "The only way you are going to solve the problem is by bringing in new capital and new management. The merchant marine industry today is the product of five generations of incest; sons and sons-in-law inherit firms. The industry has never known anything but subsidized shipping."

That the whole present system adds up to hurting America's transportation system, including the merchant marine; that it degrades the political process; that it turns organized labor's political friends away from it; that it creates skepticism, if not downright disbelief, in the free-enterprise system—all this strikes the merchant-marine industry as beside the point. All that is important to the industry is that the government system of subsidy guarantees high wages to the men who sail the ships, good profits to the companies that operate and build the ships. A genuine free-enterprise system might offer more income, greater profit. But it also includes some risk, and risk is something alien to the members of the guaranteed society.

The industry and its friends do not accept that indictment. During the Second World War, Admiral Emory S. Land had been in charge of the merchant marine and he continues through the years as one of its staunchest allies. "We have subsidized most of our civilian activities, the most expensive at the moment is space," he said in October 1966. "Why should the merchant marine and shipbuilding be the whipping boy?"

And that is a favorite theme of the maritime industry. When anyone suggests cutting back on the subsidy or hints the subsidy is not earned, the merchant marine cries it is being flogged unfairly. In 1965 Edwin Hood of the Shipbuilders Council of America said: "I have never been able to understand why it is that our shipbuilding industry is a favorite whipping boy—a favorite target for elimination. No such attitudes exist, to my knowledge, with respect to the procurement of foreign-made space vehicles or missiles—or with respect to foreign-made military aircraft for our defense establishment. What is the differentiation? So long as the national interest is served, there should be none."

Mr. Hood answered his own question when he said, "So long as the national interest is served."

OIL SHALE: 3
Gushing Dollars

One

THE SUPERSONIC TRANSPORT belongs in the guaranteed society because it violates the traditional standards by which subsidies are measured. There is great doubt about its need. There is little doubt that it will destroy competition by handing a monopoly to one or two companies. And its underlying motivation is to bolster a dying industry rather than widen opportunity for an industry.

The merchant marine also joins the guaranteed society. The national defense was the justification for it to receive a subsidy. But once the maritime industry refused to respond to the nation's defense needs, the necessity for hundreds of millions of dollars in subsidy to the merchant-marine industry fades. Certainly the subsidy does nothing to foster competition. Also it violates, as does the SST, the standard that federal aid should widen an industry's opportunity, not guarantee that industry's future.

For the same reasons, the oil-shale industry as it is developing is a candidate for the guaranteed society. Again opportunity will be decreased rather than increased. Competition will be discouraged. National defense is not a justification. And while it is acknowledged that some federal action is necessary, a very good case can be made that the course chosen by the government is the wrong course.

Compared to oil shale, however, the SST and the merchant marine are penny-ante stuff. Instead of hundreds of millions of dollars being involved, as with the merchant marine, or the several billions the SST will cost the taxpayers, there are, with oil shale, *hundreds of billions* of dollars, even trillions of dollars, at stake.

Shale is a rock. In that rock is oil. The federal government owns so much of this shale that its value is staggering. More money is involved than people realize exists. More money is involved than perhaps does exist. As a minimum the value of the oil shale is enough to give every one of the 200 million Americans a grant of $25,000. To use another example, Senator Philip Hart of Michigan has said, "The value of this oil shale at present rates is enough to pay off our national debt and present a check of at least $11,000 to every man, woman and child in the United States." At the time he made that estimate, in the spring of 1967, the national debt stood at about $330 billion, and giving $11,000 to each person in the United States would have cost an additional $2.2 trillion.

"It is hard to realize the magnitude of this resource," Secretary of the Interior Stewart L. Udall has said. "This is a great natural resource..." he continued, "and it can certainly be, when one looks ahead two or three hundred years—as we have to in the conservation field—probably the greatest national asset we have, in terms of energy and raw materials."

As the Secretary's words suggest, the importance of the oil shale may be far greater than its cash value. It may very well be the source of the nation's fuel and energy for the next several hundred years. And the decisions being made now will determine how that source is used in the future.

"Competition here is of vital concern to every consumer in the country," Senator Hart has observed. "How much competition is injected into the oil-shale development will be reflected in consumer prices for the next hundred years. Not only the obvious products will be influenced—such as the cost of heat and light for homes and gas for cars—but thousands of items being developed by the rapidly growing petro-chemical industry, including clothes and household furnishings."

But oil shale will not be a competitive industry. Because of decisions made by the federal government it will be a member of the guaranteed society—a society in which competition and the benefits of competition are strangers.

It was about a hundred years or so ago that a settler, as the story is told in northwest Colorado, decided to build himself a home in the multicolored mountains of that state. White rocks he found at the side of the Piceance Creek would make, he thought, a dramatic-looking fireplace. They made a more dramatic looking fireplace than that unnamed settler anticipated. When the cabin with its fireplace was finished, the settler built up the logs in his fireplace, lit a match and then watched dumbfounded as the logs, fireplace and finally the cabin all burned down. Those white rocks with which he had built the fireplace were the first clues leading to the discovery of the Green River oil-shale formation.

The Green River forms in western Wyoming, snakes south to the northeastern tip of Utah, where it cuts to the east; gorging its way into Colorado, it joins up with a number of small creeks before finally turning west again to run south through Utah. Where the three states meet, tied together by the Green River, are 16,000 square miles of land containing the largest known concentration of hydrocarbons in the world. Formed forty million to sixty million years ago, this region contains enough oil to supply all America's needs, at the nation's present rate of consumption of three billion barrels a year, for the next 866 years.

Oil shale is a popularly accepted phrase describing marlstones. They are brittle, lightweight stones that are weathered white on the outside but brown inside. They contain kerogen. This, in turn, is a bituminous matter from which the oil is manufactured. Some of the oil shale is a thousand feet in depth. Some of it juts abruptly from the surface of the land, its riches crying to be taken. Other shale is hidden by a thousand feet of covering earth. Still, its presence is no secret.

The most profitable oil shale is considered to yield a minimum twenty-five gallons of oil for each ton of shale mined, but some of this shale yields a maximum of one hundred gallons. In the Green River formation there is enough of this top-grade oil shale to yield 600 billion barrels of oil. A barrel is the equivalent of forty-two gallons of oil. The second grade of oil shale, not as profitable but still worthwhile, produces ten to twenty-five gallons of oil for each ton of shale mined. In the Green River formation is enough second-grade oil shale to produce 2,000 billion barrels of oil. In some parts of this formation a single 5,120-acre plot contains eighteen billion barrels of oil. That is equal to more than half of all the oil reserves known to exist in the United States from other sources. So there cannot be much argument with Secretary Udall's statement that this region may be "probably the greatest national asset we have, in terms of energy and raw materials."

The problem is, of course, to extract the kerogen from the shale and transform it into usable oil and to do it economically. At the present time and for many years to come, economically means producing the oil at a cost cheaper than, or certainly no more expensive than, producing oil by the more conventional methods, such as wells in the ground.

Mining of oil shale is not a new concept. The industry was developed in Europe in the last century, and shale has been mined in Europe, Africa, Australia and Asia. The nations that sought to produce oil from shale were those that could not get oil from regular wells, or, if the oil was available from regular wells, then its cost was so high, perhaps because of transportation costs, that it was cheaper to mine shale. The Geological Survey, an agency of the Department of the Interior, estimates that between 1850 and

1961 approximately 400 million barrels of oil had been mined from shale in various places around the world. The principal producers had been Scotland, Estonia and Manchuria. In the early 1960s Scotland and Sweden closed down oil-shale industries that were producing between 500,000 and 750,000 barrels of oil a year. At least as late as 1965 it was believed that Manchuria had an oil-shale industry turning out forty thousand barrels of oil a day.

In the United States, however, production of oil from shale has been a neglected industry. The nation appeared rich in underground and offshore pools that could be reached by conventional wells. Oil was readily available from Mideast and Latin American sources. Also—and this is the most important point in this story of the guaranteed society's hottest prospect—most of the land containing the rich shale is owned by the United States government. Eighty to 85 percent of the recoverable oil is located on government land. The remaining 15 percent is located in privately owned land.

Even this 15 percent in private ownership is so valuable that it contains an estimated 200 billion barrels of oil. Large oil companies alone own about 170,000 acres known to contain about thirty-one billion barrels of oil. That is enough oil to supply America's needs for ten years, at present rates for consumption. How these private owners develop this fabulous wealth is, of course, their business. They can ignore it, promote it, sit on it, rush it, research it. It is their land and it is their choice.

But the future of the larger section of land, containing the 85 percent of the oil which is owned by the federal government, is not a question for private industry. This land belongs to the federal government, meaning its benefits should accrue to all the American people, not to a few people. How this land is developed is a matter of public policy.

Public policy is expressed through laws enacted by Congress and signed by the President or through regulations developed by the bureaucracy in Washington. The first law governing the Green River formation was a mining law enacted in 1872. This law enabled a prospector to pay a small sum and gain the rights to mine all minerals in a designated tract of land. In 1920, however, the law was changed. To mine oil shale, said the new law, a prospector must agree to pay a royalty to the federal government on each barrel of oil produced from the shale. With this law the government was making certain it would not give away its riches too cheaply.

The oil industry did not protest that 1920 action seriously. The oil industry then was still very much the wildcatters who struck it rich in Texas and Oklahoma. The pools of oil beneath the ground they tapped seemed bottomless. The problem for them was not finding new sources of oil such as shale but changing the government's attitude toward the industry. And the 1920s were the years when the industry persuaded the federal government to give the oil companies their biggest tax breaks. In 1930 President Herbert Hoover closed off the oil-shale land to further development. Again there was not a great deal of interest at the time. The cost of extracting oil from shale continued too exorbitant, when compared to the cost of extracting oil from underground pools, for private industry to be interested.

Up until 1944 there was hardly any serious experimentation with extracting processes or with retortings. (Retorting is the process of removing the kerogen from the extracted shale.) During the Second World War, however, the government became concerned over a possible shortage of oil; the war had closed down regular foreign sources. Oil from shale was a long-shot possibility as an alternate source. No one anticipated that a process of producing oil from shale could be developed before the war's end. It was assumed that the lead time—the time from the birth of an idea to the working of an industry—would be too long. But there was concern for the future, concern that another war might catch the United States without adequate oil supplies. In 1944 the Bureau of Mines, another Department of the Interior agency, opened up an experimental plant at Anvil Points, near the community of Rifle in Colorado. Its cost was $17 million.

The object of the plant was to develop an inexpensive extraction and retorting method, and then to make that method available to private industry. This was in line with the government's approach that it was not supposed to be in the mining business. It owned the land. It would lease the land. It would collect a royalty. It would also watch over the development of this publicly owned resource to see that the public interest was best served.

During the 1950s, however, interest in shale oil diminished. The oil companies were not concerned. They visualized oil from shale more as competition for them rather than as an opportunity. In 1954 the Interior Department asked the National Petroleum Council, representing private industry, for an opinion on the future of the Bureau of Mines plant at Rifle. The council answered that the work on oil shale at Rifle "should be discontinued at present and that the facilities now on the site be maintained in a standby condition." That is just about what happened.

By the 1960s, however, there was a sharp change. The oil companies began to realize that their domestic reserves would eventually come to an end. They had always figured the United States would run out of oil from conventional sources by the next century. The next century, always before so far away, had moved much closer. It was within the lifetime of many of the young executives within the oil industry. Also there was a change in the Interior Department. Secretary Udall has come under much criticism for the subsequent role he played in the oil-shale program and will certainly come in for more. Still, he recognized that the problem existed and attempted to solve it. He did not believe in ignoring challenges, although he sometimes did attempt to obscure them, as his predecessors in the 1950s had done.

The plant at Rifle was reopened. It is being operated by the Colorado School of Mines Research Foundation with support from six oil companies—Socony Mobil, Humble Oil and Refining, Pan American Petroleum, Sinclair Oil and Gas, Phillips Petroleum and Continental Oil. In 1964 a group of private companies opened their own experimental plant. That plant now is being managed by the Oil Shale Corporation of America (TOSCO). After decades of neglect, oil shale has become a very attractive commodity.

Now the major questions are when the oil-shale industry will come and how big it will be. The Denver Research Institute estimates that one million barrels a day will be produced from oil shale within eleven years of construction of the first commercial plant. The Bureau of Mines predicts, "There will be an oil-shale industry within ten years."

There still is another question. Is the public interest going to be protected?

The oil industry wants to lock up the future development of this land and this resource. The industry wants the future of this publicly owned resource and its role in developing and profiting from this resource guaranteed. The days of the wildcatters are over. The days of the guaranteed society are here.

Following tradition, the publicly owned lands will be leased to private industry for commercial exploitation. There is no dispute over that. No one suggests the federal government itself mine the shale. The dispute, instead, revolves around this question: Should research and development leases be granted to private industry or should the federal government do the research and development itself and then make the results available to the oil industry? How that question is answered will determine how the oil-shale industry is developed, if the public will be protected.

The dispute first became a matter of public knowledge in 1965. Secretary Udall had appointed a six-man committee to study the various policy aspects of the oil-shale problem and report to him. This advisory group had an interesting makeup. There was Orlo Childs, head of the Colorado School of Mines; H. Byron Mock of Salt Lake City, a former Interior Department official; and Milo R. Perkins of Tucson, a former New Dealer. From the very beginning it was believed these men were friendly to the oil industry and their views would coincide with the industry's—let industry take over this public land to develop this resource and keep the federal government out of it.

On the other side were John Kenneth Galbraith, the former diplomat, Harvard economist, New Frontiersman and popular writer; and Benjamin V. Cohen, one of the chief architects of the New Deal. Again from the very beginning, they were expected to argue for a government involvement. The sixth member was Joseph L. Fisher, who is president of Resources for the Future, a serious and respected organization concerned with the quality of American life in its coming years. It was not, however, expected he would go along with Cohen and Galbraith. The expectation, from the beginning, was that the committee was stacked in favor of the industry.

Nobody was disappointed.

The first three—Perkins, Mock and Childs—argued for the oil industry dictating the future of this resource. Otherwise, the three men claimed, the industry could not be expected to invest its money, its time and energy if it did not have a guarantee of what the future held.

Galbraith and Cohen, on the other side, argued that the big oil companies suddenly were interested in oil shale not because they wanted to develop the industry but because they wanted to control the land and then dominate the oil-shale industry that would grow from that land. Galbraith and Cohen's plan was to have the government do the necessary research and development, then turn over its results to all oil companies. This would prevent a few big oil companies from controlling the industry. This would insure more competition, they argued, if offer fewer guarantees to the big oil companies.

Mr. Fisher, as expected, was in between. He advocated leases to private industry for research and development with the prospect that those limited leases could eventually be expanded into commercial arrangements.

The arguments involved in that report and in the fight that led to the final decision are another illustration of how an industry joins the guaranteed society, why the Congress and the Administration goes along, how the public loses and also why the public is so ill-informed.

Galbraith and Cohen were most concerned that the government would be taken for a ride. They pointed out: "The cost of development is unknown. The cost of production is unknown. The recoverable value of oil in the land offered for lease is imperfectly known.

"Given these unknowns," they continued, "the government would be offering a subsidy of unknown value for a development of unknown cost promising a return of unknown amount. This amounts to dispersing public property while wearing multiple blindfolds. It would be justified, if at all, only by the absence of orderly procedures or the need for greatest haste. Neither justification exists."

Galbraith and Cohen are not alone in their concern. A couple of years after their report, Charles H. Stoddard, who had headed the Bureau of Land Management within the Interior Department when the oil-shale decisions were being made, wrote a letter to Senator Hart. Mr. Stoddard's job at Interior had been to watch over all publicly owned lands, including those in the Green River formation, to make certain they were not abused. Permitting the oil companies to take over leases in the Green River area, he believed, would be an abuse. In his letter, which was made part of the record of Senator Hart's antimonopoly subcommittee, Mr. Stoddard posed many of the problems pointed up previously by Galbraith and Cohen.

Once these problems had been solved, Mr. Stoddard said, "then the leasing policy can be developed and plans for overall development of all the resources prepared." He then warned: "To commit large areas in the heart of the richer areas through rights to specific acreage for commercial development tied to research and development leases or contracts would be a mistake."

These unresolved problems involve several specific areas, and they demonstrate how much is at stake for the public.

The first unresolved problem concerns the presence in the shale of other minerals in addition to oil. The principal one is dawsonite. This is a rare mineral containing aluminum and is found in varying amounts in the oil shale. Its presence and its potential as a source of aluminum is important because less than 15 percent of the United States' aluminum requirements are produced domestically. Still, there is a suspicion that the interest in dawsonite is really a cover to grab the oil shale. There are several reasons for this suspicion. First, no one yet has figured out how to remove the dawsonite from the shale at any kind of reasonable cost. The Bureau of Mines and several aluminum companies, including Kaiser

Aluminum, have started research work. But that work is only beginning.

The second and more important cause for suspicion existing is the sudden interest in dawsonite by the oil companies. The oil could not be removed from the shale under the 1930 order of President Hoover closing those lands for development of oil. However, the dawsonite in the shale could be mined under the 1872 mining law. The prospecting company simply stakes a claim and pays a small fee: $2.50 an acre. There are no other charges; there is no royalty payable to the federal government. It is impossible to remove the dawsonite from the shale without removing the oil also. Secretary Udall has conceded that "for the most part dawsonite and nahcolite exist as an integral part of oil-shale deposits; they cannot be removed without removing the shale." So a company with a claim to mine dawsonite could legally mine the oil—or could it?

No one in the Interior Department was quite certain. "The claims based on presence of dawsonite must be resolved before the oil-shale resources can be made available for extensive development," Secretary Udall conceded to a Senate committee. A number of companies and individuals seemed, however, to believe they could. In the mid-1960s thousands of claims were filed on the oil-shale lands, ostensibly for the purpose of mining dawsonite. The exact number is in dispute. This dispute arises because different people use different boundaries when counting claims and, more importantly, because the Interior Department always has been short of a central repository for information on claims filed on public land. Such claims are filed with local officials.

According to a Bureau of Mines paper issued in December of 1966, "About forty thousand claims on this mineral have been made in only a very short period of time." Two months later, when Secretary Udall was appearing before the Senate Interior Committee, he reported: "It is thought by many that the oil-shale lands, although withdrawn, are open for location of deposits of metalliferous minerals under the mining law of 1872. A very large number of claims estimated to exceed seven thousand have been filed in the last few months for dawsonite—on the theory the aluminum in dawsonite is locatable."

In April 1967 Edward Weinberg, then deputy solicitor for the Interior Department, was appearing before Senator Hart's antimonopoly subcommittee. Mr. Weinberg estimated that ten thousand claims covering approximately 1.4 million acres had been filed. These claims could have been filed anytime since a change in the law in 1954, said Mr. Weinberg, but "no claims were located until the spring of 1966." Appearing with Mr. Weinberg was Robert Mesch, an Interior Department official from Denver. He said the claims of which Mr. Weinberg spoke "generally cover the interior of the Basin."

"So this is where . . .?" asked Senator Hart.

"The thickest deposits of oil shale are found," said Mr. Mesch, continuing the Senator's thought.

According to Mr. Weinberg, "The recent flurry of location activity [claim filing] appears to have been instituted and controlled by a relatively small number of parties, some sixty to seventy. . . . In some instances the locations were undoubtedly made in an attempt to obtain an interest in the dawsonite of the Green River formation for possible future mining purposes."

Because the purpose of Senator Hart's subcommittee is to uncover and end monopolistic practices, its members are not as responsive to the desires of the oil and mining industries as is the Interior Committee. So Senator Hart could seize on Mr. Weinberg's last point, that "in some instances" these claims were filed with the purpose of mining dawsonite. This was the dialogue:

> SENATOR HART: You have left unsaid what I take is obvious, too, that some of these claims could be described as filed for the purposes of clouding title to the shale lands in the hope of obtaining some kind of right on the oil shale.
> MR. WEINBERG: We do not know.
> SENATOR HART: Would you quarrel with me if I made that statement?
> MR. WEINBERG: I suppose I would have to say that in the absence of any proof one way or the other, I cannot affirm and I cannot disaffirm.

Mr. Weinberg is, of course, a cautious federal official. Within

the Interior Department the belief was widespread that the dawsonite claims had been filed to tie up a huge chunk of the oil-shale
land, cloud the federal title to that land, raise the possibility that
in their ostensible search for dawsonite the claimants can produce
oil from the shale without even paying a royalty to the federal
government. In January 1967 Secretary Udall froze such claims.
No more could be filed. This action did not affect those claims already filed the previous year. It was acknowledged that the Secretary's order should have been issued earlier, to have saved some of
those 1.4 million acres. It was explained, however, that the built-in
drawbacks of the bureaucracy delayed the order.

So this is one objection: the status of these dawsonite claims. A
legal battle is in prospect. If the individuals and companies which
filed the claims win, they will control more oil shale than the federal government does. More oil shale, that is, that had belonged to
the American people until those claims were filed in 1966. And
these claimants will profit from that oil shale without paying any
royalty.

The second unresolved problem, and the second question that
should be answered, revolves around the oil depletion allowance.
Depletion allowances are the pots of gold at the end of the rain-
bows. And the oil depletion allowance is the biggest pot of the
shiniest gold at the end of the brightest rainbow. The allowance is
part of the federal tax law, and the theory behind it is that a producer should get a return on the capital assets he uses but is
unable to replenish. Many years ago, long before the movement
toward the guaranteed society began, producers received a return
for their products in the market place. But the depletion allowance gives them an added return, an added guarantee of profit.

In its very basic form, here is how the oil depletion allowance
works: A well produces in one year oil that sells for $100,000.
That $100,000 figure then is the gross income from the property.
At this point the owner of that well deducts the 27½ percent
depletion allowance, or $27,500. That means income from that
well—for tax purposes—is $72,500. If the ordinary expenses of
operating that well amounted to $80,000, then that well operated
at a loss of $7,500 (the $80,000 cost minus the $72,500) as far as

the Internal Revenue Service is concerned. Of course the well did earn a profit. It produced oil that sold for $100,000 at a cost of only $80,000, a clear profit of $20,000. The owner of that well can do anything he wants with that $20,000. It's his. He just doesn't have to pay any tax on it.

How well the oil companies have done with this depletion allowance is illustrated by a speech Senator William Proxmire of Wisconsin made in 1964. Speaking in Wichita, Kansas, before a group of oil men, he said:

> We had a federal corporation tax rate of 52 percent in 1963. Yet the seventh largest industrial corporation in the country, Texaco, with a net income of over $500 million, made provision for income taxes in 1963 of only 13 percent.
> Standard of Indiana, the fourteenth largest corporation, with a net income of over $180 million, paid in all income taxes, Federal and other, only 14 percent of its net income. Shell, the sixteenth largest corporation, paid only 18 percent in all income taxes.
> Atlantic had over $46 million in net profit and yet paid no income taxes, and has apparently not paid any income taxes since 1956. Pure Oil ended up 1963 with virtually $30 million in net profit and yet had a tax credit. It received several hundred thousand dollars of refunds.

Should this oil depletion allowance be extended to oil produced from shale? Orlo Childs, a member of the six-man advisory committee on oil shale, answered "Yes," explaining:

> When a lease is given, the lessee becomes the owner of the asset he has leased. The public interest is served by the bonuses and royalties paid for the lease. It is a cardinal principle of our tax law that the tax fall only on income and not on the capital that produces the income. Historically and traditionally the depletion allowance has been aimed at providing for the return, to the owner, of the value of the capital asset that is used and not replenished as it is produced and sold. In an oil-shale industry this depletion concept must be taken into consideration.

In the same report John Kenneth Galbraith answered "No," saying:

> When the development is on government land, it is obvious no privately owned wealth is being depleted. In the absence of discovery costs and assuming that private firms need not be compensated for the depletion of public property, there is no conceivable justification for a depletion allowance apart from the fact that the recipients, like all citizens, would enjoy the exemption from taxes.

Professor Galbraith's point is a reasonable one. Why should the oil-shale producer be given an allowance for depleting a publicly owned resource? There may be a justification for granting an allowance for depleting a privately owned resource, but certainly no tax break should be given when a company is granted the privilege of making a great deal of money from publicly owned resource.

There is another aspect of the depletion allowance. If the oil shale is considered to be a mineral that is mined, then the allowance is only 15 percent, the rate for minerals. However, if it is considered an oil, then the rate is 27½ percent.

Obviously the oil companies want as much of a tax break as they can get. That means they want the depletion allowance and they want it at 27½ percent. And so the depletion allowance, along with the problem of the other minerals in the shale, is among the problems that should be resolved before a decision is made on how to parcel out the oil-shale land. Another is conservation.

The area where Colorado, Utah and Wyoming meet and which is underlain by the rich oil shale also is one of the most attractive physical assets the United States has. The sun-blanched mountains and the rushing streams, still in an almost untouched state, are a reminder of the primitive beauty that was once the land on which the United States now exists. Should there be a reasonable effort to conserve most of this region in its natural state?

Conservation is an emotional word. It means preserving. And most conservationists believe in preserving the countryside in its original form when such preservation suits their convenience. The history of conservation in the United States largely is the story of activists in Washington exploiting the desires of local officials to avoid paying the costs of maintaining land by having them turn over the land to the federal government. Whatever its history, however, the people of the United States have benefitted greatly by conservation efforts made in the past. Once the land, once the natural grandeur has been destroyed, it never can be replaced.

The most common method of mining oil shale is by strip mining. Giant shovels move across the land, leaving it with ugly scars, digging frightening chancres, taking all the riches out of the land—the riches found in the land's oil and the riches found in the land's beauty.

Should this land be left untouched? Should the United States ignore the oil to preserve the natural beauty? To answer "Yes" is to be unreasonable. The island of Manhattan may have had more natural beauty when the Indians sold it to the Dutch three centuries ago, but not very many people today seriously regret the change. However, that does not mean that Manhattan, once the change is accepted, should not be made as attractive as possible. The automobile offers many blessings, but that does not mean that society should not try to curb its devastating effect on air and land. And likewise with the oil shale. It offers many advantages: a large source of income for private oil companies, a source of revenue for the United States Treasury, a means to transform a quiescent area into an active one. Most importantly, the oil shale offers a source of fuel and of raw materials for the petro-chemical industry for the next several hundred years. It can neither be ignored nor stifled. At the same time, however, it cannot be allowed to grow unwatched. Lands owned by all the American people are involved, and they should be protected.

Present methods of mining shale are to remove it from the ground and then to extract the oil from it by crushing the rock and heating it until the oil is liberated. This not only produces the giant strip-mining scars on the land but it also produces two other problems. The first is water. This kind of process—or retorting, its technical name—will require a great deal of water, in an area which has a shortage of water. It will also produce a great excess of spent shale, literally hundreds of thousands of tons. A ton of shale producing twenty-five gallons of oil also would produce fifteen hundred pounds of excess rock. This is the rock after the oil has been taken from it. Where will this spent shale be dumped? Into the valleys and ravines. The area's natural beauty, its wildlife, its recreation possibilities—all will be destroyed. Strip mining is a raping of the land.

It does not have to be. Experimentation has been going on with a new mining technique, referred to as *in situ*. In effect, it is mining underground. In this method, a huge explosion, perhaps with an atomic device, is set off within the oil shale beneath the land's surface. The explosion creates an underground cavity that will fill with broken oil shale as the roof of the cavity collapses. Heat then would be applied to the broken shale to liberate the oil. The oil then would be brought to the surface.

There is no disagreement that, if the *in situ* method can be perfected, it would cause the least damage to the countryside. The land surface would not be affected except for a relatively small shaft sunk into the cavity. Nor would great supplies of water be needed. The *in situ* method also would be cheaper, meaning that more oil companies would be able to participate in the industry, in turn meaning greater competition with the benefits of lower prices and better service for the public. And, last, the *in situ* method, because it is a cheaper production technique, would mean that the federal government could collect larger royalty payments from its leases.

Perhaps industry should be expected to push development of the *in situ* process. It is not. Industry has expressed more interest in the conventional strip-mining technique. The Denver Research Institute has reported its expectation that the oil-shale industry will be built around above-ground retorting methods. Among officials of the Geological Survey, the Interior Department agency that would actually oversee the shale mining, the assumption is general that strip-mining techniques will be used rather than underground mining and retorting.

Industry is shunning the *in situ* method, preferring the conventional strip mining, a technique they know something about. Also, strip mining requires expensive retorting facilities above ground—costing between $100 million and $150 million. Only a few big companies can afford this kind of outlay. Thus, with above-ground mining and retorting, the oil-shale industry will be locked up—guaranteed—as a preserve for the big companies.

The Interior Department can, of course, require the oil companies that receive shale leases to take conservation measures. Past records, however, do not indicate that such measures would be very successful. Nor does the Geological Survey, which would be in charge of enforcing such regulations, have much of an interest in conservation. In the Survey offices, conservation means the wise development of natural resources; it does not have any meaning in the Geological Survey in relationship to preserving natural beauty. The pertinent regulations are found in Title 30 of the Code of Federal Regulations. Part 231 of that Title explains "Operating and safety regulations governing the mining of potash; oil shale, sodium and phosphate." Nowhere in Part 231 is there any reference to rehabilitating land, conservation, preservation of wildlife, anti-pollution or any such measures to preserve as much of the natural beauty of this geographical area as possible. Rather than reasonable precautions being taken to prevent a rape of the land, no precautions are being taken.

Should the federal government itself perfect the *in situ* method of mining and then insist that private industry use only that technique? That, along with the problem of other minerals in the area and the problem of the depletion allowance, is one of the questions that should be answered before a final decision is made on the oil-shale land leases.

The final problem that should be resolved concerns the amount of royalty the federal government should collect from its lease. The answer to this question depends a great deal on the answers to the other questions. A royalty should be a share of the oil company's profits. Profits depend on costs. Oil shale mined on the land surface, then crushed and retorted, has a different cost than oil shale mined by the *in situ* method. Will conservation measures be insisted on by the federal government? How much will such measures cost? Should that cost come from the federal government's royalty or should it come from industry's profit?

Should the cost of producing oil from shale be figured in the same manner that the cost of producing oil from underground wells is figured? There are serious differences. A major cost feature of producing oil in the conventional way from underground wells is the cost of wildcatting. Digging this kind of well is an expensive gamble. There may be a pretty good chance the well will produce oil, but there is no certainty. A lease for a parcel of federally owned land in the Gulf of Mexico has been sold to oil companies for $2.6 million. The cost of drilling a well on that leased property in the Gulf might be another $1 million. And all this money must be spent without there being any assurance the well will produce oil. That gambling feature does not exist with oil shale. Its presence and its value is known.

Other factors in the production of oil from shale, however, add to its cost. One is that more money is needed for mining and retorting—whichever method is used—than is needed for drilling a well. Also, oil-shale deposits are located farther from the major markets, meaning higher costs for transportation. If strip mining is used, there is the cost of dumping the spent shale. Although oil from shale has been produced in the past, it never has been produced in the scale envisioned for the Green River formation, meaning its cost continues to be an estimate.

With all these unknowns, however, the estimates still look pretty good. "The general opinion that prevails," said Joseph Fisher in 1965, "is that the cost of producing usable liquid products from shale is fairly closely approaching the cost of getting it from conventional underground liquid sources."

Some estimates even suggest that producing oil from shale now is cheaper than producing oil from conventional wells. Experimental plants guard their cost figures very closely. But one person involved with their work has estimated that current techniques could produce oil from shale at about two thirds the cost of producing it from wells. Several other estimates also suggest that even in the mid-1960s it was cheaper to produce oil from shale than from traditional underground wells. One estimate was that a barrel of oil from a well cost $4.15 to produce, including a $2.08 "finder cost," which is the wildcatting cost. This compared, according to the estimate, with a total cost of $1.46 for a barrel of oil produced from shale. That estimate probably is overly generous to the oil shale; full-scale production would cost more perhaps than experimental production under ideal conditions. At the same time, however, as conventional underground pools dry up and new ones become more difficult to find, the wildcatting cost will rise—making oil shale a more attractive resource.

These cost factors are items that should be considered when

the federal government determines how much royalty it should receive from its leases. Once that is determined, the government then must decide what it should do with those royalties. Under the mineral leasing act, passed in 1920, royalties from federal leases are split three ways. Fifty-two and one half percent goes to the reclamation fund, meaning the money is used primarily to bring water to the arid West. Thirty-seven and one-half percent is given to the state in which the lease is located. This is done even though the lease is on a federal holding and the state has no ownership nor any other kind of right to the property. The final 10 percent goes to the federal treasury.

In the half century since that law was passed, the revenues have not reached a large enough total—not yet $1½ billion—for much concern to develop over that split. In contrast, the oil-shale leases easily can produce royalty payments in the neighborhood of $1 billion a year. Should 90 percent of that money be divided between reclamation projects in the West and the three states—Wyoming, Utah and Colorado—and only 10 percent go to the federal treasury to benefit the entire nation which does own the land? Under present law the federal treasury would receive only the 10 percent. There is a precedent for changing that split. In 1953 Congress passed the Outer Continental Shelf Act. This concerned federal leases on submerged oil wells beyond the ocean limits reserved to the states. Revenues from those federal leases go entirely to the federal treasury—the total in less than two decades is approximately $1 billion. The man most responsible for that change in 1953 was Lyndon Johnson, then a Democratic Senator from Texas.

And so the list of questions to be answered before a decision can be made on how to develop the oil-shale lands owned by the federal government is a long one. There is the problem of the claims for other minerals, the problem of the depletion allowance, one of conservation and the question of royalties. And within each of these major questions are many minor ones.

With none of the problems yet resolved, the Department of the Interior in January 1967 announced how it planned to hand out the oil-shale lands to private industry. And that handout may eventually become the biggest giveaway the United States government has ever participated in.

Why did the Interior Department go ahead with its decision when so many unknowns remain to be answered? The answer is simple. The industry wanted to join the guaranteed society.

Two

The decision the Interior Department reached was to make leases available to private industry. Government research would be kept to a minimum. Industry would develop oil shale as it saw fit.

"Let us concede," explained Secretary Udall, "that we are in no immediate danger of a national petroleum shortage. Our known reserves, according to present technology, are adequate to carry us into the next century at or about present costs. However, as a recent interdepartmental energy study reports, oil and gas now supply 73 percent of our total energy requirements, and we have the potential for developing additional reserves through advanced discovery and recovery technology. Conventional sources of these fuels represent the smallest known potential reserves, worldwide, of all the fuel resources. Thus, unless we are to be forced by possible shortages within half a century into radical dislocation of our heating, power generation and transportation systems, we must begin now to plan for substitute sources."

He continued, "We have the lead time to plan the development of shale oil on a systematic, economical and sound conservation basis. Past history tells us that the difficulties are formidable. Prudence therefore dictates that we utilize the time available to us now to phase shale oil into our long-range forecast. . . . Deferral of development measures now could easily result in the need for a 'crash' effort later with attendant increased costs and sacrifice adequate conservation planning."

That very lengthy explanation by Secretary Udall to Congress is not disputed. Anyone who has delved into the possibility of future fuel shortages and into the value of oil shale would agree that the time is past due to begin the long process of turning the oil shale into a commercial product. And that is the justification for the government assistance. The country eventually will need this source of fuel and the government itself owns so much of this fuel. This necessity is one of the traditional standards under which the United States government has given assistance both to individuals and industries.

Before, however, when this standard of necessity was raised, the ultimate result was intended to be the national good. With oil shale the ultimate result appears to be the good of the oil industry. The product's future has been turned over to that industry when in reality the explanation offered by Secretary Udall is more a valid reason for the government keeping a close watch over the oil shale's growth.

The kind of leases the Interior Department is making available to private industry—approximately five thousand acres in size for research and development work and eventually commercial production—never before have been granted. The concept of development leases was created by the Interior Department for oil shale.

When criticism of the Interior Department's action grew loud, Secretary Udall made a second attempt to justify it. "I am keenly aware," he said, "of the view held by some that it is unnecessary and unwise to embark on an oil-shale development effort now. This, of course, has been the attitude of the past half-century and, if the sole test were the immediate need for additional energy sources, I might agree. It would certainly simplify things for my department if we were just told to forget the whole thing and sit on the resource until actual need could be shown."

The paragraph is an interesting one. The criticism had not been directed at the Interior Department's embarking "on an oil-shale development effort now," as Secretary Udall said. The criticism had been directed at the Department's turning this resource over to private industry before the public's interest could be adequately protected. But Secretary Udall seemed to suggest that anyone who made such a criticism was almost unpatriotic. "This is a national asset of great potential value that belongs to all the people of the United States," he said. "They can gain nothing from it, either in public revenues or a more vigorous national economy, while the resource sits in the ground. And who knows what developments will occur in the energy and petro-chemical fields in the next century? Is there today any reason to deny oil shale the vigorous research efforts that have gone into unlocking the energy potential of uranium?"

That last question is a fascinating gambit. The Secretary turned his opponents' arguments against them. The federal government took on the responsibility for developing uranium into a form of energy. That is exactly what Secretary Udall's critics wish him to do with oil shale, have the federal government take over its early development.

On occasion the standard of national defense is raised for oil shale; private industry must hurry and become involved with the program to produce a large and readily accessible reserve of oil, in the event a war or another emergency shuts off foreign supplies and creates a greater demand for oil. Even this argument falls. No matter who develops the oil shale, be it private industry or the government, the oil produced will be a relatively minor part of the country's total oil production for decades to come. The percentage of total production represented by oil from shale probably would tend to go up faster if controlled by the federal government rather than by private industry as Secretary Udall proposed. Such national security arguments, John Kenneth Galbraith and Benjamin Cohen charged, "appear to reflect only the common effort to find a national security justification for action that individuals or groups would find in their economic interest."

The real reason why the decision was made to turn over the leases to private industry is that the large oil companies wanted the leases. They wanted to control land. The more land they controlled, the more of the oil-shale industry they controlled. The more of the industry they controlled, the more they could guarantee that the industry developed as they wished—with as little competition and as assured a profit structure as they desired.

If the oil companies were interested in the industry's development, they could go ahead and develop the industry without waiting for the federal government's blessing. They own 170,000 acres, including some of the richest oil-shale lands. In 1967 Professor Galbraith talked before a Congressional committee about some of the early meetings of the oil-shale advisory board:

> At our first meetings we were enormously impressed by the seeming fact that this great reserve was being held out of use by the federal government. And I am forced to say that a considerable snow job was done on us in those first meetings as we heard how federal ownership was holding up the development. . . . As the evidence accumulated of the enormous wealth of holdings already in private hands, that argument disappeared. We began to hear that these very rich private holdings were a bit scattered, that they weren't close to service stations, hot dog stands, water supplies and motels. They needed blocking up. But the suggestion that there was not in private hands sufficient oil lands of sufficient richness disappeared from our discussions.

Despite owning this land with its oil-shale potential, "there is the undeniable fact," conceded Joseph Fisher in 1965, "that in the past, industry as a whole has not been especially aggressive in its R and D activities regarding shale oil."

That same year Senator Gaylord Nelson, Democrat of Wisconsin, put this question to John A. Carver, Jr., Under Secretary of the Interior:

> Since the private holdings involve one hundred and fifty billion to two hundred billion barrels by estimate, what would be added to the acceleration of a program of developing a better method of exploiting by throwing in the one trillion, seven hundred billion, or thereabouts, barrels that the federal government owns? In other words, there is more oil in these private shale holdings than in all other known holdings in the nation. We have these great oil companies who understand their business. Why don't they proceed to go right ahead and develop their oil lands and when they have developed a high-quality, efficient method of exploiting this shale oil, then we ought to proceed, I assume, to lease to them to extract this resource. What is wrong with that approach?

Mr. Carver, obviously embarrassed, hunted for an answer, could not find one, then finally acknowledged: "The question is a good one." It was an extremely good question. And the only reasonable answer to the query of why the oil companies did not develop the shale land they owned was that they were more interested in controlling the federal land as well as their own land and in locking up the industry's future than in developing oil from shale.

Another point supporting that thesis is the size of the leases sought originally by the oil companies. Again, Galbraith and Cohen have pointed this out most effectively in their 1965 report, saying:

> The Shell Oil Company has proposed that it be granted leases of fifty thousand acres of the oil-shale lands in the central area of the Piceance Basin. They are estimated to contain one hundred and fifty billion barrels of oil. This would suffice to cover all of Shell's oil requirements at the present rate of refining for an estimated 660 years. It is the equivalent of roughly five times the total of all proven petroleum resources in the United States.
> Sinclair has made requests that would suffice that company on the same basis for an estimated 226 years. Modest requests from Humble and Continental for approximately five thousand acres would cover the total present production of each company for fifty-four and twenty-seven years respectively.

The Department of the Interior in the spring of 1967 announced that no leases larger than 5,120 acres would be permitted. Even some tracts this size in the Green River formation contain eighteen billion barrels of oil. Walter J. Mead, a professor of economics at the University of California, Santa Barbara, made a study of the oil-shale situation. Such a 5,120-acre lease, he reported, could mean "694 years of oil production from a presently assumed optimum size plant." Even if Professor Mead has overestimated by two the oil production rate, such leases still are giving away a great deal. Professor Mead commented that if such leases were made, "they would probably become either scandalous or ruinous and the former is more likely than the latter."

Theoretically, at least, any oil company or, for that matter, any responsible individual or company can apply for a lease to mine oil shale. And the defenders of the Interior Department's policy point this out, saying it means that a great number of companies will enter the area and that great number will increase competition within the industry. That argument, intended to support Secretary Udall, actually supports his critics. If the government assumed the cost of research and then made its results generally available, a large number of companies could use that research. Competition would indeed be increased. Prices of the produced oil would be pushed to as low a point as production costs and the need for a reasonable profit would permit. Also, the more companies involved in producing oil from shale, the more innovation within the industry, the more desire to find new products—the more desire, in effect, to be better than the next guy. That is called the free-enterprise system.

Professor Mead, who presented his study of the oil-shale situation before Senator Hart's subcommittee, explained why that competitive factor will be missing under the Department of the Interior's policy of giving our research and development leases to private companies. Said the professor:

> In at least the early years of an oil-shale industry, the potential participants will be few in number. The number will be limited by two factors: First, there are only about twenty firms, at most, that have sufficient technological background to be considered serious contenders for oil-shale leases. Nine of these are presently partners in two joint research ventures. The Colony Development Company is a joint venture organized by The Oil Shale Corporation (TOSCO), Standard Oil Company of Ohio, and Cleveland Cliffs Mining Company. The Anvil Points group operating under contract with the Colorado School of Mines is a joint venture made up of Mobil Oil Company, Phillips Petroleum Company and Continental Oil Company. Second, the capital requirement for entry, including a retort and an upgrading plant to produce synthetic crude, but not including the cost of the resource itself, is estimated from one hundred million to one hundred and fifty million dollars. Thus the barriers of entry at least initially are relatively high. Further, the bonus cost of the resource itself will add to the capital cost and the bigger the unit of sale, the greater will be this additional barrier to entry.

Professor Galbraith, appearing before the same subcommittee, said much the same thing, if in more colorful language. "It is fantastic to suggest," he charged, "that individual or small companies would be able to incur the kind of developmental expenditure that is involved here. This is a multi-million-dollar operation but much more than that. It is something which can only be the extension of the very large research organizations, very large technical apparatus of the very large oil companies. So that to suppose that one is going out and give developmental leases to Tom, Dick and Harry, to a small independent oil company, and suppose that they are going to undertake the kind of research that is relevant to the development of the process of extracting this oil is beyond the range of any reasonable imagination."

The professor concluded: "These leases, if they are given, will be a device for getting a grip on the lands. They will not be a prelude to any sort of development."

Nor will there be much competition within the oil-shale industry, if past history is a guide. The big companies already have combined, as Professor Mead's study pointed out, to develop oil from shale. Professor Mead's study also discloses that when two oil companies combine together in a joint venture, they then are reluctant to bid against each other.

Among officials of the Geological Survey, the agency within the Interior Department watching over the oil-shale leases, the assumption is that when the big companies gain their leases, they will work together. The anticipation is that four companies would each acquire a 5,000-acre lease and then combine them into one giant 20,000-acre operation.

Senator Hart visualizes the development of the federally owned oil-shale lands as "a unique opportunity for new sources of competition to penetrate the petroleum industry." Maximum competition, the Senator continued, means "the fastest development" of the oil-shale industry. But the policy the government chose is not one to foster competition. It fosters, instead, an industry with its development, its corporate structure and its profits all guaranteed for a few companies.

Even the friends of the oil companies concede a guaranteed industry is what the companies are seeking, although that is not the phrase the companies would use. One of the members of the advisory board, whose position coincided with that of the industry, summed it up in that board's report when he said: "Certainly all must be able to foresee every possible economic aspect of an emerging industry before it is possible to face the enormous initial costs of commercial scale development." Another way of phrasing that statement is to say that the oil companies want a guarantee.

They got it. They have been able to achieve their guarantee because the oil industry wields a great deal of political power. In 1957 the late Estes Kefauver, Democratic Senator from Tennessee and Philip Hart's predecessor as chairman of the Senate antimonopoly subcommittee, charged: "In the recent past there has been no lack of instances in which the policy of the United States government has been directly geared to promoting the interests of the oil companies, even at times at the expense of our national security." Former Senator Paul H. Douglas, Democrat of Illinois, has called the oil interests "the most powerful force in the country." And another former Senator, John A. Carroll, Democrat of Colorado, commented once that "those of us who come from states where there is a very sparse population find that oil groups have great financial and economic strength . . . so in such areas we are faced with great difficulty."

The story of the oil interests' power begin usually with Teapot Dome. This was a federally owned oil reserve in Wyoming. In 1921 President Warren G. Harding turned Teapot Dome over to Interior Secretary Albert B. Fall to administer. That was done secretly. Fall then sold oil-drilling rights at Teapot Dome to two oil companies for $400,000. Secretary Fall undoubtedly did not place a high enough value on his hanky-panky. He was receiving a payoff of hundreds of thousands of dollars for helping with what was in effect a theft of hundreds of millions of the public's dollars. When newsmen finally broke the story, the resultant exposé made Teapot Dome synonymous with corruption by public officials.

But the Teapot Dome affair was crude. It involved illegal acts, the nature of which could easily be understood by the public. The oil industry became more sophisticated as the years went by. This was evident during the 1940s and 1950s in the dispute over the tidelands oil. This is oil directly off the shores of the continental United States. Does it belong to the federal government or to the states? Whichever owned it would collect a royalty on leases. The industry wanted the oil to be owned by the state legislatures. Perhaps the oil operators figured that state legislatures and governors would be more easily manipulated, meaning smaller royalties to the states than the federal government would collect and other more pleasant regulations. The issue came to a head during the Second World War. Several companies began drilling off the California coast. In Washington the Justice Department considered bringing a legal suit that would settle the question of ownership of the offshore oil riches. Harold L. Ickes, then Secretary of the Interior and one of the toughest and most honest officials to grace a Washington chair, charged a Democratic Party official with advancing "the rawest proposition ever made to me." A party official who was also an oil man offered to deliver $300,000 to the Democratic Party's war chest if Ickes sided with the states in the struggle for the control of the offshore oil lands, or so Ickes claimed.

Harry S. Truman was President at the time. The party official was a loyal Democrat and a friend of his, and President Truman publicly scolded Ickes, suggesting Ickes must have been wrong about the proffered arrangement. Ickes then resigned. Despite his support of the official, Harry Truman believed very strongly that the tidelands oil belonged to the federal government rather than to a few individual states. When the Congress bowed to the pressure of the oil lobbyists and passed legislation turning the tidelands oil over to the states, President Truman vetoed the bill. That veto stands as the high-water mark of the resistance to the power of big oil.

Harry Truman paid for that veto, if not as high a price as the oil industry wanted. The cost exacted was the Dixiecrat bolt from the Democratic Party in 1948. Strom Thurmond, the Dixiecrat candidate for President, talked about "states' rights" in that campaign and most people understood his reference to states' rights to mean so many fewer rights for Negroes. But the real motivation for his candidacy was tidelands oil. Ellis Arnall, a former Georgia governor, has reported: "The oil lobbyists staged and controlled the Dixiecrat convention at Birmingham, and manipulated its steering and platform committees like puppets." The oil industry directed the bolt from the Democratic Party in an effort to defeat Harry Truman and replace him with a Republican who would go along with giving the tidelands oil to the states. Strom Thurmond and his cause of white supremacy had been used. The effort to dislodge Harry Truman from the White House almost succeeded.

During the 1952 presidential campaign Dwight D. Eisenhower came out in support of giving the tidelands oil to the states. Immediately his campaign was enriched by heavy financial contributions from the oil industry and by the political support of Texas and the Gulf Coast states' Democratic parties. When he became President, General Eisenhower signed legislation giving the tidelands oil to the states. The legislation was similar to the bill Harry Truman had vetoed.

For the oil companies this lesson had been learned: Don't piddle around with illegal acts such as happened with the Teapot Dome scandal; there are enough benefits to be won legitimately if one can persuade the political powers. And the political powers can be persuaded with money. Senator Proxmire pointed up one such persuasion attempt when he told a group of oil-industry executives: "I understand that your industry operates more aircraft than all U.S. airlines put together. These planes are used in many ways, one of which is to carry influential politicians." A politician who must make a trip may be grateful for a free ride.

Another way is the use of large contributions to state political parties as a means of influencing that state's Representatives and Senators in Washington. In the 1950s Sam Rayburn of Texas, the Speaker of the House of Representatives, and Senator Lyndon Johnson of Texas, the Democratic Party leader in the Senate, used their power to make certain the tax-writing committees in the Congress were responsive to the pleas of the oil industry. Persons appointed to those committees usually came from states which had oil and gas interests and would never vote to lower the 27½ percent depletion allowance. Coming from Texas, there was nothing else Senator Johnson and Speaker Rayburn could do. Texas was their constituency, meaning their responsibility was to protect its interests if they wanted to be re-elected, and oil was its biggest industry. Oil also was the biggest financial contributor to the state's political party.

In the 1960 presidential campaign Richard M. Nixon, the Republican candidate, hoped to gain the oil-industry support that

General Eisenhower had and came out strongly against reducing the depletion allowance. John Kennedy, the Democratic candidate, in a rather quiet tone of voice, suggested that all depletion allowances should be studied. Lyndon Johnson, then John Kennedy's running mate, quickly assured his fellow Texans that the Democratic Party's platform did not recommend any change in the depletion allowance. The Democrats needed Texas to win that election, and Lyndon Johnson understood that the party moguls in that state would not give the "okay" signal for the Kennedy-Johnson ticket if they believed there would be any tampering with the depletion allowance. When he was President, John Kenendy did recommend to Congress that the depletion allowances be reduced somewhat. But the tax-writing committees were so stacked in favor of the oil industries that the proposals quickly died.

When Lyndon Johnson became President in November 1963 he still was considered the oil industry's "top man" in Washington. He understood this, and one of his first actions, after he had taken the reins of the Presidency, was to try to erase that reputation. On December 9, 1963, he called Interior Secretary Udall to his office and assigned to him the "basic policy decision on oil matters," or so Mr. Udall explained it to newsmen in the White House lobby. The oil depletion allowance, being a Congressional matter, was not involved in the assignment. The principal matter at the time was the oil import quota. The domestic industry wanted as little oil as possible imported; the less imports, the bigger the market for domestically produced oil. The states on the East Coast wanted greater imports; they could buy Venezuelan oil more cheaply than they could buy American oil from Texas.

How much President Johnson kept his hands off the oil industry and the oil-shale dispute after that is a matter of conjecture. When Secretary Udall was asked by reporters if the President was involved in the oil-shale deliberation, he answered: "I have had no discussion with him on the work of the Advisory Board. As far as I know, he may be following the press but he has not participated in any way." Later, the Secretary was asked: "Is this ultimately President Johnson's decision?" The Secretary answered: "No." He added: "I don't think so. Certainly not considering the responsibilities he delegated to us."

Within the Interior Department, however, there has been a reluctance to accept such statements at face value. Several of the Secretary's top aides have commented privately that they would imagine that the Secretary would discuss the matter with the President. Nor is there much feeling of assurance at Interior that Lyndon Johnson completely severed his relations with the oil industry. On one occasion the oil industry raised its prices, and the Council of Economic Advisers girded for a battle in hopes of rolling back the inflationary move. Interior was notified to be ready to lend a hand with the many administrative acts that could have made the domestic oil industry retreat. But the Council of Economic Advisers, which is a presidential agency responsible only to the occupant of the White House, never followed through. The price increase stayed. Whether Lyndon Johnson had bowed to the political persuasiveness of the oil industry's campaign contributions, whether he simply lost interest because the Vietnam war consumed his time and energy, or whether his "consensus" approach to domestic politics made him avoid a battle with a major domestic industry—whichever of these was his reason, the battle never was fought.

Actually the position on oil shale taken by the man who is President is of negative interest. There is not really much he can do—except to stop what others might wish to do. The real pressure for turning the oil shale over to the oil industry comes from the Congress. In this matter the shots are called primarily by Representative Wayne N. Aspinall, Democrat of Colorado. Representative Aspinall's Congressional district covers the western half of the state and includes all the oil-shale land lying within Colorado. Elected to Congress in 1948, Mr. Aspinall, a lawyer, peach-grower and state legislator, joined the House Interior Committee. Through the seniority system which rewards members of Congress who have longevity, Representative Aspinall became chairman of that committee. As such, he wields tremendous authority over the Interior Department. Any legislation that department wants first must be approved by Mr. Aspinall's committee. Considering the power a committee chairman has if he wishes to exercise it, that means proposed legislation must first be approved by Wayne Aspinall. Any funds the Interior Department wants must first be authorized by the House Interior Committee, which means the funds must first be authorized by Representative Aspinall. And so the most important consideration of the future of the oil-shale lands is what Representative Aspinall wants done with them.

Galbraith and Cohen reported: "We have been told that the Congress will not authorize appropriations for contracts for the development of oil-shale processes. Rather it will succumb to pressure from some oil companies and aspiring lease holders to resist such a course of action."

The other side of their statement is that Congress—meaning the House committee headed by Representative Aspinall—would insist on leases being given to private industry, rather than allow the federal government to finance the needed research and development itself and then make the results generally available.

Northwestern Colorado, where the oil shale lies, has a population of about seventy-two thousand persons. If the oil companies moved into the area to establish an oil-shale industry, the population would triple within a decade or so. In addition to the oil companies investing some $2 billion for capital assets, they also would spend locally $200 million a year on services and materials. An oil-shale industry would make northwestern Colorado a boom area.

Already the boom has begun. Entrepreneurs are buying up land around the edges of the federal reserve, hoping to sell the land off to the oil companies at a substantial profit. In one case talked about within the industry, an individual has acquired mining claims for twenty-one thousand acres. If the individual can pass clear mining rights—which he obtains by paying $2.50 an acre, a total of $52,500—he has an offer for the land from a mining company, at $2,000 an acre or a total of $42 million. Stockbrokers are touting stock on the basis of "New Shale Oil Rush," to quote their advertisements. And once the commercial companies move in, the boom undoubtedly will be an explosion. There is no doubt that the immediate development of a shale-oil industry by private oil companies will have a fantastic financial impact on Representative Aspinall's Congressional district. That the over-all benefit to the nation would be greater if the federal government watched over the development of the industry in its early years is not a factor of much significance in northwestern Colorado— understandably perhaps.

So there would be no doubts, Representative Aspinall has made clear his attitude toward the oil-shale industry. First, he has sponsored legislation to insure that the depletion allowance for oil shale is at the higher 27½ percent for oil rather than the 15 percent allowed for minerals. "No study of the public lands and their resources would be complete without considering all of the tax implications bearing thereon," he has explained. He continued: "From what I can gather, for example, the gap between an uneconomic oil-shale industry and one that could produce products competitive with those produced from traditional sources might well be found in the depletion allowance permitted under the tax laws."

Contrary to that statement, the profit "gap" may well be found in the growing shortage of oil from traditional sources—meaning the price of such oil goes higher—and may also be found in a less expensive *in situ* method of mining the shale, if the federal government were allowed to do the necessary research.

Representative Aspinall also has made clear that he expects the Interior Department to turn over the oil-shale lands to private industry. In a statement of his, widely read within the department, he said: "I would not want to be in charge of any other agency which anyone could say had contributed to a delay in opening shale lands for development. The fact is that anyone who does delay this development is not only ignoring the existing law, but is . . . exposing himself to the possibility of having endangered national security."

Possibly Secretary Udall should have tried bucking the Congressman from northwestern Colorado. He might have succeeded somewhat; he may not have. Without strong presidential backing it is doubtful that Mr. Udall could have done anything. Also, the price Secretary Udall would have had to pay would have been a high one. Undoubtedly any other proposal wanted by Secretary Udall would not have been received in a friendly fashion by Chairman Aspinall and the committee he controls. Actually, Secretary Udall and Representative Aspinall make a curious partnership. Mr. Aspinall is interested in promoting mining, timberland usage and the like. These industries often have found him responsive to their wishes. Mr. Udall has been more interested in the development of recreational areas, the creation of national parks and seashores and the like. So industrial development gets traded off for recreational development, and vice versa. Probably each of the two men feels he is in partnership with the devil.

And that is why the oil-shale industry is entering the guaranteed society. Wayne Aspinall is one with Senator Magnuson, who has the most to say about the SST and whose constituency would benefit most from the SST, and with Representative Garmatz, who has the most to say in Congress about the merchant marine and whose constituency benefits greatly from what he does say. Representative Aspinall, who has the most to say about oil-shale development, represents the constituency that will benefit most from that development. The President and the Secretary of the Interior, who should speak for the entire country and protect the entire country's interest, either are quiet or powerless. Perhaps they are just unwilling to fight. The battle is lost by default.

In the advisory committee report John Kenneth Galbraith pointed out:

> The American people are not presently aware of the wealth they own in these deposits. It is important both for the conservation and wise and equitable development of these resources that there be the widest public knowledge of this endowment and the issues concerning their exploitation. An informed public will be a major source of strength to officials seeking sound conservation policies. We urge that all conservation-minded members of the Congress and the public inform themselves fully on this vast resource and policies concerning its use.

This is not happening, however. Oil shale is like the SST and the merchant marine. It is so complicated, at times so difficult to grasp, that the public is not aware of the money and the issues involved. The responsibility should be shared with the news media that will not devote reportorial energy and space to inform the public and with the public which often acts as if it prefers not to be informed. It was much easier to alert the public when industry was less sophisticated and engaged in illegal activities in order to get federal funds. A juicy theft always attracts newspaper space and readers.

Perhaps aware of this, Professor Galbraith has resurrected the Teapot Dome case. On two occasions, in 1965 and 1967, he has suggested that the oil-shale lands "would seem certain to stimulate recollections of past experience with Teapot Dome." The second time he raised that specter, Senator Clifford P. Hansen, Republican of Wyoming, accused Professor Galbraith of "pure demagoguery on your part, sir." Whether demagogic or not, Professor Galbraith was reasonably successful in both references. Both produced news stories, some of the few about oil shale to make the newspapers. But that kind of interest could not be sustained. There is nothing illegal in the oil-shale policy developing.

Because it is legal, however, it is not necessarily correct. The giveaway of the fantastically valuable oil-shale lands meets none of the standards, traditional in America, for the granting of subsidies. It is not humanitarian. No one suggests the policy will serve any welfare purpose. It does not serve the national defense. Government supervision would better serve the national defense. It does not encourage competition. The policy agreed on actually discourages competition because it makes the oil-shale lands the preserve of a small number of very large oil companies that have a tradition of cooperating with each other; the policy freezes out the small company. Nor is the policy necessary. A policy for the development of the oil-shale industry is a necessity. But it should be the one that gives the most promise of protecting the public interest, of insuring adequate conservation methods and reasonable royalties to the federal government, of making certain that the industry's development is orderly and—most importantly—that competition is encouraged.

Instead the policy chosen leads oil shale into the guaranteed society along with the supersonic transport and the merchant marine.

PATENTS: 4
Golden Grants

One

EARLY IN 1962 the United States Public Health Service began using a simple blood test on newborn children to detect PKU. PKU is a chemical imbalance in the blood that causes mental retardation. If the test showed positive, a special diet could correct the chemical deficiency and one of the more serious forms of mental retardation could be prevented.

Soon several states—Massachusetts, Louisiana, New York, Rhode Island among them—began using this test either on a mandatory or voluntary basis, and its use showed signs of becoming so widespread that eventually the retardation caused by PKU (more formally, Phenylketonuria) would be eliminated. At the same time the widespread tests showed PKU to be one to three times more common than had previously been suspected. It affected four hundred newborn babies a year. Science, it seemed, had cut down another enemy of man. Those hundreds of babies born each year, previously doomed to the troubled shadow life of the retarded, now could be saved.

Then a hitch developed. The hitch was part of the movement toward the guaranteed society.

The test had two advantages. One was its simplicity. In its main part, a few drops of blood are taken from the infant's heel. The blood is examined and the disorder can be identified. The second advantage was its apparent low cost. Dr. Robert Guthrie of the State University of New York at Buffalo, the developer of the test, estimated the total cost for a kit to test five hundred infants at just six dollars. That is 1.2 cents cost for each test. According to Dr. Guthrie, that price included "all costs—labor, materials, rental and maintenance of space, etc.—[but did not include] materials for collecting blood spots or urine-impregnated paper in the hospitals."

However, Dr. Guthrie assigned manufacturing rights to a drug manufacturing company. He and his associates believed the best way to quickly bring about widespread use of the test was by having a respected company with a worldwide organization manufacture the test kits. This decision produced problems. In a letter dated December 4, 1963, to an official in the Department of Health, Education and Welfare, Dr. Guthrie conceded the company was charging $262 "for the same kit to test five hundred infants."

That is almost forty-four times the six dollars it cost Dr. Guthrie to produce what the doctor described as the "same kit," or fifty-two cents to test a single child compared to Dr. Guthrie's own price of 1.2 cents.

When an individual or a corporation develops a product with its own talent, its own resources and its own money, it has the right under the American free-enterprise system to patent that product.

The patent guarantees the developer of the product the right to sell it on the open market exclusively if the developer chooses and to charge for the product whatever the market will bear. A patent is a guarantee of a reasonable reward to a participant in the free-enterprise system.

As such, patents are a creation of the free-enterprise system. In Europe during the Middle Ages the creator of a new product was not automatically able to secure a patent. Patents were royal grants. An invention, even when the product entirely of a private individual's energy and funds, was considered public property unless the ruling sovereign determined otherwise. This principle still holds true somewhat in Europe. In many countries there, for example, a drug cannot be patented; many firms can produce the medicine and competition drives down the price. In contrast, the United States permits the patenting of drugs, meaning one firm can control the production of the drug and its price. One result of this difference is that a drug sold in the United States may be ten to fifty times more expensive than the same drug sold in a European country.

In America, the right to secure a patent was a deliberate part of the economic system as structured by the nation's founding fathers. The right is included in the Constitution. Its purpose was to provide an incentive for the growth of industry. That it did. By guaranteeing an inventor a reward for his discovery, the patent system is a major contributor to the United States's becoming the leading industrial nation in the world.

But what happens—or what should happen—when the inventor receives a considerable amount of assistance from the federal government? Should the government have some influence on the price charged in the market for the resulting product? The public, acting through the federal government, helped develop the product. Should the public not be able to use that product at its lowest reasonable cost? Or should private industry have the same guarantee that would have come if it had financed all of the product's development without any assistance from the federal government?

Again, as it was with the SST, the merchant marine and oil shale, the question is whether federal funds should be used to offer a guarantee to private industry. And again private industry is angling to enter the guaranteed society. It wants the public to pay the research cost, but industry does not want to surrender or share the patent rights; it wants a guarantee.

In developing the PKU test Dr. Guthrie received some nonfederal assistance. About $100,000 came from associations and corporations interested in making a contribution to public health. But the largest share of the cost of developing Dr. Guthrie's test came from the federal government. The Public Health Service had contributed a total of $251,700 from January 1, 1959, until December 31, 1963. The Children's Bureau, like the Public Health Service, an agency within the Department of Health, Education and Welfare, contributed another $492,000. That is almost three quarters of a million dollars of taxpayers' money. In addition to helping finance the research leading to the successful development of the test, the federal funds paid for the testing of more than one-half million infants in thirty-three states and in six hundred hospitals. Not only did public money pay for these field tests, but it was the prestige and the reputation of the federal agencies which persuaded many of the doctors and hospitals involved to cooperate in the giving of the tests.

With its own rather heavy investment in Dr. Guthrie's test, the federal government did not believe a single company should have the right to manufacture the kit and establish its selling price. Katherine B. Oettinger, then chief of the Children's Bureau, said, "It is our feeling that the rights to this screening kit should be retained by the government in view of the investment of public funds." She also pointed out that the $262 price for the kit "appears somewhat exorbitant in view of the fact that these kits have already been developed, promoted and tried." She called the commercial price "out of line."

More was at stake than the question of how much profit one firm should make. If the test became too expensive, it could not be widely used. After pointing out that a number of states planned to give the test on a statewide basis if they could manufacture their own materials, Mrs. Oettinger said of these states: "Financially they feel that they could not carry out a statewide

program unless they manufactured the necessary materials themselves." Science may have knocked down an enemy of man, but
economics had propped him up again.

One Public Health Service official, in late 1963, wrote officials
in Massachusetts, where the PKU test was mandatory, asking for
their comments on a single company receiving manufacturing
rights to the Guthrie test. In that letter the Washington official
summed up the justification for the resulting higher price. Said
the letter:

> Such time and expenditure is warranted and justified in order to
> have the company produce the product under the most exacting
> conditions of quality control in order to insure a high order of qual-
> ity and consistency of reproducibility from batch to batch, also the
> company will have to continue development research on the prod-
> uct to the point of developing modifications or even substitution in
> order to provide a better diagnostic aid and that it will have to con-
> duct an extensive education and promotional effort to obtain the
> widest possible distribution and usage of the product.

Among officials in Massachusetts those justifications of quality
control, additional research and promotion were nonsense. Dr.
Robert A. MacCready, director of the diagnostic laboratories for
the state's department of public health, formally replied to the
Washington official. He said:

> We have not found it particularly difficult to purchase and set
> up the various ingredients which go into the media used, nor the
> other supplies to complete the testing kits. We would feel that any
> properly qualified and reasonably resourceful laboratory would be
> able to adjust and standardize the reagents used and quite economi-
> cally, as they perform the test according to the published directions
> of Dr. Guthrie. Furthermore, a considerable educational and pro-
> motional effort has already taken place in one way or another
> resulting in more than half the states now trying out the test.

Dr. MacCready continued, explaining that Massachusetts
found "it most efficient and economical to make up our own kits
in our laboratory here. We would be very strongly opposed, and I
think with good justification, to the granting of any license which
in any way prevented or curtailed our making up the ingredients
and supplies into laboratory assaying kits."

He also made clear his opinion that a commercial price of $262
for five hundred tests was outlandish. He said:

Our entire cost of running the PKU tests, including professional, subprofessional, and clerk salaries and the costs of making up both the laboratory kits and the hospital collecting kits, we estimate as about fifty cents per baby tested. Of this total cost only a quite small portion goes into the laboratory assay kits. Dr. Guthrie, for instance, has told me that his costs have been six dollars for producing kits to do five hundred tests in the laboratories—i.e., 1.2 cents per test, and our costs would be roughly comparable.

Actually, the Department of Health, Education and Welfare has a policy of not permitting the assignment of manufacturing rights on products the department helps finance. The applicant— Dr. Guthrie, in the case of the PKU test—must refer any products developed with such federal assistance to the Surgeon General of the United States, who is head of the Public Health Service, to determine how the patenting of the product should be handled. The two grants Dr. Guthrie had received from the Public Health Service, totaling $251,700, required Dr. Guthrie to so notify the Surgeon General by filing an "invention report."

The process leading to Dr. Guthrie's filing that report began on January 5, 1962, when Dr. Guthrie wrote the Department of Health, Education and Welfare. In that letter he explained that he and his associates were considering having a commercial company develop the test kits. The letter explained that such a company might be reluctant to develop a new product without a patent protection, fearing that other companies might compete with them after they had made their initial investment. Five days later, on January 10, the Department responded with a request that Dr. Guthrie file an invention report. According to a memorandum within the Department's files, after the first request there were "four follow-up letters and innumerable telephone conversations" before the invention report was finally received on December 14, 1962—eleven months and four days after it originally had been asked for. (In fairness to Dr. Guthrie, it should be pointed out that much of this delay was the government's fault. Necessary questions and forms were sent by the government to the wrong person or sent only after weeks of delay. Once the necessary forms were supplied, Dr. Guthrie filed the invention report within a reasonable period of time.)

Meanwhile, on April 16, 1962—this was four months after the government first made known its interest in having the invention report filed—an application was filed in Dr. Guthrie's name for a patent on the PKU test he had developed with public funds.

Shortly after his patent application had been filed, Dr. Guthrie entered into an agreement with the Miles Laboratories, giving that commercial company rights to manufacture the kit. Actual production would be done by a subsidiary, the Ames division of Miles, located in Elkhart, Indiana. Miles, which had done considerable work itself in PKU testing, had been approved by two of the nonfederal agencies which had contributed modest amounts of money to the development of the test. The Public Health Service, still waiting to receive its invention report from Dr. Guthrie, did not approve the agreement.

If that licensing agreement held, the Public Health Service feared, any agency wanting to use the test would have to buy the kits from the Ames plant and pay whatever going price Ames charged. The prospect was that a number of public agencies interested in giving the test on a widespread basis would cut back on their testing plans.

A Public Health Service memorandum says that "upon disclosure of the amounts that Miles intended to charge for the test kit, Dr. Guthrie became helpful in attempting to destroy his existing, though non-Public Health Service ratified, agreement with Miles." That agreement did not include any provision for Dr. Guthrie personally to profit from the test he developed. The doctor was not interested in a financial reward. Years later he commented on the lengthy process he had to go through with the government in this way: "How did Tom Swift, the boy inventor, succeed? He never had to fill out 'invention report forms': the key to his success!"

Ames division of Miles Laboratories, stung by the implication it was making an exorbitant profit, hired the respected accounting firm of Price, Waterhouse & Company to go over its books. The audit showed the drug company's cost to manufacture each test was 17.4 cents. The company also insisted that its price never had been fifty-two cents but closer to forty cents at its highest (compared to Dr. Guthrie's 1.2 cents a test). The company continued that the price was dropping continually and, at the time of its statement, was down to twenty cents a test. The company also insisted it was producing the test as a public health service and that it was not profiting from test sales.

Actually, whatever the cost to Ames to manufacture the test and whatever the price charged by Ames were beside the point. As long as one company controlled the manufacture of the test, there was no competition, either in price or in quality. That one company had a guarantee. Public laboratories, such as Dr. Mac-Cready's in Massachusetts, could not manufacture the test kits themselves, being forced to assume higher financial burdens by purchasing the test from outsiders. And this with a device that had been developed with funds supplied by the American public.

Whether a test like Dr. Guthrie's should be given is a question to be answered by doctors and political leaders after proper consideration of all the medical, social and economic problems. Once a positive decision is reached, however, then the federal funds invested in the research on the test should assure that public agencies can purchase the test kits at the lowest possible price. Federal funds should not be used to provide a toehold for private industry in the guaranteed society.

Partly because of the aggressiveness of officials within the Department of Health, Education and Welfare, and partly because of the efforts of Senator Russell B. Long, Democrat of Louisiana, to publicize the PKU story, the federal government was able to break the monopoly on the PKU test. In this one instance the guaranteed society lost a member. In most other instances, however, when patents developed with public funds were involved, the guaranteed society gained members.

In the late 1950s the Department of Health, Education and Welfare was soliciting bids from drug firms to do research in the field of cancer chemotherapy. If this research eventually produced positive results, the patents on the final product would be valuable financially—if held privately. HEW's policy, however, is to make any patents developed with federal funds available to the public without charge, as it eventually was able to do with Dr. Guthrie's PKU test. This policy allows any reputable firm to use the patents without paying a royalty. The theory behind this approach is that with more than one firm using the patents, competition drives the price down to its lowest level. And this low price is the reward to the public for having financed the original research. There had been only one exception to that basic policy. Nonprofit organizations could retain patent rights if they expected to make the product readily available without an excessive royalty charge.

The research in the field of cancer chemotherapy led, however, to a second exception.

When HEW solicited bids for the work on cancer chemotherapy, a startling thing happened. Of all the pharmaceutical and chemical firms that ordinarily would be expected to seek such contracts, not one offered a bid. Such contracts would be profitable even though they would not result in exclusive patent rights. The firm would make a profit on the research contract itself. And if the product developed was marketable, the firm would have a head start on production. Still, no bids.

HEW officials were astounded at first, but soon they caught on. Because they wanted to push the work along, they changed their policy to allow the drug firm to retain the patent rights.

"I suspect that the industries with which we dealt were in many instances accustomed to patent policies more liberal than our basic policy," Parke M. Banta, then HEW's general counsel, said later. "Maybe it is enough for me to say," he added, "that we did not get any contracts for a considerable length of time, and I believe none under our basic policy."

Senator Long summed up that case in this way: "In simple terms, the drug manufacturers went on strike until they got what they wanted, and what they wanted was a monopoly to any of the patentable inventions which might arise from the government-financed work."

There is no arguing with the Senator's summation. The industries involved feared competition. They wanted the public to assume all risks by paying the research and development costs. But the industries involved wanted for themselves a guarantee of profits. No risk. Great reward. That is the cardinal principle of the guaranteed society.

The industries could get away with it because the federal government was anxious to go ahead with the research on the cancer drugs. That was not the only such case.

Another case comes from the files of the General Accounting Office—GAO. This is the official watchdog agency established by the Congress to keep track on how the executive branch of the government spends money. During the 1950s the National Cancer Institute, a part of the National Institute of Health, which is, in turn, an agency of the Department of Health, Education and Welfare, began a large-scale testing program of drugs to use against cancer.

As part of this program the government purchased drugs known as 5-fluorouracil (5-FU) and 5-FUDR. The second is a derivative of the first. The drugs were to be used by the government only for testing. If the tests showed positive results, the financial benefit that could be gained would, of course, be great. The government would test these drugs in government laboratories and with public funds, but without any charge to the manufacturer of the drugs. In effect, the public was assuming the obligation of testing the drugs. It was offering a reliable test to the manufacturers and then not even charging them for it.

Despite this assistance offered, the government still was willing to purchase the drug from the manufacturer rather than seek free samples sold at cost. The public would pay the manufacturer for doing the manufacturer a favor. There are three types of purchase contracts the government can make with a private firm. The one used with the 5-FUDR drug illustrates how an industry angles itself into the guaranteed society.

The first type of contract is a "cost-plus" agreement. The government pays all the contractor's legitimate costs plus a reasonable profit, such as 6 or 8 percent. This type of contract is used for such situations as the 5-FUDR drug purchase. The manufacturer explained it had no prior experience making the drug in large quantities and could not accurately predict its price. A cost-plus agreement would have assured the manufacturer making a reasonable profit on his sales contract. This type of contract, however, was not used in the 5-FUDR case.

A second type of contract calls for the item to be sold for a fixed selling price but also includes a "price-redetermination" clause. If the selling price turns out too high, meaning the manufacturer is making an exorbitant profit, or too low, meaning he is not making enough profit or perhaps even losing money, the selling price can be redetermined accordingly. This kind of contract can be a protection both for the government and for the private contractor. However, it was not used in this case either.

The third type of contract is a straight fixed-price agreement. The cost is agreed on—high, low or just right. It cannot be changed. This type of contract usually is used only for standard items with a predictable production cost. To use it for an item with an unpredictable cost, such as 5-FUDR was supposed to be, is unique. This is the type of contract, however, that was used for the purchase of the drug.

From June 19, 1958, until June 26, 1959, there were four separate fixed-price contracts for the purchase of 5-FUDR. The cost ranged from $60,000 a kilogram in the first contract down to $29,000 a kilogram in the last contract. A total of seventeen kilograms was purchased for an over-all price of $715,150. That averages out to $42,000 a kilogram.

The price was the price sought by the company. Was it taking a risk? Without any price redetermination clause in its contract, the manufacturer was chancing that its production costs would overshoot its selling price. If that happened, the manufacturer would have no recourse but accept its loss. When the GAO accountants examined the manufacturer's books, however, they discovered there was very little risk involved. On one of the contracts, the GAO men found, the company's profits easily could have reached a phenomenal 32.6 percent. On a later contract the profit was 31 percent. With this contract, partly as a result of the GAO investigation, the company's profit was whittled down to 8.5 percent.

The drug had been developed with some federal financial assistance. The testing by the government was free to the manufacturer, even profitable. Yet the government was stuck with a contract guaranteeing the manufacturer almost a one-third profit.

Why did the government enter into this fixed-price agreement?

It wanted to test 5-FUDR. The patent on the drug was controlled by a single company. In a letter to the General Accounting Office in 1960, a government official involved in the working up of the contracts explained: "The contractor refused a cost type contract and might have refused a price-redetermination arrangement." For the government, it was a case of take it or leave it.

In 1965 Dr. Austin Smith, president of the Pharmaceutical Manufacturers Association, was appearing before a Senate subcommittee studying the question of patents on products developed with federal funds. Senator Quentin N. Burdick, Democrat of North Dakota, was skeptical of Dr. Smith's assertion that patents on drugs developed with public funds should be held privately. "I am just trying to find out," he said, "what Uncle Sam gets for his money, that is all."

After Dr. Smith searched for an answer without finding one, Senator Burdick came back with "You believe the contractor should have the exclusive right to that patent . . . and the government gets a report from you . . . ?"

Dr. Smith answered: "Yes."

"That is all they get?" asked the unbelieving Senator.

"Well," replied Dr. Smith, "I think that in substance, to give you a quick one-word answer, yes . . ."

Patents involving drugs are just one area in which federal policies and practices combine with industry's blunt refusal to take a risk, resulting in the guaranteed society. Patents in many other areas also are involved. The federal government is spending approximately $17 billion a year on research and development. That is seventy cents of every research dollar spent in the nation. No single person, no single agency, no single Congressional committee knows how this money is being spent, where it is being spent, on whom it is being spent. Nor is there much interest in the impact of this research and development work on the American people. Seventeen billion dollars a year is more than was spent in the nation's history for research and development up to the end of the Second World War. And, with the exception of a few lone senatorial wolves, there is little concern expressed about the ownership of the results of that research and development.

According to the National Science Foundation, about two thirds of all the federal funds spent on research and development is done by the large aerospace and electronic giants, working under contract to the Defense Department or the National Aeronautics and Space Administration. Probably no more than twenty companies share this $10 billion-plus pot. This money is spent in the name of national defense, one of the traditional standards used to justify subsidies to American industry. There is little dispute over the validity of these expenditures. Politicians and defense analysts argue how this money should be spent—on ground forces or on missiles, on bombers or on submarines; but there is no argument that the money should be spent.

A large share of the remaining research and development funds goes for research into health. Senator Abraham Ribicoff, Democrat of Connecticut, speaking from his personal experience when he was Secretary of Health, Education and Welfare, has said: "Practically all the research that was being done for health in America was flourishing and being accomplished because of the large infusions of federal funds." Again there is not much argument over the spending of these funds. Research into the causes and cures of diseases so often ends in frustrating and expensive failure that only the government can afford to take the financial loss. So this kind of assistance meets the traditional standard of need. The government subsidy is filling a need that no one else can fill.

Although there is no argument over the expenditure of these funds for research, there is a great argument over the fruits of that research. The products of research and development expenditures can and will change the life of Americans. Dr. Guthrie's PKU test now is saving hundreds of babies a year from the fate of growing up as retarded children. Frozen orange juice and the aerosol bomb and the aluminum frying pan, common products today, are the results of government-financed research and development yesterday. From new valves for beer kegs to better bathroom tile caulking, from lightweight railroad cars to new ceramics, from minute fuel cells that can power automobiles to new sources of food from the algae of the ocean, from a cure for cancer to better reception on a television set, the shape of tomorrow's life will be influenced and altered by the government-inspired and government-financed research going on today.

The results of this research and development cannot be predicted. There is too much of it. One survey, by the Federal Council for Science and Technology, indicated that eight thousand inventions were made in the course of federally financed research and development contracts during the 1965 fiscal year. Five thousand of those inventions were made under contracts with the Defense Department.

Inventions or new processes developed by private industry with federal funds are in most cases a by-product. Defense Department research is aimed, for example, at producing the best weapons for the nation's defense. The National Aeronautics and Space Administration spends its research funds in pursuit of the concept of interplanetary travel. These two agencies, responsible for spending approximately two thirds of the nation's research dollar, are primarily interested in noncommercial applications of what is developed with the federal funds.

As a result, particularly with the Defense Department, the contractor is permitted to retain the patent rights to whatever invention he produces with federal funds. The government does retain for itself the right to use these inventions on a royalty-free basis. A new advance in radar, for example, developed with federal funds by a private contractor, could be incorporated into a military plane without any royalty paid to the developer. Incorporating that radar advance into a commercial passenger plane, in contrast, would require the payment of a royalty to the developer of the radar advance. This raises the selling price of the passenger plane and the cost to the public of tickets to fly on that plane.

That was not always the military policy. Before the Second World War the government retained the patents on inventions developed by private companies with federal dollars. The government then could permit any manufacturer to produce the item without paying a royalty. This was a spur to competition; it permitted more manufacturers to produce the item. During the war, however, this policy changed. No one seems to know exactly why.

Apparently, in the rapid development of America's defenses back in the early 1940s, private industry wanted the patents and officials agreed to change the past procedure in the interest of winning the war. The practice of handing over the patents froze into policy and has never been unfrozen.

At the Pentagon the claim is made that this policy is necessary to attract companies to government work. The profit made on the contract itself, it is argued, is not reward enough. Bureaucracies are like policies; they rarely change. There are some companies —and these are the giants of American industry—that do almost all their work with the federal government. To say they would turn down a federal contract unless they were assured ownership of all resultant patents is to say they would voluntarily surrender 75 to 90 percent of their market. As happens with other bureaucracies, that at the Pentagon dealing with contractors has become more a spokesman for the contractors than for the public it is supposed to represent.

There is no question why the industries want the patent rights. The intricacies of government contracts are often secret and difficult to fathom. But occasionally there is a breakthrough to enlightenment. Back in 1960, for example, the General Accounting Office examined Pentagon contracts with the Thompson Ramo Wooldridge company, which then was managing the Air Force's ballistic missile program. The GAO investigators paid particular attention to the patents resulting from those contracts with Thompson Ramo Wooldridge. Although the Pentagon permits private industry to retain patents developed under government contracts, it does require that the nature of these patents be reported to the Pentagon. Only when it has such reports can the Pentagon determine whether it should exercise its option to use those patents without paying a royalty. At the time of this particular study, several hundred inventions had been developed under the Pentagon contracts with Thompson Ramo Wooldridge but patent applications were filed or were about to be filed only for ninety-five.

Of those ninety-five, two were classified by the company as marginal and thirteen as speculative. That was the company's way of

THE GUARANTEED SOCIETY 140

saying that those fifteen did not offer much chance of commercial exploitation. Sixty-nine inventions were described by the company as secondary, meaning, again according to the company, "one of several developments relating to a major commercial program." Those sixty-nine could lead to important commercial developments. The prospect of money existed there. The company classified the remaining eleven as "primary" ones. The company defined "primary" as relating "to a development believed to be sufficiently basic and important to provide a basis for a new industry or an entirely new product line; or one which may have a major effect on the expansion or conversion of an existing industry or product line." There is no other way to read that company definition except to say that those particular eleven inventions promised to be big moneymakers.

There is a moral question: Should one company have a monopoly on products developed with public funds? Such a monopoly means controlling the development of an industry and the prices charged to the public. That question is at the heart of the guaranteed society.

There is a second question with defense contracts: Do such monopolies actually harm the national defense they are supposed to serve? The GAO study of the Thompson Ramo Wooldridge contracts suggested they could.

In its work developing the ballistic missile system, the Thompson Ramo Wooldridge company was required to deal with a number of other private companies. All of these companies were working in areas that could lead to valuable patents. A successful ballistic missile program required all these companies to discuss their work together, required a free exchange of ideas. Were these contractors reluctant to exchange their ideas with Thompson Ramo Wooldridge, afraid that company would steal the information and then patent it?

GAO gave the company a clean bill of health. "We have no indication," the investigators said, "that [Thompson Ramo Wooldridge] took advantage of its privileged position by applying for patents based on inventions disclosed or conceived by the associated contractors." There was no theft.

"However," the GAO men continued, "the opportunity for such action obviously existed and we believe that this is another factor that can reasonably be expected to be a deterrent to the full flow of information in the ballistic missile program." The fact that Thompson Ramo Wooldridge was honest, the GAO men were saying, did not alter the strong possibility that other companies might suspect them of being dishonest. And this fear might restrict the desired free flow of information.

GAO pointed out that if the government retained the patents on inventions discovered with federal funds, "the natural reluctance of participating contractors to making information available . . . probably would be reduced."

In other cases the defense contractor has delayed informing the government about patentable inventions until the contractor actually has secured the patent. Such delays took place even though the government is supposed to be notified immediately of any such inventions. Again, such delays can be harmful to national defense because the Pentagon does not know what specifically is available to it. Another possibility is that the government may have to pay a royalty to use a patent when it rightfully should be allowed a royalty-free license.

The Lockheed Missiles and Space Company, for example, delayed reporting 340 specific inventions to the Pentagon for periods ranging from six months to forty-seven months. When General Accounting Office investigators queried Lockheed, the company replied that the delays were unintentional and that a loss to the government could not be demonstrated. The GAO men, in their 1964 report, agreed that loss to the government could not be shown; only the possibility of such loss was shown to exist. The possibility in that one case raises the probability that such losses do exist in other cases, the GAO men asserted.

But all the blame does not belong to the contractors. Senator Long has described the giveaway of patent rights as "a complete rape of the public interest." If that description is accurate, part of the fault is that the government agencies are not doing their chaperoning job. The Pentagon bureaucracy has made clear it is not interested in whether the private companies comply with the requirement that all inventions be reported. In the Lockheed case, the GAO investigators found one reason "the government's patent rights were jeopardized" was that "the military's local plant representatives did very little with respect to surveillance of the contractor's patent policies and procedures."

In another case, involving the Lockheed Aircraft Corporation and government inertia, the federal government got stuck paying $82,500 in royalties. The royalty was for use of a wing-tip auxiliary fuel tank developed by Lockheed. Lockheed claimed the invention was produced outside of any government contract and the Air Force was not entitled to a royalty-free use of the patent on airplanes it contracted for. The Air Force then determined that the invention had been developed as part of an Air Force contract. It claimed a refund of $82,500 in royalties. The royalties had been collected by Lockheed from the Republic Aviation Corporation when Republic built an Air Force plane incorporating the wing-tip auxiliary fuel tank. Republic had, of course, been reimbursed by the federal government. The Air Force reached its decision, that it was entitled to a refund, in 1958. When the General Accounting Office investigated the situation in 1964, six years later, it found the government had made no effort to collect the royalty. "Apparently each Air Force office waited for the other to initiate the action to recover the royalties," said the GAO report.

Lengthy delays by defense contractors in reporting inventions to the federal government appear to be the standard. In another 1964 report GAO reported that Thompson Ramo Wooldridge delayed more than a year in reporting 113 inventions. Again there was no specific loss that could be pointed to, only the probability of loss. And again a principal reason was Pentagon indifference. "We also found," said the GAO report, "that the government administrative personnel had not established the necessary surveillance to assure that the contractor was complying promptly and completely with contractual patent provisions."

Although the GAO did not demonstrate any loss to the government in those two 1964 reports, Senator Long of Louisiana was not so certain. His charge, made before a Senate subcommittee, is a description of possibility rather than actuality. Still, it is an interesting possibility. Change some of the names and Senator Long has painted a grim picture of the possible cost to the national defense of the guaranteed society. He said:

> The best things these fellows were discovering they had been keeping secret from the other guys for more than four long years. In other words, when Lockheed gets a good fuel to put a missile in the air, they say, for Pete's sake, don't let Ramo Wooldridge know about this. When Ramo Wooldridge finds out what is the best metal, they say, for Pete's sake, don't let Lockheed find out. Here is a fellow, if he knows what is the best metal, he doesn't know the best way of welding it. It is the blind leading the blind, a Tower of Babel, financed by extortion and is a complete outrage of the public interest, all for the hope that each one of these guys is going to get rich because he is the only one that knows something. They withhold knowledge even though they all signed contracts promising they would divulge their discoveries to the government.

As far as can be determined, the intent of Congress was to retain patent rights on federally financed discoveries for the public. At least whenever Congress specifically has legislated on the matter, it so retained patent rights. Such retention is written into legislation governing the Tennessee Valley Authority and the Atomic Energy Commission and into such programs as the Coal Research and Development Act and the Saline Water Act. Only when Congress has failed to write such legislation and the agency granting the contract can exercise its discretion do the contractors end up with the patent rights. While the Pentagon, incidentally, claims it must offer the patent rights as an additional incentive to attract contractors, such agencies as the Atomic Energy Commission and the Tennessee Valley Authority have no difficulty finding contractors—even though they refuse to grant exclusive patent rights.

As for assisting American industry, evidence indicates making the patents available to all comers on a royalty-free basis is a much more beneficial practice. TVA, for example, does considerable work in developing new fertilizers. TVA retains the patents on these fertilizers, then makes the patents available on a royalty-free, non-exclusive basis. Anybody with the money to establish a company can go into the fertilizer business. And the competition between the various companies serves to keep the service high and the price low. Most of these companies—170 out of the 207 licensed to use TVA patents by a count made in the mid-1960s—are in the category of small business. The free use of the government-owned patents keeps them in business.

The relationship between TVA and the small businesses that use its patents is a good example of how government can assist in the development of a free-enterprise society. The government assumes the burdens of searching for new products that are needed, and then makes the fruits of that search available to industry. The public is served because the competition within an industry assures good products at a low price.

But that is not the way of the guaranteed society.

Two

Senator Long once explained why the Defense Department's policy of giving away patent rights is not changed. "To change that policy is beyond my power. It is beyond the power of any member of the Senate, of any member of the House of Representatives to change," he said. Then asking "Why?" he answered himself, saying: "Because both large political parties depend for financial support upon people connected with big business and such people are numerous in both parties.

"They have friends. They have votes. They are powerful and influential," he continued. "I make that statement because I know the realities of public life. Whether we like it or not, politics is the name of the game."*

*Without in any way discounting the sincerity of Senator Long's remarks, the same statement could be used in describing the oil industry's ability to defend the oil depletion allowance against all attacks, as well as big business defense of patent ownership. Senator Long is one of the oil industry's warmest friends in Washington.

Those federal agencies dealing with large companies do give away patent rights. There is no legislation to stop them. In contrast, those federal agencies dealing with small companies are guided by legislation in their patent policies, and generally the contractor does not receive patent rights. There is, in effect, a dual policy. If a large company is involved, it can be pretty certain of receiving the exclusive patent rights; it can lock up the future development of the product developed with public funds; it can lock up that product's entry into commercial areas and the product's profitability. If, however, a small company is involved, then the patent on the product developed will be generally available. No single company will be able to lock up that product's future.

In 1963 President Kennedy issued a memorandum; its purpose was to establish a code of practice governing federal agencies and their patent policies. Its object was to provide greater protection for the public, to give away fewer of the valuable patents. Although that was its object, its accomplishment was considerably less. The memorandum—actually a directive to federal employees—allowed the federal employees a considerable amount of discretion. And these members of the federal bureaucracy were again responding to the industries they were dealing with rather than the public they were supposed to be representing. Legislation then was in order.

Legislative proposals had been before the Senate's subcommittee on patents for some years. Hearings had been held at various times, but no definite resolutions had been reached. For the public there was a compelling need for resolution. The public needed its rights protected. But there was no compelling need from the standpoint of industry. From its point of view, the informal arrangements worked well. A handful of contractors were receiving the large Pentagon contracts and the patents that went with them. Although the National Aeronautics and Space Administration once had a policy of retaining patent rights rather than surrendering them to private contractors, the policy had been seriously eroded by actual practice. So the large industries did not wish change.

But Senator Long had begun an onslaught against them. As an

authorization bill for a federal agency would come before the Senate, he fought to have an amendment attached to it—the amendment directing the agency to retain patent rights. He was successful in a number of cases affecting the smaller federal agencies and the smaller federal programs. But when he began to zero in on the large agencies, particularly the Pentagon and NASA, he hit trouble. As he had said previously, "Politics is the name of the game."

The issue came to a head on the floor of the Senate in June 1965. The Senate was considering President Johnson's proposal to establish a public health program to combat heart disease, cancer, stroke and other major diseases. Again, Senator Long came up with his proposed amendment. Any patents produced with federal funds under the proposed program should, his proposed amendment said, belong to the public and no single company should have exclusive rights to them. His drive to change federal patent policy on a piecemeal basis showed signs of becoming too successful. An old dodge was used.

The Senate's subcommittee on patents is part of the Judiciary Committee. The subcommittee chairman is John L. McClellan, Democrat of Arkansas, a highly respected member of the Senate. Senators often forget that the committee system in the Senate is a tool to be used. They sometimes tend to think of the committee system, instead, as an objective in itself to be secured and enshrined. And so Senator McClellan argued that the Long amendment should be rejected, not because of any demerits it might have but because Senator McClellan's subcommittee should consider it before the full Senate did, to protect the committee system. He said:

> The real issue involved in the amendment—arguments can be made on either side—is whether we shall now abandon the committee system, do away with it, and make an assault upon the committee system in order to get an amendment agreed to. No hearings have been held on the amendment. The amendment has not been examined by the committee process. No opportunities for hearings have been offered. The amendment deals with a vital problem confronting this country.
>
> Do we want to agree to abandon a tried and valuable system that has been established and has worked over the years? In commit-

tee hearings, we have the advantage of having both sides present their cases, and then we can let the Senate resolve the question.

Are we to resolve this question in an *ex parte* fashion? If we should agree to the proposed procedure at this time, we would be abrogating every precedent that we have followed in the committee system of the United States Senate for so many years.

Every chairman of a Senate committee has something at stake.

The Senate leaders—the committee chairmen and their close associates—and those in the Senate who hope someday to benefit from the largess of the Senate leaders respond to such appeals on cue. They agreed the committee system should not be tampered with. A few members of the Senate, however, refused to go along. One of them, Ralph W. Yarborough, Democrat of Texas, challenged the assertion that a proposal should not be brought up on the Senate floor without having committee consideration first.

"We heard the statement made last Friday that the floor of the Senate is no place to legislate," he told his colleagues. "If the floor of the United States Senate is no place to legislate, why in God's name do we have it? The criticism we hear around the country is that decisions are made in smoke-filled rooms or in the little groups of subcommittees, and that the Senate has lost its savor, and fails to legislate."

Senator Yarborough's comments were striking home and proving embarrassing. The members of the Senate felt uncomfortable as he continued. Some left, to hide in the cloakrooms at the back of the chamber so they could pretend they were unaware of his indictment; others glanced nervously at the press gallery, hoping the newsmen were paying no attention to the Texan.

"Let us legislate on the floor of the Senate," Senator Yarborough continued. "Let us take this bill out into the light of day, and let the American people see how we legislate. It is time we legislated on the floor of the Senate if the fruits of $650 million of the people's research money is going to be given away to private monopolies which are already paid in full, with profit, for research done."

Senator Yarborough did not want the question of patent policy left to the Judiciary Committee. In a statement he inserted into the *Congressional Record* he explained why. "If the legislation proposed," his statement said, "would drastically alter the policy of the Department of Defense and NASA, there would be tremendous opposition from a great number of business interests, and the Judiciary Committee has a rule of free debate." He was spelling out what every member of the Senate knew. If the McClellan subcommittee tried to write a meaningful bill, it must be a bill that would attack the Pentagon's and NASA's policies. Such a bill never would emerge from the Judiciary Committee. "Free debate," the phrase Senator Yarborough used, is a euphemism in the Senate, meaning the bill's opponents would talk about it in committee for as long as necessary without permitting the measure to come to a vote, until the measure's proponents surrendered in weariness.

His prediction was almost correct.

Senator Long's amendment to the public health program was rejected on the premise that the McClellan subcommittee should be allowed to write an entirely new proposal governing federal patent policy. The subcommittee produced a bill early the next year, in March 1966. Rather than create a new federal policy, the subcommittee took the practices then in existence and attempted to codify them with legislation. The government's patent policy had been a doorway to the guaranteed society. The McClellan subcommittee tried to frame that doorway in an act of Congress.

Actually there was little else the subcommittee could do. Any legislation it proposed must then go to the full Senate Judiciary Committee for action. The full committee could either reject, accept, revise slightly or completely rewrite any legislation originating in Senator McClellan's subcommittee. For that reason the subcommittee went along with a bill it knew the full committee would find acceptable. The Senate Judiciary Committee is the meeting place on the Senate side of the Capitol of what is called the conservative coalition, the amalgamation of Midwestern conservative Republicans and southern Democrats. The coalition is personified there by Everett McKinley Dirksen, Republican of Illinois,* and James O. Eastland, Democrat of Mississippi. Senator

*In 1964 when the Senate passed a strong civil-rights bill with the apparent assistance of Senator Dirksen, it was believed the Senator had deserted the

Eastland is the chairman of the committee and Senator Dirksen is the ranking GOP member. Together they determine what the Judiciary Committee does. One thing the Judiciary Committee does not do is report civil-rights bills. When the Senate wants to pass civil-rights legislation it must bypass the committee system. Another thing the Judiciary Committee does not do is report out legislation conservative Republicans consider unfriendly to the interests of American business. And trying to stop a federal hand-out to big business is considered definitely unfriendly.

The bill reported out by the subcommittee had another appeal. Since it appeared to be codifying a policy enunciated by President Kennedy in his 1963 memorandum, it was difficult for some of his followers to be critical of it. The most obvious example of this was the late President's brother, Senator Edward M. Kennedy, Democrat of Massachusetts. A member of the Judiciary Committee, Senator Kennedy voted for the bill although his past liberal record suggested he would be with its opponents. The bill, conceded the Senator, "may not be a final answer . . . but it follows those procedures and employs those criteria with which both government and industry are most familiar. Both have extensive experience operating within its framework, as it was originally formulated in the patent guidelines issued by the White House in 1963."*

But the 1963 memorandum had been only a first step, a faltering one taken against powerful and rich industries that did not want to see their arrangements with government contracting agencies changed. And the 1963 policy, allowing as it did a great deal of discretion to the individual agencies, had not been a successful one. It should have led to a second, third and fourth step until a policy favorable to the public was achieved. It should not have been locked into law—once there, more difficult to change.

---

coalition to support civil rights as conservative Republicans on the House side of the Capitol had done. Actually Senator Dirksen, posing as a friend of civil rights, gutted as much as possible a bill certain to be approved by the Senate. He was not the bill's friend.

*In fairness to Senator Kennedy, he asserted at the time that if the proposal reached the Senate floor, "I intend to offer a number of amendments designed to expand and clarify the rights of the government and thereby emphasize the public interest aspects of the legislation."

THE GUARANTEED SOCIETY 150

The subcommittee bill first would have repealed previous provisions in law retaining patent rights for the federal government. The principle that the public should own and benefit from what it has paid for would have been seriously set back. Then the proposal would have permitted most agency heads to determine their agency's patent policies. But any official who wanted to retain patent rights for the public had to assert that intention when the original contract was drawn up. In practice this would have meant the government giving up all patent rights. A three-man minority on the committee, objecting to the bill, explained why.

"The nature of the market," said the dissenters, "the relationship of the invention to the market, its effect on existing and future competition are among facts relating to the public interest which must be considered. But certainly none of these facts can be determined at the time the R and D contract is executed [which is] the precise time [the subcommittee bill] authorizes the agency to retain or give away the government's rights to these inventions."

The dissenters were Senators Hart, Burdick and Joseph D. Tydings, Democrat of Maryland; Senator Long is not a member of the Judiciary Committee. The three men also asserted that "the fruits from R and D expenditures should not be locked up in government-created monopolies." The three were, in effect, appealing for the use of federal funds to encourage free enterprise. Make the fruits of those expenditures generally available to American business so that open competition will result in low prices and high quality, and those low prices and that high quality would be the payoff to the American people for their financing the original research with the money they pay in taxes. But free enterprise is not a very salable commodity in Washington, not when the guaranteed society is arriving.

Once the bill emerged from the Senate Judiciary Committee, it ran into trouble. Senator Long termed the proposal a "giveaway" and said it would "further entrench the monopolistic positions of many large corporations." Telling newsmen there may be "a month of speeches explaining the issue" on the floor of the Senate, he raised the prospect of a filibuster. A filibuster is a prolonged talkathon on the Senate floor lasting weeks, and Russell Long—the son of Huey P. Long, one of the greatest filibusterers the Senate ever has known—has the vocal cords to do it, as he has demonstrated on several occasions.

As a result the bill never was seriously brought forward for a vote on the Senate floor. Senator McClellan on one occasion did try to have it placed on the "consent calendar," a senatorial device for passing noncontroversial measures quickly and without debate. Senator Long objected and the attempt failed, as Senator McClellan must have anticipated would happen. Nothing more was heard of the proposal. When the Eighty-ninth Congress ended in January 1967, the patent bill died.

Actually, while the bill died, the practice of giving away valuable patents, developed with public funds, continues. The guaranteed society had it both ways in this case. If the bill passed, then the giveaway was written into law. If the bill did not pass, then the giveaway was continued by bureaucratic action.

One reason why the guaranteed society succeeded so well in the case of the patent rights was its enemies. Russell Long is so vehement in his opposition that it is difficult for other members of Congress to go along with him. Opponents of the SST, such as William Proxmire, are not against the airplane. They oppose the federal government's unnecessary and intimate involvement with a private industry. The critics of the merchant marine did not become vocal until the merchant marine, refusing to fulfill its part of the bargain, did not respond to the nation's defense call. Even then the industry's critics did not wish to end the subsidy to the merchant marine. They are willing to spend federal funds to make it more competitive. With oil shale, again the critics are not against private industry making a profit. They are against the denial of the public interest. With patents, however, Russell Long goes beyond any such reasonableness.

The legislation he advocates would have the federal government retain patent rights to all products developed with federal funds. He would make only one concession to the private company that developed the product. He would give it exclusive licensing privileges for the first three years of the product's life so the private company can enjoy some profit from its efforts in the development of the product. After the three-year period ends, the patent would be available to other companies on a royalty-free basis.

In its way, Senator Long's approach is as unfair and extreme as is the current policy of giving the patent rights to a single company. His one concession, of letting the private companies have exclusive licensing provisions for the first three years of the product's life, is really not much of a concession. A new product probably will not become commercially successful for many years after its development and patenting. Just as current policy does not recognize that the public makes a contribution when it finances research, Senator Long's approach does not recognize that the private industry makes a contribution.

And of course the industry does make a contribution. A new alloy, a new missile fuel, a fuel cell or any of the hundreds of new inventions discovered each day with federal financing assistance does not just spring from the ground when the land is watered with federal dollars. Such devices are the product also of industrial know-how and a company's experience.

"Our feeling has always been," one Pentagon official explained, "that it is a question of fairness in recognition of the contractor's equity that he has already established in his prior work which was not performed for the government. We are not automatically entitled to full patent rights just because we finance a particular phase of the development work. In other words, the profit on the particular contract that may be involved is not compensation for the investment he has made in the past to be in the position where he can be chosen for research work for us."

That statement of why the Defense Department was not entitled to "full patent rights" was used to explain why the Pentagon gives away all patent rights. The explanation, offered to Congress by R. Tenney Johnson, deputy general counsel of the Army, does not justify any such giveaway. It would justify a sharing of patent rights between the public and the private contractor. But neither Senator Long nor the private contractor is interested in any such sharing. Each wants all.

Devising a formula for the sharing of patent rights would be difficult. "In some cases a fifty-fifty division might be fair," Senator Jack Miller, Republican of Iowa, once pointed out. "In other cases an allocation of one hundred percent to the federal government might be fair. In some cases it might be fair to give one third, while in other cases it might be fair to give two thirds."

But although devising such a formula would be difficult, it would not be impossible. Perhaps a Patent Board could be established to determine the public's share and private industry's share of a patent. The patents would be available to other companies. The other companies would have to make a payment of a percentage of a fair royalty equal to the private company's contribution to the development of the product. For example, if a fair royalty for use of a specific invention was estimated at one thousand dollars and the private industry's contribution to developing the patent was 50 percent, then any company using the patent would have to pay the developing company five hundred dollars.

Such a formula would serve several purposes. It would assure the private industry of a fair return for the investment of its experience and energy in the developing of a new product. It would also assure the public a fair return for its cash investment. Competition would be increased because the patent rights would be generally available. The price would not be exorbitant because the royalty would be diminished by a percentage equal to the public's contribution to the patent's development. Although such a formula would be complicated, it would not be more so than most arrangements between private industry and the government. Nor would it be impossible to administer and police.

And if the concept of a Patent Board did, in fact, turn out to be unworkable, another system can be worked out to divide fairly the benefits from patents developed with public funds and private know-how. At least reasonable men should be able to do so.

But the prospects are not good for any fair division. The present system of giving away the patent rights offers a guarantee. The private contractor can take public funds and develop a product knowing that he will control the commercial exploitation of that product. How fast it will be brought onto the market, how much it will cost, how it will be improved—all will be decisions made by a private contractor. The public will have no voice in those determinations. The failure of the Eighty-ninth Congress to change that system assures the only opportunity available to the public is that of picking up the bill.

That is the guaranteed society.

GAI: 5
Minted Moonlight

One

IT IS NOT SURPRISING that in an environment promising private businesses profit without risk, as with the SST and the merchant marine; in an economy that freely offers private industry the fruits of public property, such as with oil shale and patents; it is not surprising in such a society that the philosophy of a guaranteed society extends to the individual. The suggestion is that he receive a guaranteed income and become a member in good standing of the guaranteed society.

Some students of the subject profess to find the origins of the guaranteed annual income in the various biblical injunctions to be charitable to one's neighbor. Various nineteenth-century philosophers suggested it in one form or another. But most historians agree that the modern history of the guaranteed annual income begins in September 1933 when Dr. Francis E. Townsend of Long Beach, California, wrote a letter to the editor of the local newspaper. In his letter Dr. Townsend recommended a cure for the depression then tearing apart the economic fabric of the United States. His suggestion: a monthly pension for all persons who retired at age sixty. The only reservation the doctor added was that the recipients of the pension "spend the money as they get it."

A thin, gray-haired man in his sixties, Dr. Townsend appeared much too benign to become the leader of a national crusade that at times verged on exploding into a major political movement. But the simplicity of his idea had enormous appeal to the men and women who found their "golden years" tarnished by the lack of financial security. Using something called a "transaction tax"—a 2 percent levy on an item every time it moved from one commercial point to another—Dr. Townsend's plan would have each retiree receive $200 (the doctor's original proposal had been for $150 but he later raised it) from the federal government.

Soon thousands of "Townsend Clubs" sprang up around the country. They appealed to millions of older persons and also to their dependents. These younger persons saw the Townsend plan as a means of relieving them of the financial obligation of supporting their aged relatives. Dr. Townsend and his followers helped elect several members of Congress, who promptly introduced legislation modeled after the Townsend plan. Townsend himself later joined with some other movement leaders to pose a threat to the Democratic Party in the 1936 election.

Dr. Townsend was not alone in advocating a guaranteed income in the 1930s. Senator Huey P. Long, Jr., Democrat of Louisiana, was willing to go one better even than Dr. Townsend. His "share-the-wealth" plan promised every American family a guarantee of a $5,000 stake to begin with and a $2,000 annual income. He was not limiting the concept of a guaranteed income only to pensioners; instead, in the phrase of his movement, "Ev'ry man a king." Within a few short years Huey Long claimed his plan had seven million supporters.

The plans were obviously more unworkable, demagogic appeals to persons afflicted by the depression than rational attempts to solve the nation's economic problems. Still, these plans fostered movements which developed political power or at least the threat of political power. New Deal historians consider the widespread support of the Townsend plan as the immediate impetus for the passage of the Social Security Act in 1935.

Despite this accomplishment, the Townsend plan and Huey Long's dream of shared wealth met ridicule from thoughtful persons in the 1930s. This ridicule was summed up best at the time by an English visitor. The Townsend plan, said Winston S. Churchill, is an attempt to "mint the moonlight into silver and coin the sunshine into gold."

Now, less than four decades since practical men ridiculed Dr. Townsend and respectable men sneered at Huey Long, the moonlight is about to be minted and the sunshine is about to be coined. Within the nation is developing a powerful movement for a guaranteed annual income, or the negative income tax, as it is sometimes called. Its impetus derives from the fact that its supporters are neither the far-out kooks nor the extreme demagogues of the 1930s; instead, they are eminently respectable economists, businessmen, social scientists and government officials. Members of both political parties are among the guaranteed annual income's supporters.

How fast this movement had developed can be traced in statements made by some federal officials. In 1964 the President's Council of Economic Advisers, in its annual report for that year, definitely seem to be saying "no" to such proposals as a guaranteed annual income or a negative income tax. Said the report:

Conquest of poverty is well within our power. About eleven billion dollars a year would bring all poor families up to the three-thousand-dollar income level we have taken to be the minimum for a decent life. The majority of the nation could simply tax themselves enough to provide the necessary income supplements to their less fortunate citizens. The burden—one-fifth of the annual defense budget, less than two percent of GNP—would certainly not be intolerable. But this "solution" would leave untouched most of the roots of poverty. Americans want to earn the American standard of living by their own efforts and contributions. It will be far better, even if more difficult, to equip and to permit the poor of the nation to produce and to earn the additional eleven billion, and more. We can surely afford greater generosity in relief of distress. But the major thrust of our campaign must be against causes rather than symptoms. We can afford the cost of that campaign too.

Only two years later, however, the Council was not quite so certain that eliminating the roots of poverty would be "far better" than buying it out of existence with some form of guaranteed income. In its 1966 report the Council said:

> Increasing concern about [poverty] is producing a variety of new income-maintenance proposals. One approach would make public assistance coverage more comprehensive and assure all recipients more adequate benefit levels. Another approach is the institution of uniformly determined payments to families based only on the amount by which their incomes fall short of minimum subsistence levels. Such a system could be integrated with the existing income tax system. This plan is now receiving intensive study by many scholars. It could be administered on a universal basis for all the poor and would be the most direct approach to reducing poverty. In future years, these and other proposals deserve further exploration.

A few months after that report, a citizens' committee with semi-official status, known as the Advisory Council on Public Welfare, also spoke positively about a guaranteed annual income. It suggested to the Secretary of Health, Education and Welfare a plan in which "a floor of required individual or family income would be established for each state in terms of the cost of a modest but adequate family budget for families of various sizes and circumstances as established by objective methods of budget costing. This would constitute the minimum level of assistance which must prevail in that state."

Taking the proposal for a guaranteed annual income from the disrepute of Huey Long's share-the-wealth scheme to the trial balloons of reputable government studies produced no cry of public protest. In the absence of any serious opposition, President Johnson felt able to advance the proposal one step forward. In his 1967 economic report he said:

> Completely new proposals for guaranteeing minimum incomes are now under discussion. They range from a "negative income tax" to a complete restructuring of public assistance to a program of residual public employment for all who lack private jobs. Their advocates include some of the sturdiest defenders of free enterprise. These plans may or may not prove to be practicable at any time. And they are almost surely beyond our means at this time. But we must examine any plan, however unconventional, which could promise a major advance. I intend to establish a commission of leading Americans to examine the many proposals that have been put forward reviewing their merits and disadvantages, and reporting in two years to me and the American people.

That commission was appointed at the end of 1967. Shortly after that the Council of Economic Advisers produced its report for 1968. This is the group that four years earlier definitely had rejected an income maintenance program in favor of equipping and permitting "the poor of the nation to produce and to earn." Now, however, the Council reported:

> Despite the prospective benefits from training programs and further economic growth, there will still be a need for income maintenance or income supplements for poor families headed by men of working age.

The guaranteed annual income/negative income tax is moving toward becoming a part of American life. A good bet is that it will be enacted into law by the early or mid-1970s. That will be approximately a decade after it was first mentioned seriously by economists. That is a relatively brief period of time for a major economic change. Medicare, for example, required almost a quarter of a century of discussion, debate and advocacy before it was accepted and became a formal program of the federal government. And the Keynesian approach to national economics—at times deliberately courting budget deficits in defiance of the "Puritan ethic" that says all debts are bad—took even longer before winning national acceptance in the income-tax cut of 1964. But each generation moves faster than the preceding one, and only a decade is necessary before a choice is made on the guaranteed annual income. If it becomes law, it will be the sharpest break the country has ever made with its traditional welfare philosophy.

"Welfare" always has been a part of the American philosophy and of the American economy—"welfare" meaning the helping of an individual by the government. In the earliest colonial days a newly arrived colonist could acquire land often simply by applying for it and promising to farm it. Some of the huge land holdings in Virginia were amassed because the colonial government was offering fifty acres to a man for himself and for every person he brought to the new country. The young colonist built up his estate by bringing all his relatives, his friends, his wife's family and also slaves.

This welfare approach, the giving of land to an individual in exchange for his promise to develop it, continued when the colonies formed the United States of America. Perhaps the greatest welfare program the United States ever undertook was the Homestead Act of 1862. During the Civil War years alone, for example, the federal government gave away some twenty-five million acres of land to settlers, asking in return only that the land be developed. This program represented the welfare state in its truest sense: a federally owned commodity is given away to the needy. The riches of the majority are redistributed to the minority who are poor.

This kind of "giveaway" program was marked by two characteristics. One was fulfilling a welfare need by providing employment—the farming of the land—for the new immigrant to America and for the man unable to survive economically along the Eastern seaboard. The second characteristic was the resulting national benefit. The homesteader peopled and cultivated a whole new territory. He supplied the United States with wheat to export. He purchased the industrial output of the factories in the East. The homesteader accepted the nation's largess, but he paid it back many times.

This kind of welfare program succeeded so admirably because it was built on the traditional standard of offering a means of increasing opportunity.

The Homestead program lasted almost four decades, finally

ending in the 1890s when the United States ran out of public owned land suitable for homesteading. That kind of welfare ended then also. But a new kind was needed. In the years that followed, the distorted vision of America as a frontier land and the Jeffersonian concept of the individual American as a small farmer obscured the fact that a major change was taking place in the United States. That change was the industrial revolution.

When a man worked his farm he was working not only for current income but also for a security when old or sick. The farm would always exist, he believed. As his children grew, they would continue to till the land. Those children, appreciative of the contributions he had made to develop the farm land into a productive unit, the farmer felt certain, would always provide a home for him. The welfare problems of the aged and the ill were not a concern for the government. In the agricultural society of that time they were the concern of the family.

But when a man worked in the new society produced by the industrial revolution, he was working only for current income, not for his future security. Only a few companies offered pension programs in the nineteenth century. The first large company to do so was the American Express Company (now the Railway Express Agency). After that "breakthrough" in 1875, several other companies did also. These included the Consolidated Gas Company of New York (now the Consolidated Edison Company), the Carnegie Steel Company and the Standard Oil Company of New Jersey. "Pension" may be a misnomer in describing these early programs. The plans were only promises to pay by the companies. The pension money was not kept in a separate fund. The employee had no rights to the pension, no assurance he would receive a pension, other than the promise, not always kept, by a management not particularly friendly at that time to the employee. The plans were gradually strengthened but continued limited in their application. By 1920 only three million workers had pension protection at their place of employment.

But the 1920s were a time of generally high employment, and the failing of the industrial society to provide security went largely unnoticed. Problems were being created even then, of course. But most people, too involved in enjoying a national prosperity, were ignoring them. Then came the crash of 1929 and the depression of the 1930s. The problems increased. People such as Francis Town· send and Huey Long seized on them as tickets to personal power. The federal government began a mammoth effort to provide or at least organize a new kind of welfare program. The government recognized that it must provide welfare not only to increase an individual's opportunity, as it had done with the Homestead Act, but also that it must solve the problems created by the failings of the industrial society. A wide variety of programs were developed. There was insurance against an individual suddenly being thrown out of work; a program of financial aid to children-in-need was developed; and, most importantly, there was the Social Security program for older persons, persons disabled on the job and for the families of working men who die. Except for the unemployment insurance, which was to assist a person temporarily out of work, these programs were not designed to broaden opportunity as past welfare programs had been. Instead, these programs made a sharp break with the past philosophy. The United States was acknowledging that in an industrial society there are some people—the aged, the ill, the young—who cannot support themselves. Secondly, the United States was acknowledging that society in an organized fashion, through its government, must provide care for these people. That is the modern concept of welfare. At the height of the depression this new concept was best enunciated by the governor of New York. "Modern society, acting through its government," said Franklin D. Roosevelt, "owes the definite obligation to prevent the starvation or dire waste of any of its fellow men and women who try to maintain themselves but cannot."

When those programs were developed in the 1930s, they were aimed at what was the immediate problem: the financial condition of the poor visible then, the lower middle-class Americans. That group was hit hardest by the depression. Unable to cope with a situation not of their making, the members of that economic group needed help. The welfare programs of the New Deal hit their targets very well.

The working man, suddenly without a job, found income in

temporary "make work" projects. He had something of value to do until the economy improved and he could secure a regular job. The skilled worker found a new power in unions because of the New Deal's support of organized labor. This power would offer him economic protection in the future by giving him and his fellow workers an organized strength. These programs largely succeeded.

The children of the people who benefited most from the New Deal are today the college graduates, the young executives, in most cases members of the top half of the middle-class. And even their parents, the specific targets of the welfare reforms of the 1930s, are living with a reasonable amount of dignity and comfort.

But the solving of one problem often only reveals the existence of a second problem. Raising one group out of poverty reveals that another group remains. The New Deal welfare programs helped the middle class, those persons experienced at working, capable of working and guided by their environment to be interested in working. Unemployment insurance, for example, assists the worker who is thrown out of work for a few months. The aid-to-dependent-children program helps a mother and child who suddenly lose the man in their house, the breadwinner.

But there are many people for whom such programs are of either no assistance or are actually harmful. Unemployment insurance offers no help to the man who has not worked, who has no training for a job and whose environment has guided him away from working. The aid-to-dependent-children program is of no value to the family where the man in the house is unable to earn an income. This program actually is detrimental to the man and to his family. Because of the requirement that aid cannot be extended to a house in which there is a man in residence, the program forces a man to desert his family in order to assure the family's receiving a welfare income.

It is people with these kinds of problems—not the members of the middle class who were temporarily unemployed in the 1930s—who need assistance today. The New Deal welfare programs, as revolutionary as they appeared to be and as generous as some thought they were, basically were an extension of the old practice of the rich giving the poor a turkey every Christmas. Franklin D. Roosevelt always was the benevolent master of Hyde Park, making certain that none of his poor neighbors went hungry. But that kind of welfare has served its purpose. Now it no longer works.

Senator Robert Kennedy of New York explains why. "We have created a welfare system," he has said, "which aids only a fourth of those who are poor, which forces men to leave their families so that public assistance can be obtained, which has created a dependence on their fellow citizens that is degrading and distasteful to giver and receiver alike.

"We must understand what we have done," he continued. "We have said, 'Here. Here is what we are going to do for you.' And in our generosity we have created a system of handouts, a second-rate set of social services which damages and demeans its recipients, and destroys any semblance of human dignity that they have managed to retain through their adversity."

And the situation will become worse, much worse. There are three groups entering the welfare rolls in ever-increasing numbers.

The first group is the half-million Negroes a year who are pushed, persuaded to leave, enticed out, chased or somehow encouraged to exit from the rural areas of the South and come to the ghettos of the North. A four-year study by the Twentieth Century Fund reported in 1967 that the trend of migrants from the South, both poor whites as well as poor Negroes, may decrease somewhat through the 1970s as more industrialization comes to the South and more jobs are available there. But the report, titled *The Advancing South: Manpower Prospects and Problems*, cautioned with the obvious.

"The employment outlook facing the Southern Negro is a discouraging one," it said, "so long as he is undereducated, lacks industrial experience and is subjected to racial discrimination." Unless the South alters its way of life dramatically, the exodus of Negroes to the North will continue in great numbers.

Immigrants have invaded the ghettos of the Eastern cities before. But there are two differences between the waves of the Irish from Ireland, Italians from Italy, Jews from eastern Europe and the waves of Negroes from the South. The members of the earlier groups had rudimentary educations, at least. In the South the rural Negro has been and is denied even that. The impact of education on a family's chance to escape from poverty is great. If the head of a Negro family has less than eight years of schooling, the chance is less than one in two that his family will escape a life of poverty. If that breadwinner has graduated from high school he has a 7 to 3 chance of seeing his family live above the poverty line. And if that breadwinner has managed to obtain some college education, then the odds have risen to 4 to 1 in his favor. Unfortunately, the average rural Negro in the South still is back where the chance is less than one in two.

The second difference involves the jobs waiting for the earlier immigrants. They could run the elevators in the office buildings and roll the cigars in their tenement flats while they and their families absorbed enough of the middle-class American culture eventually to become part of that culture. But today the elevators are automatic and laws prohibit the rolling of cigars at slave wages in tenement flats. And so those half-million Negroes a year who come to the Northern cities will be either candidates for welfare or worse.

"All around our nation," Senator Kennedy has said, "Negroes and Puerto Ricans, Mexican-Americans and Indians, poor whites in Appalachia and in blighted inner-city areas, are waking up to what we have done. They are demanding what the rest of us take for granted—a measure of control over their lives, over their own destinies, a sense of communication with those whom they have elected to govern them. If we do not yield, if we do not work a virtual revolution in the organization of our social services, the result could be the ripping asunder of the already thin fabric of American life."

Senator Kennedy concluded: "The stakes are indeed high."

The second group of welfare candidates comes from the people who eventually will retire, only to find their income then is inadequate. The Social Security program of old-age payments is not meant, and probably never will be meant, to insure financial security in a person's old age. It is, instead, a floor on which such security can be built. Wilbur Cohen, the Secretary of Health, Education and Welfare, explained the concept this way:

> The concept there [in the old-age program] is that you provide x dollars for old-age retirement, then a private employer adjusts his private retirement system on top of that. The private pension is the second layer. The third layer is whatever the individual wants to do on his own.

There are two reasons why Social Security never will be more than a basic floor. Robert M. Ball, the head of the Social Security Administration, offered one reason in testimony before a Congressional subcommittee. He said:

> There is widespread acceptance of the idea that our retirement arrangements should consist of a universal government plan with private pensions and certain government plans supplementing the universal system. A single approach [that is, relying on Social Security solely for retirement income] may seem at first glance to have considerable attraction, but even if Social Security benefits were to be considerably liberalized, as they should be, it is extremely doubtful that a generally applicable system would pay benefits high enough to satisfy management and unions in the more successful companies or industries. Moreover, in some occupations and in some industries special types of provisions, such as lower retirement ages, may be desirable. And, for those in top executive positions and for supervisory personnel many managements want to facilitate retirement or shifts to another job by paying retirement benefits much higher than will be paid by a general system.

Mr. Ball's point is well taken. A system run by the government must be a uniform system. Social Security largely is. An individual making $15,000 a year will earn no more in Social Security benefits than a person earning $7,800. But in a private-enterprise society, retirement programs must be flexible. Otherwise there would be little incentive for a worker to wish to become boss.

The second reason why Social Security probably will never become the single retirement system in the country is a political one. If the government were to enact such a program, figuring the dollar amount needed would be a simple arithmetical problem. Social Security is dispensed as a matter of right, not as a matter of need. All the government statisticians would have to do is check the census reports for the number of people over sixty-five, multiply that number by whatever benefit figure is used, and the answer is how much the government has to pay out each year. But federal programs never are decided that way. The dollar amount the federal government spends is established by the ballot box and not by a statistician with pencil and paper. When Alf M. Landon, the former governor of Kansas in the 1930s and the unsuccessful Republican opponent of Franklin Roosevelt in the 1936 presidential election, observed his eightieth birthday in 1967, he commented to a newspaper interviewer that he could see no reason why he should be receiving Social Security. Such money, he argued, should go instead to people who need it. His argument has not had a lot of political support and will not have as long as Social Security remains a basic floor and politicians can claim it costs only a "small amount each payday," as President Johnson did when he signed the Medicare provisions into law in 1965. But broadening Social Security into a uniform and the sole retirement system would require a much greater increase in taxes—one that the ballot box probably would not accept.

So for persons entering their retirement years, Social Security will not be enough. Can they rely then on pensions to make up the difference? The answer is mixed, but the prospect is bleak rather than bright. Presently more than one fourth of the poverty in the United States is found among the aged. If anything, that percentage may grow in coming years. In the late 1960s about one out of six persons over age sixty-five was receiving a pension. By the 1980s that figure will rise to slightly less than one out of three. It will continue to improve in subsequent years, but only very gradually. Decades will pass before even half the retired people in the United States have pensions.

Many people currently working who think they will retire with a pension may be disappointed. Most company pension plans require, for example, that the employee reach a specific age and work for the company a specified number of years before being eligible for a pension. In some cases that is not desirable; an employee is better off if he seeks new employment. In other cases it is not possible.

"I work as an engineer in the aerospace industry and every two or three years I end up working for another company," said one worker, explaining why his pension credits are nonexistent. "Each time I move, I lose money on the sale of my house and I lose any retirement benefits I might accrue. In essence, I have become an itinerant defense aerospace worker. Mind you, I don't mind the changing of jobs. However, I am now thirty-seven years old and it is almost impossible to go into some other industry."

That situation is not unique. Many workers must change jobs every few years either because the Defense Department shifts contracts or because one domestic industry loses out to another, or one company fails while another succeeds.

And when a company fails, its pension program fails, at least partly, with it. Willard Solenberger, a United Auto Workers official, has said: "Available government statistics indicate that in each of the years 1964 and 1965, some five hundred pension plans in the United States were terminated. Although data are not available on the numbers of employees affected or on the funding balance sheets, there can be little doubt that the discontinuance of these plans cancelled the pension expectations of many thousands of persons."

A couple of examples illustrate how unsure a promise of a pension plan is. When the Packard automobile company closed down in the late 1950s, those employees already receiving a pension had their benefits reduced to 85 percent of the promised amount. Those workers about to go on pension—that is, men age sixty or over and with ten years of service in the company—received nothing. There was a provision in the pension plan for them to receive some funds. While there was a provision, there was no money.

When the Stubebaker plant closed down a few years later, the results were better—but not by much. At the time of the closing approximately eleven thousand employees could be identified as ones to whom some pension rights had been promised. Of these employees, there were 3,600 who were at least sixty years old and who had ten years' employment with Studebaker. They received their full pensions; there was sufficient money in the pension funds to purchase annuities for them from insurance companies. There was a second group of 4,500 employees, with ten years' employment at Studebaker, but ranging in age from forty to fifty-nine. They received lump-sum settlements equal to fifteen cents on the pension dollar owed. These men were, on the average, in their early fifties and had just under twenty-three years' employment with Studebaker. One man was fifty-nine years old and had forty-three years' service at Studebaker. These men had given up part of their hourly salary in exchange for what they believed would be financial security in their retirement years. Instead of that security, they received lump-sum payments ranging from $150 to $1,600. The average was $600. There was a third group, its members either under forty years of age or with less than ten years' service with Studebaker. What did they receive? Nothing.

Pensions, then, are a promise, but only a flimsy one. The United States cannot count on these privately operated plans to provide anyone with security. They obviously will assist some people, but they will not solve the problem of the aged person.

The welfare system, then, still must be relied on. It must assist the aged who either do not benefit from pensions or whose pensions may be too low, as well as assisting those new immigrants from the South and from other depressed areas.

The third group of candidates are those underemployed or underpaid. The farmer is one example. Almost one out of two farmers is poor. He has been left behind in the wake of the agricultural revolution. The revolution is a mechanical one. Its result is that the financially profitable farm is, in reality, an agricultural factory, huge and mechanized. The farmer who perhaps did not have the initiative or the daring, certainly the one who did not have the education and the assistance, has been crushed into a life of abject rural poverty by federal policies that reward industrialization of the farm. Politicians traditionally pay homage to the "family farm." They extend financial aid to the industrial farm.

Actually one out of five poor persons in the United States is like that family farmer. He is working but does not earn enough money to pull his family above the poverty level. He may be the victim of prejudice. He may lack skills. He may be a bad bargainer when he sits down with his boss. Whatever the reason, he does not make enough money.

To ignore these three groups—the immigrant to the industrial cities who comes almost as a member of a feudal society crossing five hundred years into the modern era, the aged and those who will move into retirement without adequate security, and those who work but earn inadequate incomes—is to risk what Senator Kennedy has said "could be the ripping asunder of the already thin fabric of American life."

The answer generally being presented to the plight of these people is the guaranteed annual income or the negative income tax, its sometimes other name. In this context the guaranteed annual income is being suggested as a replacement for the welfare programs that have been kicking around since the New Deal days and that have generally proven themselves unable to meet the problems of today's destitute. The degree of unanimity on the guaranteed annual income as a replacement for welfare is surprising.

Late in 1966 the A. Philip Randolph Institute, an organization created to give direction to the civil-rights movement and the struggle against poverty, issued a "Freedom Budget" to achieve "freedom from want" by 1975. The report was signed by practically every Negro and white person prominent in the civil-rights movement. After examining present welfare policies, the "Freedom Budget" said:

> This summary cannot detail all of the deficiencies in the nation-wide medley of welfare services. Many of them are both inadequate and degrading. They institutionalize poverty instead of fighting it. The largest group of those dependent upon organized public payments are our senior citizens. About two-thirds of them live in poverty, and receive benefit payments—upon which most of them depend almost entirely for their livelihoods—averaging somewhere between one-third and one-half of the income required to lift them above poverty. With large federal contributions to offset in part the undesirable features of payroll taxes which take away with one hand in order to give with the other, the average old-age insurance benefits should be approximately doubled within five years. Other types of welfare payments should be increased in similar manner. As already indicated, we should start working now toward replacing this medley of inadequate efforts with a more universal and unified system of guaranteed incomes for those who cannot or should not be gainfully employed.

The "Freedom Budget" was developed and supported primarily by those classified as "liberal" along the political spectrum. But the concept of a guaranteed annual income as a replacement for the "medley" of welfare programs has also been endorsed on the conservative right. Dr. Milton Friedman, professor of economics at the University of Chicago and considered the dean of conservative economists in the United States, was addressing a United States Chamber of Commerce symposium a few weeks after the "Freedom Budget" was issued.

"No doubt," Professor Friedman conceded, "the taxpayer who pays the bill to support people on relief may feel that he has the moral as well as legal right to see to it that the money is spent for designated purposes. But," Professor Friedman insisted to the assembled businessmen, "whether he has the right is irrelevant. Even if he has, it seems to me neither prudent nor noble for him to exercise it."

Why should the givers of money not watch what the takers do with that money?

"The major effect of doing so is to weaken the self-reliance of the recipients, diminish their humanity, and make them wise in the stratagems for evading the spirit of the restrictions imposed on them," answered Professor Friedman. "And the effect on the administrators is no more salutary. Instead of welfare workers bringing counsel and assistance to the poor, they become policemen and detectives, enemies to be outwitted."

But would the poor spend their guaranteed annual income in "proper" ways?

"It would be far better," said Professor Friedman, "to give the indigent money and let them spend it according to their values. True, they may spend much of it in ways we disapprove of—but they do now, and not all the red tape in Washington will keep them from finding ways of doing so."

Professor Friedman then insisted that the present "grab-bag" of welfare measures is a guaranteed income in reality but that "the negative income tax would be vastly superior to this collection of welfare measures. It would concentrate public funds on supplementing the incomes of the poor—not distribute funds broadside in the hope that some will trickle down to the poor."

The proposal has had some support from business and union leaders. Early in 1966 a group of them, organized into the National Commission on Technology, Automation, and Economic Progress, supported a guaranteed annual income as a means of pulling the low-paid and the welfare recipients out of poverty. The commission members included business leaders such as Thomas J. Watson of IBM, Edwin H. Land of the Polaroid company, and Patrick E. Haggerty of Texas Instruments. Among its union members were Walter Reuther of the United Auto Workers and Joseph A. Beirne of the Communications Workers of America.

Within the federal government, Sargent Shriver, the former head of the War on Poverty, also subscribes to the philosophy of a guaranteed annual income in place of welfare, as recommended in the "Freedom Budget" and by Professor Friedman. "There always will be in any country," said Mr. Shriver, "some people who are so old or physically disabled or who for other reasons are not able to maintain themselves completely without the help of others. The idea behind the negative income tax I believe . . . is that these people deserve to have the assistance of the whole community so that they are not in destitution. I subscribe to that personally."

The guaranteed annual income is referred to as the negative income tax because it would work through the income-tax system. Presently, a person who expects to pay more income tax during a year than is withheld from his salary is required to file a "Declaration of Estimated Income Tax." He then pays the excess tax in quarterly installments. The negative income tax would work the same way, only in reverse. The federal government would guarantee that each individual or family will have a minimum income. A person who reasonably anticipates his income will fall below that guaranteed figure files a claim for a cash benefit. The amount of that cash benefit would be the difference between his income and the federal guarantee. Adjustments or any changes necessary could be made during or at the end of the year in the same way a person who files a "Declaration of Estimated Income Tax" now does. In a computerized society administering such a system would not be difficult.

Would the system be "cheat-proof"?

Probably no more so than any system devised, including the present one. But that is not much of a consideration. The welfare cheat does not measure up to his publicity. No one favors the welfare cheat. When a politician or a newspaper base a campaign on ferreting him out, the campaign usually is a surefire winner. Everyone supports it. Such campaigns, then, are popular, and their popularity creates the impression that cheating the welfare system out of money is widespread. The evidence does not support that impression. The classic case, of course, is Newburgh in New York State. It received national fame in the early 1960s when it launched a campaign aimed at forcing the welfare "cheat" to go to work. After all the newspaper editorials had been read and all the television programs ended, Newburgh was unable to produce one able-bodied welfare recipient physically and mentally capable of working. The town had no welfare cheats.

There is no mystery about who receives welfare. The money goes to about seven million persons. That is 3 percent of the total population. Many more persons are poor, but only the seven million receive aid.

Of these seven million, about two million are elderly, over sixty-five. Most of them are women, and the median age is seventy-two. One million of the seven million are the blind or disabled. There are three and one-half million persons receiving welfare who are children and whose parents cannot support them. There remain about one million persons left on the welfare rolls. These one million persons are the parents of those three and one-half million dependent children. Of these one million parents, nine hundred thousand are mothers. The traditional picture of the heads of these dependent-children families is that of a Negro mother in a large city slum. Actually the recipients of this aid are almost evenly divided between Negro and white families. And the growth in the number of recipients has been more rapid in rural areas than in urban areas during the recent past.

It often has been asserted that the heads of these aid-to-dependent-children families should be compelled to go to work. At the end of 1967 Congress did pass such legislation. It gives local welfare agencies some discretion in determining if the head of the welfare family should be compelled to work. The legislation also requires that day-care centers be established for the working parents to leave their children and also requires that job-training centers be established. In many cases it would be valuable to encourage the head of aid-to-dependent-children family to work, but it is very bad policy to compel that person to work. Such a policy decrees that a dependent child is denied necessary welfare funds unless the mother bows to the local bureaucrat, who may or may not be interested in helping the mother, who may or may not be an honorable person, who may or may not provide the day-care facilities for the children, who may or may not provide decent job training.

In addition to these mothers there are between 100,000 and 150,000 male parents of dependent children also on relief. Of that number about two-thirds are incapacitated. The remaining 50,000 have potential to become self-sufficient. If any "cheats" exist on welfare, they are among those 50,000—not all those 50,000, just among those 50,000. A fraction of 50,000, out of more than seven million, is not a very high figure. Those figures were compiled after an exhaustive study by the Department of Health, Education and Welfare. They are supported by local studies.

In the annual report titled "Public Welfare in New York State," published in 1967, the breakdown is roughly similar. Three out of four people in New York State receiving welfare are children and those taking care of them. The sick, the aged and the disabled constitute 20 percent of the welfare recipients. According to the annual report, "Adult recipients employable in today's labor market represent less than five percent of all recipients and costs." Even among these 5 percent, the report continued, "many are employed full-time or part-time. Some hold two jobs. But in either case, their income is so low that they need supplementary welfare help."

Actually if there is any significant "cheating" going on in the welfare program, it is not being done by the recipients but by those who dispense welfare. The present welfare programs, although largely bankrolled by the federal government, are administered by state and local governments. These local officials operate these programs with a minimum of federal supervision. And in some cases they cheat by running the programs to suit their prejudices rather than to help the welfare recipient. In many Southern communities, for example, welfare programs are deliberately operated stringently to drive Negroes out of the state and to the Northern ghetto. The federal government distributes food to the needy—but such programs operate through local agencies. About one out of two counties in the South refuses to operate such programs, permitting the poor Negro to starve. Or a state like Alabama pays a woman with dependent children $12.75 a month for each child on welfare, most of it federal money. In New York City that woman would receive $56.40 for each child. The motivation for the woman to take her family and move from the rural land to the city ghetto, even if it is a journey from the known to the unknown, is understandable.

The legislation passed by Congress at the end of 1967, compelling the mothers of children receiving aid-to-dependent-children payments to go to work, contains a gimmick for this kind of cheating. The gimmick is the provision giving local administrators discretion in determining who must work and who should not work. If the welfare officials in the South continue as they have done, they will operate their programs in a manner designed to chase the poor out—demand the mother work even if there are persuasive reasons for her not working—giving the poor even more reason to travel to the city ghetto. Such action may alleviate one local problem but it aggravates a national problem.

And this migration will continue for other reasons. The Southern Negro is predominantly a rural person. He grew up on a farm; usually he was a sharecropper. But it is this kind of small farm that is losing out to the automated agricultural industry, and the Southern Negro is being cut off from the only way he knows to make a living. In addition, the schools and other social services in the rural parts of the South do not equip the farm Negro there for any other kind of life. The result when the Negro does move to the Northern ghetto is the racial explosions that are becoming part of every city's summer activities.

And that "cheating" by the dispensers of welfare is another argument for a guaranteed annual income to replace the present collection of welfare programs. The GAI, being operated out of Washington, would dispense benefits uniformly. It would help in Alabama and Mississippi as well as in Northern states. There would be little financial reason for the Negro mother in the South to take her children on that long bus ride to New York City.

As a replacement, then, for the welfare programs available to those unable to earn a living, the guaranteed annual income is probably the best answer available. It may be the only answer available. Certainly the present system of welfare is not working. The people of the United States should pay the cost, learning to accept that responsibility of helping those who cannot earn a living as they learned to accept the responsibility of subsidizing American industry when it needs assistance.

If this were where the proposal for a guaranteed annual income ends, as a substitute for welfare, there would not be much serious argument against it. Politicians would battle the pros and cons for a few years and then enact it. But the proposals for a guaranteed annual income go far beyond using the device as only a replacement for present welfare. And that is the danger of the guaranteed annual income.

Two

The guaranteed annual income now is not only being proposed as a substitute for welfare but also as an inviolate right for the individual physically and mentally capable of working. The guaranteed annual income would be a payment, large enough to assure a decent life, made by the government to the individual who chose to receive it. That individual would not be required—really not even urged—to work in return. Robert Theobald, an economist, who is perhaps the guaranteed annual income's most zealous supporter, proposes the GAI as a device "to break the link between jobs and income." As such, the guaranteed annual income is to the individual what the SST is to industry because the SST breaks the link between corporate risk and corporate profit.

Mr. Theobald wants the guaranteed annual income to be offered by the government "as an absolute constitutional right." To place any restrictions on the government's promise of a minimum income for every man, woman and child, to allow an official any discretion in determining who is entitled to that minimum income would be to place every American at the mercy of a bureaucrat, much the way welfare recipients often are at the mercy of their case workers. That, at least, is Mr. Theobald's argument.

The traditional concept of an individual contributing to society in a positive way—whether it be as a street cleaner, industrialist or artist—would be a thing of the past. No matter how valuable an individual's work might be to society, to the individual it would not be necessary. The world indeed would owe him a living, even if he be healthy, intelligent and capable.

It is Mr. Theobald who, through books, lectures, articles and talks during the 1960s, has done the most to give the guaranteed-annual-income concept a respectability that neither Francis Townsend nor Huey Long could. The 1966 book of essays on various aspects of the subject, *The Guaranteed Income*, which he edited, is the authoritative volume on the subject.

He is, of course, not alone. Although his concept of the guaranteed annual income is much broader than replacing welfare or bolstering low incomes as recommended by Milton Friedman, Thomas Watson and Sargent Shriver, it has received a push from their more limited endorsements. The name is the same even if the game is different. And Mr. Theobald's concept has caught the imagination of many economists and other persons genuinely concerned as he is with the economic plight of the individual in America. Through such organizations as the Ad Hoc Committee on the Triple Revolution and through a wide range of lectures and popular articles—such as "Washington Should Pay Taxes to the Poor" in *The New York Times Magazine*—they have managed to give the concept a wide currency.

The social workers also have picked it up. They argue that the definition of poverty is to be without money. Providing money, therefore, eliminates poverty. Elizabeth Wickenden, one of the most noted authorities in the study of the poor, has explained:

> For the average person poverty is simply a question of not having access to enough money to meet his basic needs and expectations. The reasons for his condition may be highly varied—no job, inadequate earnings, small children without means of support, disability, old age, heavy expenses, social isolation, ostracism, discouragement or some other form of personal or social disaster—but the common element is lack of wherewithal to meet his needs. In our society that "wherewithal" generally takes the form of cash.

Congress has accepted this assertion, if in a modest way. In early 1966 the Congress approved legislation authorizing a pension for every elderly person in the United States who is not already receiving Social Security payments or a federal pension of some kind. In scope, this program is much less generous than traditional proposals for a guaranteed annual income. It offers $35 a month for individuals and $52.50 for married couples. But the principle is the same. No requirement of need is to be shown to gain the pension. The program distributes its benefits to all, regardless of need, to the rich and to the poor. It is not a welfare program but a guaranteed annual income.

The "minted moonlight" is almost here.

A strong boost for the concept of the guaranteed annual income, if not the specific plan, has come from Daniel Patrick Moynihan. He is the former New Frontiersman who eventually became director of the Joint Center for Urban Studies of the Massachusetts Institute of Technology. Anyone who has come in contact with him or his work considers him brilliant. Theodore H. White, author of *The Making of the President* series, in 1965 described Mr. Moynihan as "one of the most luminous and perceptive of the younger American officials in Washington." Of those persons suggesting some form of income guarantee or maintenance program, he is one of the few who speaks with a personal knowledge of poverty. He himself is a former shoeshine boy who pulled his way out of the slums.

His proposal differs from Mr. Theobald's. Mr. Moynihan would have the government pay a fixed allowance to every family for each child in the family. In one respect it is more liberal than Mr. Theobald's. The guaranteed annual income would not go to persons who earned above a certain dollar amount. Mr. Moynihan's family allowance would go to every family, despite its income level. Whether the income was high or low would be incidental. The only requirement would be the fact of the child's existence. "The very well-to-do," he explained at a Senate committee hearing, "will normally pay back most of their allowance through income taxes. In other words, a small inequity is paid for a universal system that does not separate the poor from the rest of the population, and does not require an army of investigators and accountants to administer."

This family allowance system exists in many countries, and Mr. Moynihan estimated it would cost about $9 billion a year to implement in the United States. "And," he told the Senate committee, "I can't imagine a more sensible way to spend the money.

"A family allowance for the United States roughly equivalent to Canadian or Scandinavian levels," he explained, "would suggest payments of perhaps eight dollars a month for all children under six years of age, and twelve dollars a month for children between six and seventeen. At present [1967] population levels this would cost nine billion dollars a year, just over one percent of the gross national product. For a family of four children this would increase income by, say, forty dollars a month, or roughly five hundred dollars a year."

Compared to his estimate of a $9 billion cost for a family allowance plan scattering its benefits to the rich and middle-income as well as the poor, the cost of the guaranteed annual income would run between $2 billion and $20 billion, depending on what income levels are used for the guidelines. That is Mr. Theobald's range of figures. Others have suggested the costs would be higher. No one, or course, can be certain.

Although Mr. Moynihan's proposal for income maintenance differs in detail from the proposal for a guaranteed annual income, it is based on the same rationale: Some persons cannot make enough money to support themselves.

"In a modern industrial society," said Mr. Moynihan, "wages are geared to production, not to need. Hence, a forty-year-old man responsible for a growing family will often find himself earning no more than the young bachelor or older married woman working alongside him, although his family's needs may be much greater. He has four kids around the house and they all need shoes, dentists, clothes, piano lessons, and he is still only making $2.40 an hour."

And according to this argument, the situation will become worse, necessitating some form of income maintenance. Society, the argument continues, just cannot create enough jobs paying decent salaries to absorb the growing manpower pool. This pool of men capable of working grows not because of population increase. The fact of a population increase itself can mean more jobs; more people mean more automobiles and more workers to build them, more houses built by more construction men, more supermarkets with more clerks. Instead, the reserve of men in search of work is growing, so the argument runs, because of increased technology. Whether called automation, cybernation or whatever, this increased technology seems to threaten vast numbers of people with the specter of perpetual unemployment. The Ad Hoc Committee on the Triple Revolution summed up this argument succinctly when it said that, in the future, automation will enable a relatively few workers to produce limitless abundance, making the industrial productive system "no longer viable" as a basis to operate society.

"The fundamental problem posed by the cybernation revolution in the United States," said the thirty-two-member committee's report, "is that it invalidates the general mechanism so far employed to undergird peoples' rights as consumers. Up to this time economic resources had been distributed on the basis of contributions to production, with machines and men competing for employment on somewhat equal terms. In the developing cybernated system, potentially unlimited output can be achieved by systems of machines which will require little cooperation from human beings." The committee was top-heavy in its membership with liberal economists, but it also included a sprinking of businessmen who joined in advocating a guaranteed income as a matter of right. "We regard it as the only policy," said the committee, "by which the quarter of the nation now dispossessed and soon-to-be dispossessed by lack of employment can be brought within the abundant society."

Not all the job displacement is due to automation. "In New York City," Mr. Moynihan has pointed out, "it was recently reported that thirty-one percent of nonwhite teenagers in the area work force were unemployed. Now if thirty-one percent are unemployed at $1.25 an hour, what will happen with a two-dollar minimum wage?"

In Washington, D.C., during the summer of 1967, a ruling came from somewhere in the bureaucracy of that city decreeing that shoeshine boys who worked in barbershops and dry-cleaning stores were not self-employed entrepreneurs. They were, instead, employees of the establishments where they worked. As such, they were entitled to $1.40 an hour, the prevailing minimum wage at the time. Immediately, the cost of having a pair of shoes shined went from fifteen cents to thirty-five cents. Shortly after that, dozens of young Negro men who had been earning between forty dollars and fifty dollars a week as shoeshine boys were out of work.

For many, of course, that specter of perpetual unemployment is not a dark promise of the future but a grim reality now. The sharecropper in the South, whether Negro or white, is a victim of the mechanization of farming. From the late 1940s until the mid-1960s the production of farm goods in the United States more than doubled. But the number of people actually working on farms dwindled to less than half in that same period. With the help of technological improvements and other scientific advances, then, one man on a farm today is producing four times as much as a man on a farm less than two decades ago. Americans are buying more automobiles, about nine million a year compared to five or six million a decade ago. But for every ten men who once worked in the automobile industry, now only six men are needed. And they produce more cars. The Puerto Ricans who came to New York City looking for their pot of gold began their search as elevator operators. Now the elevators are automatic.

When a person is displaced by a machine, he can generally anticipate that his job potential is ended. If his skill, competence and knowledge were such that they could be replaced by a machine at one job, then they are such that they will be replaced a second time. For a few years he keeps one jump ahead of the machine, but eventually it overtakes him. That the machine wins ultimately is a certainty. The machine is a slave, and slave labor always is cheaper than labor by a free human being. The shoeshine boy who must be paid thirty-five cents plus tip for a shine is replaced by a shoeshine machine that collects only a quarter in its slot. Even the janitor who sweeps out a building for a few dollars a week in wages and a dirty basement apartment to live in is replaced by a crew of men in uniform equipped with automatic sweepers and floor polishers who clean a series of buildings more efficiently, faster and cheaper. The janitor's apartment is retitled a "studio" and is rented.

But it is not only a saving of money that makes machines so attractive. Many other reasons add to the allure of the mechanized worker. Mr. Theobald has pointed out some of them, saying: "Machine systems do not get tired, they can carry out a particular task with a continued precision that cannot be demanded or expected of a human work force; they are incapable of immorality, they do not lie, steal, cheat, or goof off; they do not claim that their rights as human beings are being violated by factory work practices; they are not class-conscious; above all, they are not vocal in their criticism of management and they do not go on strike."

In New York State this has led to a situation where there are one million men, women and children dependent on the public's largess, and the largess they receive amounts to $1 billion plus in welfare. George K. Wyman, commissioner of that state's public welfare department, warns: "No economy, however affluent, can afford the rising social and financial costs of a situation in which the resources of great numbers of its people are not developed and not used, in which the promise of a decent, wholesome, self-sufficient maturity is virtually denied to millions of its children."

Increasingly that promise of a decent life goes unfulfilled. Mr. Moynihan, in his study "The Negro Family," made when he was with the Labor Department, estimated that perhaps two million adult, able-bodied Negro males had disappeared from the statisticians' figures. They could not be found by the takers of the census. They were untouched by the welfare and War on Poverty programs. They were the victims of a past prejudice that had denied them an adequate education and a respectable culture. They were the victims of a modern society which has no use for the uneducated. They were hidden in the alleys of the slums, not really a part of modern-day America. And even of those Negroes who are found by society's counters, the promise in many cases is not much better. One out of twelve adult male Negroes—again these are the able-bodied, in their prime working years—have given up even seeking work. The mountain of dismissals, rejections, disappointments, and frustrations has become too great.

Although the problem is most pronounced among Negroes, because of the past discrimination leveled at them, it is not confined only to Negroes. It cuts across all races and all regions. A Labor Department study of job training and educational backgrounds of adult American workers concluded that some twenty million Americans lack the minimal training required for the jobs of the 1960s. And there was little prospect of reducing that disturbing statistic.

"If the nation continues at its present pace in the fields of education and training," the study warned, "it could anticipate having some thirty-two million adult, non-high school graduates in the labor force by 1975. Again, twenty million of these would have no formal job training experience."

In the mid-1960s a series of frightening statistics were beginning to be developed about the nation's potential unemployment problem. The statistics can be transformed into two lines. One is a familiar one: the increase in population. That line rises steadily, as expected. But the next line rises sharply. This represents the number of jobs being eliminated by automation, perhaps two million or more a year. What the two lines mean is that there will be more people and fewer jobs. The lines actually move in opposite directions. A reasonable estimate is that in the early 1970s, for example, more than ten million persons, interested and able to work, will be unable to find work. That is an unemployment rate of approximately 12 percent.

Even that statistic is misleading. A 12 percent unemployment rate means that at one specific time the rate of unemployment is 12 percent of the men and women working and looking for work, and the actual number of persons unable to find work at a specific time is ten million. During the year, however, some of those ten million find work and then are replaced on the unemployment rolls by others. An annual unemployment rate of 12 percent would mean easily that during a single year some twenty million persons experienced some unemployment. And even among those who are working, if the present situation is any guide, there will be those forced to work part-time because they could not find a full-time job, some who will be holding two jobs because one job does not pay them sufficient money to survive on, some unable to earn an adequate income.

Gardner Ackley, when he was chairman of the President's Council of Economic Advisers, summed up the significance of those two projections when in 1965 he expressed his concern that the "foreseeable gains in output are not sufficiently large to sustain our recent progress in reducing unemployment." The fighting in Vietnam obscured those statistics. War, with its increased demand for men to fight and workers to build the tools of war, distorts the unemployment picture. But when the Vietnam hostilities end, or when the fighting is de-escalated, that unemployment picture will return to its sharp, ugly shape.

Progress should not be knocked. The revolution on the farm means cheaper food prices. A rise in the minimum wage means more income for those persons working. These kinds of changes are inevitable and are beneficial to the nation and its people. Still, although necessary and valuable, these changes cause much trag-edy. Although out of a total population of two hundred million people only between seven million and eight million actually receive welfare, many millions more live in poverty. Figures vary on just how many persons dwell in what Michael Harrington aptly called "The Other America" where "tens of millions of Americans are, at this very moment, maimed in body and spirit, existing at levels beneath those necessary for human decency."

Although the figures vary, there is no disagreement that the number of people in America without the means for a minimally decent standard of living is large, whether the figure is twenty mil-lion or fifty million. Both estimates have been used. These people may make less than the standard a family of four needs to remain above the abject poverty level—about three thousand dollars. Or they may make between that amount and what is considered an income capable of providing a decent standard of living for a family of four—about six thousand dollars.

And these people are the motivation behind the proposal for some form of income maintenance as a matter of right. If millions of persons—other than those eligible for welfare—are unable to find work paying a decent income, why not separate the concept of work from income? The government then would provide an income, perhaps not very large but adequate for a decent standard of living, to each person if the individual chose to receive it. And the individual could not be refused. He, and only he, would deter-mine not *what* contribution he would make to society but *if* he would contribute to society. The government would guarantee that no matter how the individual chose, he would not want for food, clothing, shelter and a small amount of the pleasures of life.

"At the present time," wrote Robert Theobald in 1966, "we are committed as a society to the idea that we can and should provide jobs for all. This goal is no longer valid, and we should therefore provide everybody with an absolute right to a guaranteed income."

An individual capable of working is guaranteed an income even though he chooses not to work. An industry is guaranteed a profit-able future even though it takes no risk. That is the guaranteed society.

But as there are faults with this approach when it is applied to industry, there are faults when it is applied to individuals—several economic and several social faults.

Three

In the 1960s the United States government set out to prove that consumer demand could be increased. If demand is increased, so went the thesis of the "new economics," jobs are created to fulfill that demand. Despite that the economy demonstrated this thesis correct—unemployment dropped from the area of 5 percent to that of 3 percent—the advocates of the guaranteed annual income still reject it. Increased demand, their answer goes, does not increase the number of jobs. Rather, it increases the desire for more automation so more products can be turned out for less labor cost. Increasing automobile production by 10 percent does not increase the automobile labor force by 10 percent. It may increase it by only 5 percent, 2 percent or not at all.

True. But increased demand, more money for people to spend, does something else. It gives people a desire for products that did not exist before, or at least did not exist for the vast majority of persons in the middle class. The second home, for example, was once limited only to the rich. By the late 1960s there was a vast, and new, industry building summer and vacation homes, aiming its sales at the middle class. This is a highly mechanized industry also. Still, it employs more people than it did a decade earlier, when it did not exist as an industry. More money for people to spend permits them to satisfy their basic desire for entertainment with a color television set, or to satisfy their desire for convenience with processed foods. Fewer workers may be needed to manufacture more cars, but more cars on highways created the motel industry. Eight motels stand at each crossroads where none was a few years ago. Intelligent policy decisions by the government can create jobs; society can never be quite sure just what those jobs will be, but they will come.

Also, one demand creates a second. The "demand" created by the government with the tax cut of 1964 was a demand of dollars. More people had more money to spend and they demanded more and better products. This demand, in turn, created a demand for social services. As a greater number of people enjoyed the adequate medical protection of the middle class, the better schools, the better police protection, their example of their "good" life whetted the appetites of many other persons.

An example is medical care. Although in 1967 the American Medical Association argued that comprehensive medical care was a privilege rather than a right, by that time most Americans had turned those two words around; everyone has a right to decent medical care. Such medical care, however, is scarce. Richard D. Lyons, science writer for *The New York Times,* reported that the nation faces a shortage of 50,000 doctors and 125,000 nurses, and also that there may already be some five thousand communities in the nation without doctors. Even these figures may be a gross understatement. At the time they were written, the United States was on the verge of a revolution in its attitude toward medical care. That "right" was about to be extended into the slums of the large cities. People who had known medical care only in the most meager quantities were about to receive complete care. The District of Columbia is an example.

Dr. Murray Grant, the health director there, announced in late 1967 that his department planned to place "family doctor" health clinics in the city's poverty areas. Beginning with three pilot projects, the plan eventually would have fourteen clinics scattered throughout the city, each one serving 25,000 people. Prior to the establishment of the clinics, the poor in the nation's capital city, as most large cities, went to a city-operated hospital for treatment. If they could reach the hospital, the crowds were so thick that a patient sometimes had to wait three hours there for attention. The situation was a frustrating one, discouraging the poor from seeking medical care. But Dr. Grant's clinics will cause a complete change in the extent and quality of the medical care available to the poor. They will be able to receive as good medical treatment—probably better care—as the middle class or rich. What Washington is planning eventually will extend to other cities. The program is being financed by Medicaid, the program of medical care for the poor that was slipped into the Social Security program when Congress wrote legislation providing medical care for the aged.

No one can really be certain what this revolution in medical care for the poor will mean to the medical employment picture. There will be need for more doctors, nurses, medical technicians, pharmacists, record keepers, teachers to teach all of these people, builders to build schools for the teachers and clinics for the doctors. The coming revolution in medical care alone easily could employ a million people over and above those people needed by the medical profession merely to keep pace with a statistical growth in the population.

And medicine is only one area. Education is another area facing a complete revolution. Teaching will be greatly computerized in the future. But this coming computerization has been misunderstood to mean that more children can be taught with fewer teachers. Actually more people involved with instruction will be needed even to teach the same number of students. Computerization means more care for each student, not less. The student will have a program of learning created for him alone. He will learn at a pace best suited to himself. This means the student will need someone to program a training process for him, someone to give his absorbtion of that process a great deal of attention. And the student also will need the attention of a great many specialists because computerized learning will spot his faults and his problems much better than the old style of teaching. Not only will this "teaching" personnel be needed, but other persons will be needed to design the computers for school use, to design programs, to build buildings where they can be used.

Actually, in the late 1960s one could examine the United States and see many areas where problems exist which will require people to work at them. There is inadequate police protection, dirty rivers, polluted air, juvenile delinquency, cities growing uglier and uglier. Computers will work at solving all of these problems. Basically what they will do, however, is point out work man can perform. This work of the future will not be the manual labor which is associated with work even in the 1960s. It will be much more sophisticated than that. But it will exist.

The mistake made by those who predict technological change causing massive unemployment is the same mistake made ever since the beginning of the industrial revolution. Tomorrow's statistics are applied to today's world. Because automation will displace millions of workers, it is assumed that nothing else will come along to offer those displaced persons and their children new opportunities. And that assumption always has been proven wrong. New problems require new solutions, and new solutions create new jobs.

And one does not have to wait for the future. Commissioner Wyman of New York State's welfare department reports that an estimated "three million job vacancies in industry [are] going unfilled because of lack of job candidates with the needed skills." He continues: "An employment authority says if domestic service could be made 'dignified'—something that occurs when an occupation reaches a severe shortage stage—another million people could be put to work part-time or full-time." In the second half of the 1960s the computer industry itself had need for fifty thousand additional employes, primarily the processors who feed the information into the computers. In late 1967 the volunteer Citizens Committee for Metropolitan Affairs in New York City made a test survey of the automobile mechanics in that city. The committee concluded that New York City had "a shocking scarcity of well-trained mechanics." What is true of New York is probably true of other cities. What is true of auto mechanics is true of other trades.

The jobs exist. They will continue to exist. The problem is not automation. It is education.

The real challenge of the computer revolution, if it can be called that, is not to find some way of guaranteeing idle millions an income source. The real challenge of automation is to put those idle millions to work at the jobs that need to be done. And that challenge is one for the present, not for the future. Tomorrow is too late. Whether, in fact, there will be enough medical personnel in the late 1970s and 1980s and beyond to meet the revolution in medical care depends on decisions made in the late 1960s. Medical schools are graduating fewer than eight thousand doctors a year. Not enough. Society—in this case the American Medical Association, the public health authorities, the government officials—must press for an expansion of medical education facilities. The government would put up the money, if necessary, and the medical profession would supervise the development of such facilities. But it takes years to build a medical school and to educate a doctor. That means that although the problem of a shortage of medical personnel will be a reality in ten years, the solution is a reality now.

Perhaps the most important part of that solution is the developing of potential students. Students are needed not only for the medical schools that must be built but also for the colleges that must produce twice as many nurses as are now being graduated. Students must be found for the engineering schools that will train the personnel to cope with the sophisticated problems of the coming decades. Students must be found to attend the teachers' colleges that must produce educators of a quantity and quality superior to that existing in the 1960s. Students must be found to learn the skills with which they can cope with tomorrow's problems.

These students must come from the slums. The children of middle- and upper-class families already are going to the medical schools, becoming engineers and teachers, nurses and lawyers. If these areas are going to be greatly expanded, a new source of personnel must be found. And that source can only be the children of the poor. They are the only persons remaining. By the millions these children now grow up to be either the unemployed or the underemployed. That is a waste of resource that no longer can be tolerated.

Saving that resource requires more than merely money. "Providing the poor with added income is only one aspect of combating poverty," according to economist Sar A. Levitan. "The poor," he continued, "also need better schools, housing, training, and diverse services to improve their ability to compete for jobs in the labor market."

And Vice President Humphrey, in an interview published in *The New York Times*, spelled this out even more clearly. "One of the ways in which you can relieve the pain of poverty," said the Vice President, "is by simply writing a check, by handing out money. That will eliminate poverty, but does it really get at the problems of despair, uselessness, apathy, alienation, indifference, hostility? We're not dealing with men who simply want money handed to them. We're dealing with people who are nonparticipating, isolated members of society—who need to feel they have a place in the scheme of things. I don't think we should reject the negative income tax proposal, or similar proposals, out of hand. But money alone is not going to bring people back into our society."

What Mr. Levitan and Vice President Humphrey are saying is that the man existing in poverty exists outside the regular American society. Not only is he poor in pocket but he is poor in spirit. The War on Poverty has been of great assistance to the poor man, with such programs as the Neighborhood Legal Services, the organization of credit unions, community action centers that link the poor man with his municipal government for the first time, and such educational programs as the Headstart project to reach preschool children. But these kinds of programs, as valuable and as successful as they have been, are only means of attacking the results of poverty. They do not attack the causes of poverty. The Headstart project, for example, aims at replacing some of the cultural loss in an impoverished family. But it does not really serve a great deal of purpose if the child's home remains a cultural vacuum.

More than piecemeal nibbling at poverty from its outer edges is needed for the man in poverty to be brought back into American society. If that man in poverty is to be turned away from the guaranteed society, if this generation of Americans and the next is to be turned away from the guaranteed society, at least two improvements are needed. One is an increase in the over-all standard of education offered to the poor child. The other is to provide the poor man with a better opportunity for him to contribute to society.

The quality of education offered to slum children is abysmal; the low level of that education may be the greatest cause of poverty. The National Commission on Civil Disorders, in its March 1968 report, charged that "... for many minorities, and particularly for the children of the ghetto, the schools have failed to provide the educational experience which could overcome the effects of discrimination and deprivation." The commission, headed by Illinois Governor Otto Kerner, was not optimistic for the future. It continued: "The bleak record of public education for ghetto children is growing worse. In the critical skills—verbal and reading ability—Negro students are falling farther behind whites with each year of school completed."

Shortly after that report was issued, Secretary Wilbur Cohen of the Health, Education and Welfare Department made the same point in an interview with United Press International. Education, he said, is the "central solution" of the welfare problem. "The vast majority of these people on welfare," he said, "have no education; they're grade-school and high-school dropouts. They can't make change; they can't take a telephone message. We've got to educate these people, train them for jobs, vastly expand the education of their children."

Such comments should not come as a surprise.

Almost without exception in most large cities the children of the slums are educated in the worst buildings with the least qualified teachers. A teacher in the Boston, Massachusetts, public schools, Jonathan Kozol, wrote a book about his experience teaching there. He called it *Death at an Early Age* and subtitled it "The Destruction of the Hearts and Minds of Negro Children in the Boston Public Schools." The picture he draws in his 1967 book is a frightening one but not a unique one.

In Washington, D.C., for example, a Negro civil-rights leader went into court and proved the public school system there was discriminating against poor Negro children by denying them as good an education—as good teachers, as good textbooks, as good physical facilities—as was available to middle-class white children in the city. The court in 1967 ordered the school board to end such discriminatory practices.

In New York City a special program in the ghetto schools of Harlem produced substantial improvement in the reading and comprehension levels of the children there. As soon as the program proved itself a success the school board moved to end it.

School boards respond to the demands of parents of white children for decent educational opportunities. School boards ignore the demands of parents of Negro children. The situation became so bad in New York City that an extreme reaction was created. Negro parents in slum areas were insisting on almost complete control of the schools in their neighborhoods, wanting to be able to name principals, teachers and devise curriculum. Their move was a thrust for power, an unfortunate thrust. But even more unfortunate was the arrogant disregard of these people's needs which led them to take such action. In a section of Washington, D.C., Negro parents and liberal whites realized that white children were essential if slum schools were to be improved. They insisted on what became known as the "tri-school plan." What this plan did was to take the white children from one school and distribute them among two other schools which were almost entirely Negro. The hope was that the presence of white children in these two schools would spur officials to improve the quality of education offered there.

Obviously money is needed, a great deal of money, to correct the evils plaguing slum schools. But not only money is needed. In the mid-1960s a group of professional educators from Columbia University in New York City made a thorough study of Washington, D.C., public schools. They spent $250,000 to find out what was wrong with the public schools in the nation's capital. Their report contained few surprises. The buildings are old. The teachers are not well trained. The bureaucracy is insufferable. The report could have described almost any large-city school system. But there were a couple of interesting points. One concerned Montgomery Elementary School in what is generally conceded to be one of the worst slums in the United States—the Cardozo area of Washington.

Everything seemed to be going against Montgomery. The average pupil was Negro, came from a family with an income of less than three thousand dollars, which in Washington is far below the poverty level, and the pupil's parents probably had never finished elementary school. Of the twenty-five schools in Washington studied, the Columbia team ranked Montgomery at the bottom as far as what could be expected from it. But when those expectations were checked out, through a series of reading and other tests, Montgomery did not measure twenty-fifth. Instead, it ranked eleventh, far higher than was expected.

Montgomery has a couple of pluses. There is a tutoring program by an Urban Service Corps group. More importantly, Montgomery is one of four schools in the United States being used as a testing ground for a "Project Discovery" experiment financed by the Encyclopedia Britannica and Bell & Howell. These two companies inundate the students with audio-visual aids. But the significant factor at Montgomery, according to all those who have examined the school, is the attitude of the teachers. They want to teach. They feel that slum children can be taught as well as children of middle-class parents, and so they try. And they are succeeding. Teacher dedication does not replace money, but it is itself an essential requirement for the proper education of children. Most often, however, it is lacking.

"Montgomery was lucky to have a number of experimental projects," said one observer of the school. "But almost anything will work if you have a good staff, and almost nothing will work if you don't."

Montgomery also was lucky in that its two most recent principals believed in experimentation and in trying to reach their students. They encouraged the teachers to teach. Not all students in Washington were so lucky. A teacher in another school, with a student body almost entirely Negro, was severely reprimanded because she suggested her junior-high students read *Raisin in the Sun* by Lorraine Hansbury. The play, of course, was written by a Negro and is about Negroes; it is also considered a significant drama of the American theatre. But literature by Negroes and about Negroes was not considered valuable to Negro students. At least it was not allowed.

That particular incident involving *Raisin in the Sun* happened in June of 1967. Malcolm X, the slain Black Muslim leader, in his autobiography tells of growing up in Lansing, Michigan, before the Second World War. One of his high-school teachers, whom Malcolm admired greatly, once asked him what he planned to do as a career. Malcolm answered he was considering being a lawyer. The teacher responded, as Malcolm recalled it, that Malcolm should be "realistic about being a nigger" and think, instead, of becoming a carpenter. Ten years later in Pittsburgh, Pennsylvania, a teacher asked a group of high-school students their choice of a career. When a Negro girl answered that she wanted to teach, the teacher replied, "In the South." It was not a question. The specific reason for Mr. Kozol being released by the Boston school system in 1965 was that he read his predominantly Negro class a poem by Langston Hughes, the Negro poet.

For too many years teachers and the school systems they represent have declined to teach Negro children. They have suffered their presence in their classrooms, but they have not taught them. This is as true—perhaps more true—in the North, where equality is proclaimed, as it is in the South, which acknowledges its segregated school systems. The Columbia University study of the District of Columbia schools pointed out this reluctance on the part of teachers to teach where they will have large numbers of Negroes in their classrooms.

"The task force interviews," said the report, "suggest that teachers would prefer to travel further, inconvenience or not, to serve in middle-class schools rather than in lower-class schools." This attitude on the part of teachers was so strong, the report seemed to be saying, that it could not be dented. "Instead of trying to alter such attitudes," the report continued, "the system must turn to the early recruitment and introduction of a corps of teachers with very different training and a forward-looking kind of commitment to education in the urban school."

To many persons it always comes as a surprise that the slum schools are not at the same level as the schools catering to middle-class children. Even more of a surprise are the results of offering a middle-class teaching effort in slum schools. A study by Samuel S. Bowles of Harvard University documented what most thoughtful observers of slum schools know to be true: A good teacher makes a good pupil. The disparity between the achievement of Negro pupils and that of white pupils could be cut in half, studies by Mr. Bowles show, if the teachers of those Negro children had one more year of education. If the teachers of those Negro children had the same verbal facility as those of white children, continued Mr. Bowles' study, the disparity would be cut by one fourth.

But the best qualified teachers, as the Columbia study points out, decline the challenge of the slums for the sanitized suburbs. And so the slum children, most of whom are Negro, are the unfortunate victims. If they do happen to come across a teacher, such as Mr. Kozol, who does want to teach them, then they become the victims of school boards that will not spend the money needed for their education or will not back up the teachers who wish to teach. If a student goes to a Montgomery, where the teachers and the school administration are interested in teaching and where the facilities are available to teach, then that student is fortunate to have hit an exceptional school. Such schools should not be exceptional. They should be routine.

Admittedly, money always will be needed and finding it always has been a problem. In the mid-1960s the federal government began aid to elementary and secondary education in a massive way and it was hoped that the problem of money had ended for the nation's schools. Again, because of the Vietnamese war costs, the hope fades. Instead of the continuing expansion of such assistance programs as expected, they have developed a static quality and even have been cut back. The 1967 budget figure for such aid was $1.45 billion. The next year it had inched up to $1.61 billion. By 1969 the drop had begun; the expenditure figure was down to $1.56 billion. If the original momentum could be regained, the problem of money for education would not be a serious one.

The search for new teaching techniques is a problem, not because new techniques are not needed nor because they cannot be found but because the search for new techniques itself becomes an excuse for procrastination. The best techniques for teaching culturally deprived slum children may not yet be discovered. But that does not mean that great improvements cannot be made immediately. The best method may not be known, but much that is wrong with the present method—the untrained teachers, the inadequate textbooks, all the failings of the modern school system that are visible to anyone who walks through the urban school—is known and can be corrected. A start on improving schools should not be put off for decades while theoreticians argue over techniques. Too many school children would be lost.

Schools can be improved also by starting at the top. Any bureaucracy tends to stultify. But the channels of action can be unfrozen a little if the man at the top lights a couple of matches. Another way is to remove some of the drudgery that hangs heavily on the teacher. He is not only expected to teach but also to be a policeman, scorekeeper and accountant. A number of schools are using teachers' aides (Montgomery in Washington is one) to perform some of these chores. A third way is to insist that the teacher continue his training, particularly in learning new ways to deal with culturally deprived children.

None of this—and none of dozens of other means of improving teacher quality—will happen until a community realizes that it is responsible for the education of all the children within its borders, not only those who are white or the children of middle-income parents. It is natural for a mother and father to wish their child to go to a neighborhood school, but it is foolish to ignore the drab conditions of the school in the other neighborhood. The attitude of a teacher toward a Negro pupil is a reflection of the attitude of the community toward Negroes. When a community chooses a segregationist as a school-board member and as a candidate for political office, as Boston did, it is not surprising that the teachers and the school officials in that city give up teaching Negroes. In his book about the Boston schools Mr. Kozol tells of beginning his teaching career in 1964 and observing children, mostly Negro, sitting in a "dank and dirty urine-smelling cellar" in the school. Less than three years after Mr. Kozol first made those observations, Boston was wracked by a series of painful riots led by young Negroes. To riot is wrong, but if someone from outside the city reads Mr. Kozol's book, he cannot be a harsh judge. If a resident of the city walked through some of the schoolrooms described by Mr. Kozol, he could not be a harsh judge either, or should not be. The Negro children there were not receiving the education they deserved. The city of Boston received the turmoil it deserved. The city was paying for its neglect of those children. It probably will continue to pay in coming years. In this respect, unfortunately, Boston is little different from other large cities in the United States.

Mayor John V. Lindsay of New York City has said that the slums of America are invisible to what he described as "the insulated America." The shell of smugness with which middle-class Americans insulate themselves must be penetrated. If it is not penetrated by logic, sincerity and intelligent discussion, it most likely will be penetrated by violence. And violence once begun can rarely be contained. Educated people rarely riot. In modern American history that certainly is true. Uneducated people are much more prone to riot. The lesson should be obvious.

Improving the schools is one half the problem of turning away from the guaranteed society. To make a complete turn, for the poor man, away from the guaranteed society, the slum dweller's attitude toward work must be changed—"work" here meaning the making of a positive contribution to society. Presently the slum child grows up in an environment in which work is not available to the men who seek it, in which ambition is not rewarded and in which personal laziness seems to be a desired attribute. The guaranteed annual income would perpetuate that kind of environment. It would offer the people in that environment enough money so they would be neither hungry nor cold. But it would not offer them any reason for or assistance in climbing out of that environment.

If not a guaranteed annual income, then what should society offer to the slum dwellers?

Jobs paying a decent income. When required, job training should be supplied. If necessary, the federal government should be the employer and the trainer of last resort.

Welfare Commissioner Wyman of New York State insists: "It must be clear to everyone—those who put human values above all else, those who think otherwise, and those who have a well-balanced approach to all the factors involved—that this economic and social segregation of a huge, growing segment of the population from the main stream of living must end. We cannot afford it, from any point of view. . . . The only solution is to integrate into our economy as many of our welfare recipients and poverty-line people as possible."

Most civil-rights leaders agree with that philosophy of integrating the unemployed into the economy rather than securing them a guaranteed niche outside the economy. "The guaranteed annual income," said the "Freedom Budget," signed by almost all civil-rights leaders, "is a highly desirable goal, designed to assure a nationwide and universally guaranteed decent standard of income for all those who legitimately cannot obtain it through their own efforts. It is based on the inescapable fact that an economy as rich and powerful as ours cannot countenance widespread deprivation, much less widespread poverty. . . ."

Then, in the next paragraph, the "Freedom Budget" said: "But this proposal for a guaranteed annual income becomes excessive and unattainable when not founded upon recognition that it should be supplementary to rather than in place of a nationwide full-employment policy which embraces both adequate earnings when employed and adequate social insurance payments during such temporary periods of unemployment as may occur." Concluded the "Freedom Budget": "Indeed, it is even more important that the federal government guarantee sustained full employment than that it guarantees incomes for all."

Bayard Rustin, the Negro leader who organized the 1963 March on Washington and who now heads the A. Philip Randolph Institute, which produced the "Freedom Budget," has even suggested scrapping the whole antipoverty program for a two-dollar-an-hour minimum wage. Speaking in December 1966, Mr.

Rustin said: "In this society, one's spiritual judgment of himself has ... to be related to his role in the production of goods and services. He is someone because he does something which society puts a value upon, and therefore, while I am for a guaranteed income for the aged and the crippled and certain types of unemployables . . . I am for a guaranteed wage, not income, for others.

"A two-dollar minimum wage," Mr. Rustin continued, "would be the most important single factor of significance in American life. It would do more than the entire antipoverty program."

When Mr. Rustin spoke, the minimum wage was scheduled to hit its top of $1.60 an hour by 1968. If a man works forty hours a week, for fifty weeks a year, at that wage scale, his annual income is $3,200. For a family of four that is considered "poverty level." It is also about one half of what is considered necessary for a family of four to live a "modest but adequate" life. Should that family head work more than forty hours a week for fifty weeks? Perhaps he should. But actually the problem is not that he does not wish to work more hours. The real problem is that he cannot find work for even that limited number of hours. People at the bottom of the wage scale are frequently unemployed for periods of several weeks a year. Surveys suggest that a person at that income level will be out of work seven weeks a year. With a minimum wage of $1.60 an hour, he is fortunate to earn $2,500. So that even Mr. Rustin's call for increasing the minimum wage to two dollars an hour is not extravagant.

Any increase in the minimum wage eliminates some jobs. There comes a point when the work a person does is simply not worth two dollars an hour to an employer. So the person is fired. Eliminating this kind of cheap labor can be a good thing. There is nothing ennobling about shining shoes or washing dishes as a lifetime career.

But eliminating such jobs, without assuming some responsibility for those workers displaced, can be harmful. The usual problem of a person fired because of an increase in the minimum wage is that he does not have skills of value. He is one with those already unemployed, whose lack of education and job-training has made them "unemployable."

These persons must be trained and employed. Private industry is showing an awareness of this need. A number of business leaders and city officials organized in the fall of 1967 into the Urban Coalition. One of the Coalition's tasks will be to establish industries in the slums and then to train persons to work in those industries. After the national group was organized it spawned a number of local groups. The New York Coalition, for example, was drawing on the talents of Christian A. Herter, Jr., a vice-president of the Mobil Oil Corporation, and Andrew Heiskell, chairman of Time, Inc., plus another hundred business leaders from the city.

These business leaders seemed to sense, as Henry Ford II expressed it, that "we will need to work out a drastic reordering of our national priorities." Mr. Ford told the National Urban League that "employers are just beginning to learn . . . that equal employment opportunity requires more than the elimination of deliberate racial discrimination. Opportunity is not equal when people who would make good employees are not hired because they do not know of openings, because they lack the self-confidence to apply, or because formal hiring criteria screen out potentially good employees as well as potentially poor ones."

And then in what can be described as a call to his fellow businessmen, Mr. Ford continued:

> I believe that employers must take aggressive steps to overcome such barriers. It is not enough to provide technically equal employment opportunities. Management should be willing to go directly into the city, to seek out the unemployed, to make sure that hiring standards are not unnecessarily or unrealistically restrictive, and to lend a helping hand in adjusting to the work and the work place.

Because of private industry's strong desire to earn a profit, it may be necessary for the government to provide an incentive. One such incentive was offered by President Johnson in late 1967 when he initiated a small pilot-project program. Industries located in slums and training slum dwellers for jobs could expect some federal assistance and a better chance of selling their products to the government. The President's tactic was to mix this kind of incentive with the kind of exhortation for which he has become famous. When a new Commerce Department official was sworn in at the White House, for example, Mr. Johnson said that the official was entering a department that "once spoke only for business . . ." but "now it speaks to business about the real business of America—the well-being of all the American people, including the business people." He then directed the Commerce Department officials to work with American businessmen to "solve the stubborn problems that plague the nation," including "to try to hire and to train the half-million hard-core unemployed." In 1968 Mr. Johnson offered another incentive, subject to Congressional approval. The federal government would pay $3,500 to a company if it trained a member of the hard-core unemployed to work for the company. The payment was supposed to compensate the company for the extra costs it had in training a slum dweller to be a worker. Another type of incentive suggested by Senator Robert Kennedy was to offer tax breaks to the industry that provided jobs for the unemployed. The object of his plan is the same as Mr. Johnson's: to offer industry a financial reward for being humanitarian. Not surprisingly perhaps, this attitude of rewarding business for hiring and training the unemployed is becoming popular politically, in Republican circles as well as Democratic. And why should this approach not be used? Private industry receives many rewards and much assistance from the federal government for doing almost everything else. Why should it not receive such blessings for being humanitarian?

But it may be that only the federal government can do the job. Rather than give a man a federal handout of sixty or seventy dollars a week as his "right," as proposed in the guaranteed-annual-income concept, why not pay him that much if he attends classes forty hours a week? He could learn reading, writing, personal hygiene, how to protect himself from the money sharks that prey on the poor; and he could learn a needed job skill. It is not a one-week, two-week or three-week operation. The training program might last six months, a year, perhaps two—maybe even longer. However expensive to train one man, it would be less expensive than to support that man's family with welfare funds for decades.

Where such programs have been tried they have had great success. An Opportunities Industrialization Center opened in Washington in 1967. After six months it had graduated 176 persons. Of those 176, 154 had secured full-time jobs paying an average salary of $4,000 a year. The center has two programs. The first is a "feeder" program of basic education and job orientation that leads to the second program of job training. The Washington center is similar to centers in several other large cities which, in turn, are modeled after a program begun in Philadelphia in the early 1960s. The program is financed with federal funds but draws on private industries to assist with job training. These programs never lack for candidates, although, during the twenty-six-week course, the trainee receives absolutely no money. Said one of the officers of the Washington program: "We're not giving anything away and we're not paying our trainees anything to help themselves. We're the opportunity for the loser who hasn't been given an opportunity to show what he can do. He doesn't want a handout. All he wants is that chance to demonstrate that he can be his own man."

Another program demonstrating success in Washington is operated by the city's Welfare Department at its Work and Training Opportunity Center. The center enrolls about 150 persons every nine weeks. First the enrollee attends remedial education sessions, then receives job training, either at the center, at a vocational school or on the job site with a cooperating employer. The whole program lasts one year. In addition to paying the costs of training the impoverished person, the Center also gives him an average of $46 a week. In two years of operation the Center had placed approximately eight hundred family heads in jobs. The average salary paid by the jobs was $75 a week. Not only is that about 50 percent higher than the average welfare payment, but it is also, of course, earned money rather than given money. The program has not had complete success. Four out of ten trainees never finish the program. Three out of ten graduates are not at their job six months after graduation. But that can be said another way. Six out of ten trainees do stick out the course. Seven out of ten graduates hold onto their jobs. The program does not lack for applicants. A total of six thousand have applied; only two thousand could be accepted.

A study of graduates of the Job Corps centers showed that

65 percent were working one year after leaving the center, 7 percent were in school, and the remainder were unemployed. Considering that most entrants into the Job Corps were "unemployables"—that is, they had neither the skills nor the motivation in some cases to work—that study is proof of remarkable results. The study was made by the respected Louis Harris polling organization and was released early in 1968.

Still, as successful as these programs appear, they have not been expanded as they should. Primarily they are part of the War on Poverty. But, as such, they get caught in a political pull between statistics. The poverty war must justify itself to the politicians in Washington who appropriate the funds. The politicians, in turn, must justify their appropriations to their constituents who supply the money via taxes. The resulting pressure on the War on Poverty is to cut back or at least slow down the expansion of those programs that are aimed at training the really hard-core unemployable. These people are the most difficult to train. More significant politically, they are the most difficult to demonstrate success with. Taking people who can neither read nor write at an adult level, who have neither job skills nor work experience, training them and producing at least some who are working, this is a major accomplishment. It does not show up well on a graph, however. Americans traditionally expect an immediate dollar's value that can be seen and felt for a dollar spent. But correcting the failings of decades cannot be done quickly. The process will take decades.

That the United States faces a long, tough job of bringing the alienated and the uneducated and the culturally deprived back into society has never been fully explained or sold to the middle-class American public. It is this public which has impact on Congress. The result is that job-training programs do not have much Congressional support. In 1967, for example, the Senate defeated in a 54-28 vote a proposal to spend $2.8 billion for job training and for creating jobs in the slums. A few minutes earlier, by a 47-42 vote, the Senate killed a compromise $925 million plan. Both plans had Democratic-Republican support and also opposition from both parties. President Johnson in the White House was against both plans also; he didn't wish to spend that much money during the Vietnamese war. The Congressional opposition is more interesting because it shows a complete misunderstanding of the problems of the poor today—which are the problems of perhaps one fourth of the American people.

"Is the country ready to give a permanent job to anyone who cannot or will not find work elsewhere?" asked Senator Robert C. Byrd, Democrat of West Virginia, in leading the fight against the plans.

Obviously the nation was not ready. Only when it is, however, will it solve the national disease of poverty. To say that a need exists for ten thousand medical technicians has little meaning to the adult who can neither read nor write. To say that openings exist for computer programmers has little meaning to the residents of the Appalachian region where no computer can be found.

In some cases training might not be necessary. Daniel Moynihan, who believes in a full work program as well as the family allowance, has made an extremely practical suggestion: Have the government return to twice-a-day mail deliveries. Being a mail carrier does not require sophistication nor a great deal of education. Twice-a-day deliveries would mean, Mr. Moynihan estimated, the hiring of an additional fifty thousand mailmen. They could be drawn from the unemployed or the underemployed. True, the Post Office Department's budget would soar. But the net dollar impact on the nation might be a saving as these fifty thousand men and their families come off the welfare rolls, are persuaded to avoid a life of crime or immorality. In addition to this, the nation's mail service would greatly improve.

There are a number of services that could be increased. In most cities trash is collected once a week. Why not twice a week? Why can't streets be swept more frequently than they are? The "Freedom Budget" rejected such "dead end" jobs, as well as jobs producing doubtful products.

"Although almost any kind of employment is better than unemployment," it said, "employment cannot be the sole criterion. We do not want leaf-raking nor pyramid-building. We cannot be satisfied with a million more jobs resulting from construction of luxurious hotels on the beaches and from production of superfluous gadgets by the hundreds of millions, if this substitutes for the additional jobs which would result from creation of effective demand and markets for the things we need most as a nation and a people." The "Freedom Budget" goes on to say that it believes in uniting the "goal of full employment with the goals for meeting the other priorities of our national needs."

"Make-work" projects, however, should not be dismissed too casually. Leaf-raking is a dead-end job—unless, of course, a requisite for earning two dollars an hour at raking leaves is the attending of classes teaching reading, writing and vocational skills.

"Make-work" projects, however, should not be dismissed too training program. One fourth of the worker's day—perhaps one third or one half, whatever is a convenient figure—should be devoted to job retraining and classes trying to make up the failings of the American educational system. Leaf-raking can be ennobling when it is a step to a decent job and a greater degree of self-respect.

Whether job retraining is part of a make-work project or straight classroom time, some people would not respond. A man in his thirties or forties who never has worked may be too old to begin. He may be too old even to begin to try. He also may be too antagonistic, incapable perhaps of learning even the most rudimentary skills. These people would be relegated to the leaf-raking level of employment for the remainder of their working days. Or they may choose to hustle on the streets, to become the pimps, the dope pushers, the numbers men. They would be a serious problem but not a critical one. This group eventually would dwindle, particularly as the hustlers' markets narrowed in the disappearing slums, and the number of their replacements would grow smaller and smaller. The generations of people coming, products of a better environment and better educational opportunities, would not be forced to do menial work, could do better than street hustling, as a permanent way of life. Richer opportunities would be available and the members of coming generations would have the capability to grasp those opportunities. No plan for the eradication of poverty offers an immediate solution. The cultural and educational poverty existing in the United States at the end of the 1960s is the product of decades. The United States will be fortunate if only decades are required to end it.

Even though the problem is not a critical one, the fact of requiring some people to live off make-work projects or leaving some to the streets as a permanent way of life is a flaw in the work/training system, a tragic flaw. But it is not as tragic a flaw as that inherent in the guaranteed society: making a near-poverty level a permanent way of life for a large number of Americans.

The advocates of the guaranteed annual income, naturally, do not concede their proposal would act as a brake on the individual. They see it, instead, as a spur. Freeing a man from the concern of providing food and shelter, so the argument runs, permits him to develop his capabilities as they should be developed. Leon H. Keyserling, an economist whose credentials as a liberal date back to the early New Deal, has responded to this argument most effectively.

"Whether or not," he said, "it is better for a person who is highly cultivated to hold a job at pay or to be free instead to write poetry or paint pictures—even if he cannot do this well enough for others to pay him for the results, the Negroes in Watts and Harlem and elsewhere, and most of the unemployed, whether black or white or younger or older or male or female, do not have this kind of cultivation. The real alternative for them, in the near future, is between jobs—not the best possible job, but some decent jobs at once—and further deterioration and despair."

Do people now living in poverty wish to be returned to society or can they be returned?

There appears to be a growing debate. On one side there is the old argument that some people are naturally shiftless, disinterested in contributing to society. On the other side it is asserted that, provided opportunity and shown a decent prospect, most people will work. The debate is an idle one, perhaps even a silly one. Society should not compel a person to work, but then society should not guarantee financial security for a person who can fill a job but refuses to do so. It is a responsibility of society to care for the aged, the handicapped, the dependent children and the ones who watch those children. Others—those capable of working—should be placed in a position where they can work at a decent wage and at a decent level of employment. That is the position of the authors of the "Freedom Budget" and of Vice President Humphrey when he talks of making people feel "they have a place in the scheme of things" and of other persons who actually come in contact with the poor, who know the poor as people and not only as statistics.

The debate over laziness versus opportunity is more significant for those doing the arguing rather than for those being argued about. Welfare, the dealing with human beings who need help, has become as bureaucratized as any other American industry. A newspaper headline in the Washington *Post*, for example, proclaims "WORK TRAINING FAILS AT GETTING POOR OFF RELIEF." The story that followed, however, told about advocates of Labor Department-supervised training producing a report criticizing training done under the auspices of another agency. Government agencies, with the help of Congress, should be able to work out between themselves the best job-training techniques. Perhaps they can't because the agencies feel the pressure for quick results, for the statistics proving conclusively that they are spending their money in a valuable manner that produces great gains. Actually, even as the *Post* story conceded, as badly as the other agencies ran their training programs, as much as those agencies appeared to have botched up the job, the job training still managed to get one out of eight welfare recipients involved in the training off relief. That's 12½ percent. Although that is a low percentage, it is actually a decent measure of success considering the inadequacy of the training programs offered and the extent to which the welfare recipients had been shunned by society in the past.

As with all bureaucracies, one of the difficulties of people involved in welfare work is that they tend to become more interested in technique and agency rather than in people to be served. The argument between the Labor Department people and the other agency reported in the Washington *Post* is one example. Another was reported in *The New York Times*. The story concerned one of the worst aspects of the welfare program: It insists on a 100 percent tax on earnings. If a recipient is given $150 a month in welfare and then goes out and earns $50 a month at a job, her welfare check is automatically reduced $50. This denies her incentive to work; she receives just as much by not working as she does by working. It is the guaranteed society gone dangerously wild. It not only guarantees a minimum, but it forbids reaching for a maximum.

In 1967 New York City came up with an experimental plan. Welfare recipients could earn $85 a month at a job without losing any of their welfare benefits. As their earnings increased over $85 a month, they would lose a percentage of their welfare payments. At approximately $5,000 a year in earnings for a family of four, welfare would stop. The idea is a sound one, a reasonable way of encouraging people to get off the welfare rolls. President Johnson placed a similar proposal before Congress for enactment nationally. But the proposal has an acknowledged limited value. It benefits a narrow range of people. In New York City there were 130,000 adults eligible for the program. All of them received welfare because they cared for dependent children. For them to take advantage of the new program by going to work means they must find some way to care for their children while they work. They also must know about the program and have a job skill or be trainable. For these reasons the program got off to a very slow start. The social workers had not been trained; they did not know about the program and about how to guide their welfare charges to apply for it. The day-care centers to watch over the dependent children were inadequate.

The Times reported, in its headline, "RELIEF-JOB PLAN OFF TO SLOW START—FEW ENROLL IN CITY PROGRAM URGING POOR TO WORK." The newspaper also reported that some social workers considered the plan "miserable" because "It doesn't touch the main problem. It only helps the mothers. The real problem is the unemployed male—and he only gets on the relief rolls when he is old or physically disabled. His status doesn't change; he's still made a moocher, whether he lives off his wife's welfare check or off her paycheck."

Everything in the article was accurate and was objectively

reported. But unintentionally the account gave the impression of a program failing. Most news accounts of similar programs also are accurate and objective, but also give impressions of programs failing. For what the program was intended to do—and its intentions were limited—it was making reasonable progress. It was not failing. Actually it was society that failed with these people in the past, and it is society that is succeeding with them, admittedly only very slightly, now. The challenge is not to ignore or scoff at that small success—nor to permit it to become caught in bureaucratic arguments—but to enlarge it.

That it can be enlarged is demonstrated by the success of the training projects in Washington and other cities. There are other signs. A private consulting firm under contract with the Office of Economic Opportunity (the main War on Poverty agency) studied community-action programs in ten communities. The firm, Daniel Yankelovich, Inc., of New York, concluded that the poor, especially the Negro poor, wants to work its way out of poverty.

"Contrary to some widely accepted beliefs," said the 1967 report, "the poverty populations investigated in our research, especially among Negro segments, (A) are highly motivated to work their way out of poverty; (B) share conventional middle-class standards to an even greater extent than the middle class itself; (C) want self-help assistance to enable them to get out of poverty more than they want generalized services aimed at making their existing situation more bearable...."

The report recommended that the Office of Economic Opportunity "adopt as a major objective the support of programs aimed at breaking the poverty cycle rather than the support of programs aimed solely at mitigating poverty."

That report is not alone. Rather, it supports, and is supported by, other studies of the poor and of welfare recipients. A survey of mothers on welfare in New York City in 1968, for example, showed that 70 percent would prefer to work rather than receive welfare payments. They were unable to, of course, because there were no day-care centers for them to leave their children, because they did not have vocational training or were unable to locate jobs, or because, in some cases, there was a lack of even the minimum skills needed to apply for a job. But the strong desire was there. It only needed some help. It needed an opportunity, not a guarantee.

There is another sign, one not supported statistically perhaps but well known to law-enforcement officers. Every city has what is called its "slave corner." There line up the men who cannot find regular jobs because they lack training or because unions discriminate on the basis of color. An employer who needs some manual laborers and who will take the cheaper nonunion help drives by and hires his men. The going price is between fifteen and twenty-five dollars a day. Most of this work is outdoor construction work, pick-and-shovel work. And so if it rains the slave corner shuts down. Then the police worry. They know that these men, unable to pick up their twenty dollars at legitimate work, will pull a burglary or another crime. The men wish to do honest work, but, even more than that, they wish their families not to go hungry.

The desire by the slum dweller to work is well known to those who deal with the poor. In talking about Negro teen-agers, Bayard Rustin has said: "Whenever job programs have been announced, they have turned out in large numbers, only to find that the jobs weren't there. In Oakland, a Job Fair attracted 15,000 people; only 250 were placed. In Philadelphia, 6,000 were on a mailing list for a training program. What Negro teen-agers are not inclined to accept are dead-end jobs that pay little and promise no advancement or training. Many would prefer to live by their wits as hustlers or petty racketeers, their version of the self-employed businessman or salesman. That their pursuit of this distorted entrepreneurial ideal only mires them deeper in the slum proletariat is not the point. They want to be part of the white-collar organization man's world that is America's future, not trapped behind pushcarts."

Not to enlarge that opportunity to train these men, to place only 250 when 15,000 show up, to give the poor a guaranteed annual income, to assume that the poor's only problem is a lack of cash is to court two dangers. The first leads to the second.

The first danger is that the nation will produce a section of society perpetually doomed to living off government handout, whether that handout is called welfare, the guaranteed annual income or the negative income tax. Poor people produce other poor people. A family with a cultural heritage, a decent education and modest ambition—even though that family is without income—will produce children capable of earning a better living than did their parents. Immigrant families have been doing it in America for decades. However, a family poor in cultural heritage, education and ambition—even if it has a minimum income guaranteed by the government—will produce children like itself, completely alienated and separated from modern society.

And these poor—culturally poor, educationally poor and ambition poor—would multiply rapidly. Society would be encouraging it. Society would be saying: "Here, you do not have to work. You do not have to worry about your old age. You do not have to worry about your children. You have no worries. You have no obligations." That kind of an appeal could not help but attract persons right on the fringe of poverty to go all the way. Like the aviation industry going after the SST, the individual would say: "The guaranteed society is here; why fight it?"

Senator Ribicoff of Connecticut has pointed out: "The person earning $100,000 a year wouldn't be worried very much about someone who would be getting $3,000 a year [from a federally guaranteed annual income], even though he was not working. But how about the man who works forty hours a week for $3,500 a year and sees his neighbor get $3,000 a year for not working?"

The Senator made his comment to point up the political difficulties involved in persuading members of Congress to go along with the guaranteed annual income. But the problems would not be the political ones that Senator Ribicoff foresees. They would be of a different kind. When that man working forty hours a week for $3,500 sees his neighbor receiving $3,000 for not working, the first man would quit his job. Society would be telling him working is not valuable.

Most supporters of the guaranteed annual income concede that American society would collapse if too many persons chose the offered income rather than employment, but then it is argued this will not happen. Most Americans will choose to work, argues Robert Theobald.

"If man is inherently irresponsible and a bum," Mr. Theobald has said, "the guaranteed income is undoubtedly the most stupid idea that anybody has yet managed to come up with. If, on the other hand, you believe . . . in the long run human beings can become responsible, can rise to the responsiblity of developing themselves in our society, then the guaranteed income is the only thing in my opinion which will begin to lead us into a free society."

Man is a working animal. He always has been, most particularly in the United States, where rewards often are predicated on the amount of effort expanded by the individual. Even the slum dwellers, those most alienated from modern society—as the long lists of applications for all the work training programs demonstrate—want to work.

But that is true of the present society in which work is prized and encouraged.

What of a society in which work is said to be unnecessary and discouraged?

The results would not be noticeable immediately. However, within several decades it would be quite evident that more and more of the population would join the recipients of the guaranteed annual income. The guaranteed society would be larger and larger. And the guaranteed society would be a trap from which few would escape.

The United States does not now accept the handout as a standard way of life. Still, it does not provide the social services, the educational facilities, the job training to end the handout. In the guaranteed society, when the United States accepts the handout as an inviolate right, can anyone honestly expect that the means of ending a person's cultural and educational poverty—the decent schools with the concerned teachers particularly—will be made available?

The members of this guaranteed society, the persons trapped in a life of minimum decency, which is another way of describing a life that is one step above squalor, will be primarily Negroes. The guaranteed annual income is a means of insuring that the children of those presently poor also will be poor, and in the 1960s the poor, other than the aged poor, were primarily Negroes. Almost half of all nonwhite families with children in the United States during the mid-1960s were poor—"poor" meaning that the family's income was below approximately $3,000 a year. There were white families living in poverty, of course, but the percentage of Negro families ran ahead of them by three and one half times.

It would be ironic, in the second one hundred years after the Negroes were freed of their bondage in America, if the Negroes were to be forced into another serfdom. Rather than be based on the economic selfishness of the majority, this new serfdom would stem from the majority's economic largess.

This first danger, that of creating an unemployed class, leads to the second danger. If the United States writes off a large part of its population, then it will lack the manpower to meet the problems of the coming decades. The people to go to the medical schools, the teachers' colleges, the engineering schools are not going to be available. They cannot emerge in needed quantities from a near-poverty society, which is what a guaranteed society would be. The way to end poverty is not with a guarantee but with education that leads the child to income-earning capabilities and with an environment where work is valued and encouraged.

Achieving that kind of education and that kind of environment will not be cheap. Schools for children and job training for adults cost money, probably more at the beginning than would a guaranteed annual income. The path away from the guaranteed society is not an inexpensive one. But eventually the investment would pay off in rich dividends, not only in the individual people employed but in the society growing stronger and richer.

That is not only good morality but also good economics.

6

Toward a Creative Society

One

WHEN THE KRUPP FAMILY still personally operated the giant industrial works that bears its name in Germany, it was said of the old Kruppianer—the worker in the plant—that "you were born in a Krupp hospital with the aid of a Krupp midwife, you lived in a Krupp house, were christened in a Krupp-built church, went to a Krupp school, worked in a Krupp plant, retired on a Krupp pension and lived in a Krupp old people's home. The only thing he didn't do was bury you."

That Kruppianer lived in a guaranteed society.

It was not accidental. Almost a century before American businessmen were willing to negotiate with union leaders as equals, the Krupp family realized that a happy worker, free from financial problems, was a better and a more efficient worker. In 1967, for example, Walter Reuther, the president of the United Auto Workers, began a bitter contest with the automobile manufacturers to insure year-round income for his union members. But at the Krupp plants such a plan had been established in the 1870s, almost a century before Mr. Reuther began his campaign. Krupp had decided then that it was a bad investment to lay off and perhaps lose a talented and trained employee even if there was no work for him. After all, so went the Krupp explanation, next year there will be work and it would cost us more to train new men than to "make work" for our present employees.

Is housing difficult for employees to find? Krupp built low-cost housing and made it available to his employees at low rents. Are Krupp employees organizing cooperatives to purchase food and other supplies cheaply? Krupp took the cooperative over. Do his workers worry about illness or the insecurity of their retirement years? Krupp established insurance and pension plans that would not be rivaled for generations.

As long as the Kruppianer did his job well, did not cause difficulty and was loyal to the firm, his future was secure. He had a guarantee.

But there were problems. In exchange for its largess, the company expected its employees to act toward the company as young children toward their parents. Submission was required. The guarantee offered security but discouraged independence. Any employee who caused trouble, such as organizing a union or espousing political theories unwelcome to the Krupp family, faced the loss of his job and with it the loss of his insurance and pension. Krupp supervisors checked the newspapers the employees read, the printed political propaganda found in their trash baskets. It was not difficult. All that Krupp-financed housing brought the workers tightly together and made watching them easy. Krupp acknowledged that the company's purpose was to develop from its labor force "many faithful subjects to the state, and workers of a special race to the firm." One Krupp historian commented of that statement and of the cradle-to-grave supervision that it suggested that "a long time before 1984 Alfred Krupp pioneered also the image of Big Brother."

It is now time for the United States to decide if it wishes to enter a Big Brother society, a guaranteed society where a minimal security is assured. But with it also is banished opportunity, competition, initiative and creativity.

Does the American businessman really want the federal government to determine which company will have a monopoly on supersonic aircraft production—in effect, dictating the leading aircraft company of the coming decades?

Does the labor leader really want the government to enter wage negotiations on a non-defense industry, something the government eventually must do if the SST is to fly at a profitable price?

Does the consumer really want the federal government to dictate air fares, the selection of airlines and of schedules, again something it must do if the SST is not to nose-dive financially?

Does the American businessman who must ship goods abroad really want a group of maritime executives to peg transportation prices artificially high? And then does that businessman want to pay those extra costs through his taxes as well as his shipping fees? And is that businessman who must pay those costs really satisfied with ships that go slowly?

Do the American taxpayers really want to give away their possessions, such as a share in patent rights and the oil-shale deposits? These are precious assets. They belong to everyone. Should only a few people control the development of that wealth? Should only a few people be guaranteed a return from those assets?

Is the American worker really ready to settle for a minimal existence? Or does he wish to have the opportunity to try for better than that? Is the American individual ready to accept a society that encourages a person to remain a worker rather than encouraging that person to become a boss?

Those questions are involved in the coming of the guaranteed society. And the United States seems to be saying "yes" to them.

Before that drift toward the guaranteed society becomes too

great, perhaps it is time to turn toward a creative society. The phrase "creative society" sometimes is used by persons considered fiscal conservatives as a slogan meaning the cutting back of federal spending—usually spending aimed at assisting the poor. That is a cheapening of the concept embodied in the phrase. A creative society is not a cheap society.

In a creative society the question should not be whether the individual or the industry wants a subsidy. Everyone, from the most successful businessman to the poorest welfare recipient, "wants" something from the government. The question for society should be, instead, does the subsidy conform to the traditional standards used previously in the dispensing of federal assistance?

Does the subsidy increase competition? Does the subsidy fulfill a need that otherwise will go unfulfilled? Is the subsidy a legitimate part of the defense effort? Does the subsidy fulfill a humanitarian task? If the subsidy cannot be justified by one of those standards, then it is outside the American tradition. It is a guarantee leading to a new kind of society, a society alien to the United States.

In addition, it probably is not necessary.

Shortly after the Lockheed corporation lost out to Boeing on the SST contract, it began development of a "jumbo jet" airplane designed to carry several hundred passengers. Flying at six hundred miles an hour, the airplane will be subsonic, and its principal contribution to transportation is the expected lowering of fares, because of greater payloads, between continents and on long-distance intracontinental flights. In comparison with the SST, the jumbo jet probably is a less dramatic advance. But by lowering transportation costs it will enable larger numbers of people to travel. It also should lower air-freight costs. Those gains are in comparison to the advantage of the SST, which is only to cut what will be a negligible amount of time off door-to-door traveling while adding appreciably to transportation costs in the process. Whether more or less dramatic, the point about the jumbo jet is that it is privately financed. Lockheed raised $500 million to build it. (Because of the Defense Department's deep involvement in aviation, no airplane is built with private funds entirely. The jumbo jet, however, is still a private endeavor. The government offers no guarantee to Lockheed of its financial success.) Lockheed's ability to raise a large amount of funds privately to build this airplane suggests that the aviation industry, perhaps several companies combining into a Comsat-type operation, could have raised the money to build the SST.

Other financial means could have been used. There has been a bill before Congress for several years calling for the SST to be built with funds raised by the sale of bonds to the public. The federal government would stand behind the bonds, if the SST proved an unsuccessful venture. Representative Clark MacGregor, Republican of Michigan, pointed up the advantage of such a system.

"If the project is successful," he said, "and the contractors are thereby able to pay off their bondholders, the Government would not have to spend one dime on it. Forecasts of the future markets for the SST, relied upon today by the Department of Transportation, show that this is by far the most probable outcome."

He continued: "But even if the project failed and the Government had to make good its guarantee on the bonds, it would still be cheaper since the interest rate on private bonds is lower than that on Government short-term securities which would be used to finance this proposed deficit expenditure."

Not only would such a system be cheaper, whether the SST succeeded or failed, but also it would much more closely resemble the free-enterprise system.

Another possible financing method was suggested by Dr. Arnold Moore, an economist and former Pentagon official who had studied the economics of the SST while working for the Defense Department. In a talk before the American Economic Association he said: "It would have been preferable if, from the start, the SST program had been viewed as a purchase by the government of 'externalities.' Once a value had been placed on them—say, $300 million—the government could have said, 'Anyone who will agree to make an SST, introduce it by 1974, and sell, e.g., two hundred to commercial airlines before 1985 can have $300 million.'"

The value of such a plan, Dr. Moore said, would be to make

"the national interest cost explicit in advance" and would be to give "an element of economic competition which is now lacking." Dr. Moore explained why, however, no other plan except the one finally chosen ever was seriously considered. "Programs of this sort," he said, "are usually generated by fascination with some technical novelty. Detailed economic analysis come late, if at all. Further, it is often done by the interested agency on the theory that close knowledge of the 'industry' and the 'technology' are more important than detachment. Thus a prime need is for introducing dispassionate rationality earlier . . . merely choosing among the designs that engineers dream up is not sufficient . . . favorable statements by the President make it difficult for government agencies to entertain any but the most enthusiastic notions. Indeed, once such public positions have been taken, it becomes increasingly difficult for the President to get good advice."

There are other reasons why only one plan was ever considered. Any other financing technique would have had some element of risk, some competitive challenge, some requirement for the old element of free-enterprise daring. And nobody in the industry wanted this. After all, as long as the government can be persuaded to guarantee all the financial arrangements, why bother to seek other money sources?

The guaranteed society is with us. Why fight it?

An example of how a different approach could have worked is the program of government assistance to the railroads. In the mid-1960s, when it became obvious that the transportation arteries in the northeast corridor between Washington, New York and Boston were choking, the government offered a subsidy. Moving people by railroad in this area is the most intelligent means of transportation because it is the method that moves the most people fastest with as little discomfort to the rest of the community as possible. But while the government assists the railroad industry, the assistance is not such that the government must dominate the railroad industry. The money does not overpower. The railroad industry is putting up more money than is the government, in comparison to the SST, where the federal contribution so far is 6.5 times the private contribution. Also the federal funds clearly are limited to research and initial promotion. The industry can continue to run itself. The aid is in the national interest because it is helping unclog congested transportation arteries; the intent of the assistance is not to bolster a dying industry although that may be one of its secondary effects. With the SST the priority is reversed. The federal assistance is to save the aviation industry; the public benefit comes next.

The assistance to the railroads will increase competition—not only between railroads and other forms of transportation but also within the railroad industry itself. Any technical gains made will be available to all members of the railroad industry, not just the Pennsylvania Railroad, the original contractor. (The Pennsylvania Railroad now is, of course, the Penn Central.) The Pennsylvania will not be in a position to lock up the future development of anything—as Boeing can do with the SST. And certainly the practice of assistance to an industry, which can lead to a valuable contribution to American life, is within the national tradition.

Even the merchant marine could be made a competitive and profitable industry. Two points must be acknowledged. First, despite the merchant marine's poor showing in the Vietnam war, a defense need does exist for a merchant marine. The possibility of a full-scale war in the future cannot be ignored. If it comes, the wishes of the merchant marine in a time of total mobilization will not be significant. The fleet will be called into service as would most other members of the American economy. For that reason it is necessary to keep a fleet capable of expansion. Shipyards must be maintained to meet a demand for cargo ships in wartime. Trained merchant sailors must be available to become the nucleus of a much larger force if large-scale war breaks out. This means that some subsidy always will be necessary. It should be clearly labeled as a defense expenditure. It should be limited only to that defense need. It should not be used for bolstering the merchant marine in its old ways.

The second point to be acknowledged is that an industry which has received government assistance since the beginning of the government cannot be denied that assistance abruptly—no matter how deserving of such action the industry appears. The government does have an obligation not to cut the merchant marine adrift. This means that rather than ending the nondefense subsidy with one stroke, it must be phased out gradually.

In late 1965 an interagency committee of the federal government produced a sixty-three-page report that was designed to accomplish both those purposes—retain enough of a maritime potential to meet national needs in case of a full-scale war and also phase out the remainder of the subsidy program gradually. The interagency committee was headed by Alan Boyd, then Under Secretary of Commerce for transportation. The committee adopted many of the ideas of Nicholas Johnson, then still Maritime Administrator and a member of the interagency committee.

The committee urged the gradual end of the subsidy for America's ocean liners. No more would the taxpayers pay half the cost of a small group's transportation across the Atlantic Ocean on the S.S. *United States*. Another recommendation was the replacement of the traditional operating subsidy with new forms of payments. These would, of course, be subsidies also, but they would be designed to encourage better, faster and cheaper service. This improved service, hopefully, would make the American merchant marine more competitive with other national fleets, eventually leading to a reduction in or an end to the operating subsidy. The cargo-preference subsidy would be dropped, according to the committee's recommendations. In its place would be a program of building large, ultramodern cargo ships economical enough to compete with foreign ships for goods. Again, once the American fleet became competitive, it was expected the need for a subsidy would, if not evaporate, at least diminish.

The interagency committee also recommended that the ship-construction subsidy be sharply revised. The committee called for the building of a specified number of ships in American shipyards with a government subsidy. After that specified number had been built, however, the ship operators would be permitted to buy cargo ships abroad but still receive an operating subsidy. Under the 1936 law, if they buy ships abroad they cannot receive an operating subsidy. Maintaining some subsidy in effect keeps a cargo ship construction ability within the nation, to be expanded in case of full-scale war. But the committee proposal would have taken off the artificial limits set on the American merchant marine.

There were other proposals of less importance. They all added up to making the merchant marine a more competitive industry, to taking it out of the guaranteed society in which it was slipping before it was permanently locked in.

The interagency report had been drawn up by government officials from the Commerce Department, the Maritime Administration, the Budget Bureau and the Pentagon. When it was completed, it was passed on to an administration policy committee, made up of five members from the labor unions, five members from management and five members representing the public. That policy committee was stacked ten—the five management and the five union members—against the five public members. The committee refused even to receive the interagency report in late 1965, then rejected its proposals. One member of the interagency committee commented later on that double action, "I can't conceive of a situation where people exhibited such closed minds as they did in this case." The policy committee alternative was that the government increase its subsidy to the merchant marine. This continues the industry's cry.

Since the furor over the merchant-marine subsidy program, begun when Nicholas Johnson was Maritime Administrator, some segments of the industry have started to worry about their "image." They also are concerned that someday Washington might run out of control, that their subgovernment would be destroyed. The operators of the subsidized lines began to cozy up to the federal government, saying they would go along with plans to purchase ships abroad or to increase automation. Of course, neither of the proposals involved any risk to the operators; it made no difference to them where they purchased their ships and they could only benefit if labor costs were reduced. The shipbuilders also came up with some proposals. They would build more automated ships—at a higher construction cost, and the government paying a higher subsidy to the shipyards—to help reduce the operating subsidy. Each segment of the industry volunteered to reduce the other's subsidy.

Still the Johnson Administration persevered, in its own particular way. When Alan Boyd became head of the new Transportation Department he was directed by President Johnson to bring all the elements of the merchant marine into agreement on a new policy. That was asking the impossible. The interests of the various segments of the industry were too varied, and none wanted to give up its benefits under the old plan to help reach a consensus. The only rational solution was to develop an intelligent policy and impose it on the industry; after all, the subsidy was coming from the general revenue.

But that wasn't done. And in May of 1967 Secretary Boyd was forced to acknowledge that he had failed to bring the various parts of the industry into agreement. "I must now report," he told a Congressional committee, "that we do not have the kind of agreement that will make such a program a reality."

The Secretary, asked by a newsman to pinpoint the main problem, said, "The one thing necessary for going ahead with a program is agreement on foreign ship construction."

Perhaps that is the "one thing" necessary, perhaps not. What really is needed may be a commitment by the industry to the free-enterprise system. But the merchant marine chooses not to make such a commitment. Instead, it has chosen the *status quo*. There will be no rough waves. Smooth and subsidized sailing is guaranteed.

And the merchant marine is not alone. The critics of the Administration's oil-shale program, such as Professor Galbraith and Benjamin Cohen, have pointed out how that industry can be made more competitive and bring with it all the rich fruits of a competitive society. The same can be done with patents. All that is required is a commitment to the free-enterprise system and a willingness to help bring it about.

With such a commitment and such a willingness even the rural Negro in the South, for example, could be helped to lead a productive life where he is, in the South that he knows. William V. Shannon, a member of the editorial board of *The New York Times*, has commented, "There is no mystery about what could be done. . . . The government could buy land and sell it to ex-sharecroppers on a long-term mortgage at easy terms. A Negro family could be settled on a family-sized farm in most parts of the South for an investment of $10,000 to $15,000. This would be far cheaper than transferring that same family to the welfare rolls of some Northern city. The land reforms that should have accompanied political reconstruction a century ago still need to be carried out."

Mr. Shannon also suggested, as possibilities, that the government encourage the development of industries in the South that "agreed to hire and train Negroes," and that the government finance the building of racially integrated "new towns" around industrial plants. The point about Mr. Shannon's proposals that is so valuable is that he is suggesting ways to transform people, people pushed by society into an unproductive position, into again becoming contributing members of society.

Shortly after Mr. Shannon made his proposal in a *Times* column, Agriculture Secretary Orville L. Freeman appeared to pick up the idea, or at least a variation of it. He suggested it might be wiser to subsidize a Negro rural family on the farm with a thousand dollars a year for twenty years rather than build them a dwelling unit in the city for twenty thousand dollars.

Actually, while any program designed to stop the forced flow of Negroes from the rural South to the ghetto North would require federal assistance, it may not require permanent or even lengthy subsidies. An area not really explored is how much the Southern rural Negro's poverty may be caused by the white power structure. Near Selma, Alabama, for example, there are hundreds of Negro farmers who had been scratching out an existence on farms of fifty to seventy acres. They harvested their cucumbers, the okra, the peas, then took the crops into Selma in hopes that the white man there would buy some from them at a reasonable price. If a Negro farmer was very lucky—meaning that if the white men in Selma were very kind to him and bought some of his crop at rock-bottom prices—the Negro farmer could make maybe $1,500 a year. If the Negro wasn't so lucky, and the white man were not buying, he had to give up his farm and flee to the city. In a five-year period during the mid-1960s, one out of five farmers did so.

In 1967, however, helped by a $400,000 assist from the Office of Economic Opportunity, the farmers organized themselves into a cooperative. Now they themselves process and sell their crops to the large packagers rather than depend on the white power structure in Selma. Their crops bring the going market price, which is higher than what the Selma whites were paying. Also, the market seems unlimited. They sell as much as they grow. The power structure in Alabama has bitterly opposed the OEO grant, but the agency made it anyway. A little seed money—in this case amounting to five hundred dollars for each of the eight hundred families involved—is helping to turn people from a marginal existence toward a productive existence. They had been heading toward the guaranteed society.

That is an example of the government spending a small amount of money to shift direction from a guaranteed society to a productive and creative society. In other cases the government could do so by changing policy. An example is pensions.

These promises of security, as flimsy as they are, are the creation of the government. Without special encouragement from Washington there would be no pension system. The first such break came in 1921 when Congress exempted the income of pension funds from taxes. Then Congress exempted workers from paying taxes on money contributed to the pension fund for them by employers.

The next big government push for pensions came in the 1940s. During the Second World War industry was faced with a labor shortage. Wartime conditions imposed wage freezes, meaning that industries could not raise salaries to attract employees. But industries could in those war years offer supplementary wage benefits—fringe benefits, they have come to be called. The War Labor Board, which watched over industrial economics then, recommended the adoption of such practices. Pensions were a particularly cheap means of attracting employees. Because of the high tax rates then in effect, every dollar contributed to a pension plan by an employer allowed that employer to reduce his income tax by eighty cents. This meant the actual cost to him of contributing a dollar to the pension fund was twenty cents.

There were other factors influencing employers to go along with pensions. Such a plan is a reasonably humanitarian system enabling a company to rid itself of aged and unproductive workers. The appearance of an employer voluntarily adopting a pension plan for his employees might influence those employees to refrain from joining a union. Most important was the realization that, as work became more skilled, it was valuable to a company to keep its most talented employees on hand, even if that meant spending a few dollars.

Employers also realized that fringe benefits such as pensions are cheaper for them than equivalent amounts granted in salaries. Example: A worker earns a base rate of two dollars an hour in wages and an additional fifty cents an hour in fringe benefits, a total of $2.50. He works overtime and is paid time and a half. For each overtime hour he receives three dollars, his base rate of two dollars plus one half of that for overtime. But if he received the entire $2.50 in wages, his overtime would be $3.75—the $2.50 an hour plus one half of that.

Pensions are billed as an asset to the worker, a kind of forced saving that eventually will provide him with an economic guarantee. Actually they are a gift to the employer. By appearing to be generous, he establishes a beneficent image, retains skilled workers, saves a substantial amount of money in fringe benefits and also avoids spending thousands of dollars constantly to train new workers.

The Bank of America, as an example, takes full-page advertisements in *Fortune* showing an executive walking out of an office and the written material in the ad begins with: "Is it too easy for him to quit?" Obviously it is. The ad's answer: "One way to make your company hard to leave is to make sure your pension and profit sharing plan is more attractive than your competitors'." The Bank of America, of course, is in the business of handling such plans. The fact that it advertises its programs as a benefit to the employer rather than as a benefit to the worker should cast some suspicion at least on the fiction that pensions are a great gift to the worker. It is because of that fiction that there are so many tax breaks for pension plans.

And because of those tax breaks, the taxpayer picks up as much or possibly more of the bill for those pensions than does the employer. Of all the federal and local laws and of all the contract provisions affecting pensions, nothing is as important as the Internal Revenue Code. Secretary of Labor W. Willard Wirtz commented on these tax concessions and then concluded:

> I have tried to state the tax implications in as neutral a form as I can, because there has been concern expressed at talk about "tax subsidies." This statement is an attempt to state the facts in a most restrained way. I just want to point out that it is unquestionably true that to whatever extent there are tax benefits to a program of this kind, what that means is that the taxpayers as a whole pick up that much of the cost of these plans.

What are these tax "subsidies" currently? First, the employer deducts his contribution to a pension fund from his earnings. Since the corporate tax rate is 48 percent, the employer actually pays only fifty-two cents and all taxpayers pay the remaining forty-eight cents. The money then goes into a pension fund. These funds now are worth in the area of $100 billion. Obviously this money is invested in a number of stocks, construction projects and other commercial investments. It earns dividends. The Internal Revenue Code exempts these funds from paying any income tax on those dividends. That is the second tax break. The third break exempts the workers from paying taxes on the amount contributed to pension funds for them by employers. In contract negotiations workers argue that fringe benefits such as pensions are part of their compensation. When it comes to paying taxes, however, such benefits are not taxable.

How valuable to the pension system are these tax breaks?

If an employer wishes to create a $100-a-month pension for his worker, the employer must contribute $136 a year to the pension fund. He deducts that $136 a year from his gross income before computing his income tax. The worker who eventually will receive the pension does not report the $136 a year on his income tax. And the dividends the $136 earns each year are not taxable. If those tax breaks were not available, the cost to the employer would be not $136 a year but $194 a year for each worker.

How much does this cost the general taxpayer?

A 1965 study by a Cabinet-level group figured that the loss to the federal treasury was more than $3 billion a year. All taxpayers must make up about a $2.5-billion-a-year loss because the corporations deduct their contributions to the pension funds. The taxpayers also make up about $1 billion in lost tax revenue because the income of the pension funds is not taxed. When the pensions are paid, the recipients pay income tax, of course. This amounts to only about one fifteenth of the loss due to the tax breaks legislated for pension funds. To phrase those calculations another way: If the tax breaks offered pension funds were repealed, the nation's income-tax collections would increase by $3.5 billion. If the nation were operating at a deficit, that $3.5 billion could be used to reduce the deficit. If the nation were operating with a balanced budget, that $3.5 billion could be used to reduce tax rates for individuals and corporations.

Are these tax breaks nothing more than traditional business deductions, in the same way that rents, the cost of equipment and salaries are? The answer: No. They are special tax concessions. Stanley S. Surrey, assistant secretary of the Treasury Department, has explained why. He said:

> I want to make clear that qualified pension plans do get a special tax treatment. . . .
> With regard to an employer's contribution to a pension plan where the employee's benefits are not vested, all that is involved for the employer is the possibility that he may have to make a pension payment to some employee in the future. This possibility of future payment is not sufficient under the general principles of tax law to permit an accrual of the deduction. . . .
> Where the contribution by the employer is vested at the time made, or where it becomes vested at a later point before the employee receives the pension, the general principles of tax law would suggest that the employee should be taxable at that time. It is not controlling that the employee receives no cash money at that time. . . .
> Finally, it is clear that the investment income of a pension trust would be taxable under general principles of tax law except for the benefits extended to qualified plans.

So the cost to the taxpayer is both an exceptional and an expensive one. But as the employees of Studebaker and the Packard plants and as the employees of the hundreds of firms where pension plans are terminated each year can testify, the results are far from the security promised.

What has gone wrong with the pension system is much the same that has gone wrong with the many programs that are beginning to make up the guaranteed society. A national need is perverted to satisfy an immediate desire. What should have been developed as a means of assisting an individual to protect himself against the financial hazards of old age became instead a gimmick for industry to save some money and lock up the future of its workers.

The gimmick can be changed.

As long as the income-tax system is being used, as it is now being used to promote the traditional pension, why not use the tax system to help an individual to provide for his security? Instead of using the tax system as a device to permit industry to manipulate an individual, why not use it as a device to free the individual?

The mechanism already exists. In the early 1960s the government enacted what has become known as the Keogh plan. It encourages self-employed people to save for their retirement years by offering them a small tax break.

Why not simply extend that principle somewhat? Any person who contributed part of his income to a personal and approved retirement program—whether it be government bonds, private insurance, stocks, or whatever—would be given a small tax concession. Being less in need of a company pension, the employee would take more of his wages in cash and less in fringe benefits. That extra cash would supply him with the money to contribute to his retirement fund.

A company still could offer pensions. But they would be recognized for what they are: means of assisting the company to achieve ends it desires. The cost to the income-tax system probably would be no greater than the present tax concessions for pensions. The dollar cost to society would be much less than providing universal welfare payments to the aged.

One drawback appears. Many people might choose not to join such a plan. The growing popularity of the Keogh plan with the self-employed suggests, however, that the number of such refusals would be small.

Those who did decline to join would face the prospect of a bleak time in their retirement years. They would have Social Security benefits as a minimum, plus whatever welfare benefits political decisions make available. But this would not be as bad as the present situation in which millions of workers have no pension coverage. The best estimates indicate it will be the year 2000 before only 50 percent of the American work force can expect to retire with a company pension. (More than 50 percent of the labor force will work at companies offering pensions; but a large number of these employees will not be eligible for such pensions when they reach retirement age.)

The problem is not whether aged people should go hungry and cold. They should not. The real problem is how society can encourage people to best protect themselves from hunger and cold. Encouraging people through the tax system to create their own pension plans is the most creative way to accomplish this. It has two advantages.

The first is that the individual is not dependent on the economic health of his employer for his retirement security, as the employees of the Studebaker and Packard plants were. Particularly with defense industries, a plant may swell its employment rolls or cut them suddenly. The worker becomes an itinerant, moving from one place to another. And each time he loses his retirement benefits. He is a prisoner of economic forces over which he has no control. With his own pension plan, the individual will be dependent only on himself.

The second advantage is that the individual will have more freedom to shape his future. Should he stay with one company his entire working life? Should he change jobs when he is forty years old? Is his future brighter in another locality, working at another trade? The possibility of losing pension benefits often pulls the employee into a position of accepting the *status quo*, of staying where he is. Sometimes he should not stay where he is.

An individual, of course, can save by himself for his retirement years without the assistance of an income-tax break. Many persons do. But the question is not what an individual can do but what society should do. As of now, society, acting through its government, has adopted a policy of imprisoning an employee with one company in exchange for a guarantee, a guarantee that does not often pay off. Society, instead, should adopt a policy of freeing the individual.

Actually, in adopting any policy the government should follow a set procedure. The first step should be the identifying of a national problem. How the aged are cared for financially obviously is such a problem. Not only are the elderly people themselves affected, but their relatives are equally concerned. Anyone who does not belong to either of those two groups, the aged and the families of the aged, belongs to the third group which must decide if it will permit a person, even a stranger, to starve.

Once a national need is identified, the next step is to seek a solution within the American tradition. Having the government offer assistance is within that tradition. The United States government has been subsidizing industries and individuals since the very first Congress passed that first tariff break for the merchant marine many years ago. The crucial question is how that assistance is given. Guaranteeing a bare minimum is humanitarian and is being done, through the Social Security system and through an improving welfare system. Humanitarianism is within the American tradition. But broadening the individual's opportunity to do more than achieve a bare minimum is also very much within the American tradition. It is, in fact, the American tradition.

Another example of how a shift in emphasis could help turn the United States toward a creative society is in the area of housing. Statistics differ on how many Americans live in substandard housing, but the number is large. Probably one out of every four Americans lives in a house without proper heating and sanitary facilities. Is this a national problem? It obviously is. The tradition of humanitarianism compels Americans to be concerned by the plight of other Americans. And beyond this, bad housing is a problem because it becomes a slum, and the slums, in turn, are the environment contributing heavily to much of the social ills afflicting the United States. Eliminating slums would mean the savings of billions of dollars lost to crime and lost because of the undeveloped potential of the individuals growing up in the slums.

Identifying a national need is not sufficient. Identifying a need for government assistance is necessary. If private enterprise can eliminate slums, then the government should stay out. But private enterprise cannot do it alone, as it has frequently asserted. The cost of building new dwellings is so expensive as to mean rents higher than can be paid by the poor who live in the slums. One reaction to this situation is simply to demand that the government take over the building of low-cost housing.

In 1967 Senator Robert Kennedy sponsored legislation aimed at bringing private capital into the low-cost-housing business. His plan offered tax incentives and, by his assessments, would permit private industry to build inexpensive housing to replace the slums and still make a profit. Senator Charles Percy, Republican of Illinois, offered a bill that would enable low-income persons to purchase homes with government-backed mortgages. Still pending at that time, although far in the background, was an old idea of President Johnson's to have a private/public corporation rebuild the slums.

In an editorial *The New York Times* denounced all three approaches. "None of these plans will directly help the people in the slums who are worst off . . ." said the *Times*. "Private capital's involvement," insisted the editorial, "is not a substitute for public housing, much less a panacea. The subsidized interest rates, tax concessions, and other inducements of the Percy and Kennedy plans are a roundabout way of doing what the government could do straightforwardly if the public understood that decent housing for the poor cannot be a goldmine for private profit."

Even Senator Kennedy's friends disagreed with his proposal. John Kenneth Galbraith, in a speech to the City Club of New York late in 1967, ridiculed the idea of private industry having an impact on the problems of the cities. "Private enterprise and private investment," he said, "are being aroused to their responsibilities—as they have without result a hundred times before." A few weeks before his speech a group of insurance companies had announced from the White House that they planned to invest one billion dollars in rebuilding slum areas. "Nothing will come of it," predicted Professor Galbraith of that announcement. He continued to insist that only public funds could work any changes in the slums. Of a program being developed in the Bedford-Stuyvesant area of Brooklyn by Senator Kennedy to have private industry create jobs and build new housing, Professor Galbraith said the program "will be successful only as far as public money is available."

But is the construction of housing with public funds the answer? The record says that it is not. The first public housing was built in the 1930s. Since the late 1940s the government has had a continuing program of public-housing construction. It simply has not done the job. As the National Commission on Civil Disorders pointed out: "To date, Federal programs have been able to do comparatively little to provide housing for the disadvantaged. In the 31-year history of subsidized Federal housing, only about 800,000 units have been constructed, with recent production averaging about 50,000 units a year. By comparision, over a period only three years longer, FHA insurance guarantees have made possible the construction of over ten million middle- and upper-income units."

Why is the federal program such a failure?

First, such a program is dependent on Congressional attitudes each year. If the Congress is "liberal," in the sense of its willingness to appropriate funds, it will be generous toward public housing. If it is "conservative," in the sense of not wishing to spend money, it will be niggardly toward public housing. Also, once the money is appropriated, it must then work its way through the bureaucracy of local and federal agencies. Projects have been held up for years within that bureaucracy for the pettiest of reasons.

And there is another reason. As such programs work their way through the governmental process, their purpose becomes perverted. This was pointed up by Henry Ford II when, in a speech, he said: "The number of low-income public housing units [built with federal assistance] is much lower than the number of low-income private housing units destroyed. When the net result of public programs is to reduce the supply of housing available to poor people, something is wrong with our priorities."

There is much that the federal government can do to increase the amount of housing available to the poor, and not all of it requires large expenditures of money. For example, when the group of insurance companies announced they would invest one billion dollars in building housing in slum areas they made clear their commitment hinged on the Federal Housing Administration insuring mortgages on the new homes. It was announced at the time that FHA had made a major policy decision several weeks earlier, in August of 1967, permitting the issuing of federally insured mortgages on dwellings in slums. It probably came as a surprise to many Americans that a federal agency—the FHA—had not been offering assistance to the poor by making mortgage insurance available in slum areas. FHA, instead, was insuring mortgages almost solely in the suburbs and other economic middle-class areas. In such areas, certainly in the 1960s, conventional mortgage money was available. The FHA guarantee was not needed by most purchasers of homes in these middle-class areas. The FHA was subsidizing persons who did not need the assistance while refusing to assist those persons who did.

However, as the stories appeared in the wake of the insurance companies' announcement, the FHA now was going to start helping the poor. Actually that policy decision made in August was little more than a repetition of a policy decision made the previous year, in November of 1966. That earlier policy decision was supposed to accomplish the same thing, bring the FHA into the business of insuring mortgages on new homes in slums. It accomplished, however, almost nothing.

Born in the 1930s, the FHA has developed as a conservative business organization. Although staffed with civil servants and financed with public funds, it operates only to benefit a small segment of the public. It is reluctant to insure a mortgage unless the safety of that mortgage is a certainty. That kind of an attitude on the part of a commercial lending agency is understandable. People give banks money in hopes of making money and the banks have a responsibility to that trust. But government has a different kind of responsibility. It can afford to be a little riskier in hopes of accomplishing a public good. The trust placed in government is not to earn money. It is, instead, to improve the quality of American life.

A loosening up of its attitude by the FHA probably would be enough to produce a substantial number of new dwellings in the slums. The case history of one FHA program is offered as an example. Under a law passed in 1961, nonprofit groups can secure cheap mortgages from FHA to build low-rent housing. As the program was conceived, an organization such as a church would sponsor the construction of an apartment project to house persons in the lower economic brackets. The income maximums for such tenants are between six thousand and seven thousand dollars for a family of four. There is a great shortage of adequate housing for persons in that economic bracket.

When the proposal was first before Congress, government officials promised the program would mean the building of sixty thousand units a year. Six years later only forty thousand apartments of the promised three hundred and sixty thousand had been built. Another twenty-two thousand were being constructed. In addition there were applications for more than eighty thousand units waiting FHA's approval or disapproval. That wait lasted an average time period of eighteen months. The program was too slow.

In fairness to the FHA, its top officials realize this and are trying to change it. At a meeting in October 1967 of the FHA's insuring-office directors, Philip N. Brownstein, the agency's commissioner, laid it on the line. "We are still not doing enough," he said, "and we are not doing it fast enough." Even Mr. Brownstein seemed baffled at his agency's inability or disinterest in cutting through delaying red tape. "When I look at our loss record on many of our multifamily programs," he conceded, "I am even more baffled to understand why we take so much time. The record does not show that our long and profound agonizing over multifamily proposals has improved our judgment."

But he tried to make his speech a call to arms. "We must

eliminate the negativism, and the tortuous slowness of our processing of multifamily applications," he said. "This is our real Achilles' heel, and it has got to go." He confessed to his listeners: "It is not easy to counter the charges against the FHA when you are confronted as often as I am with case after case in which we took an inexcusably long time to reach a decision."

Whether Mr. Brownstein's words will have any impact is a matter for the future, of course. But the prospects are not good. The "multifamily" projects he talked about are mostly apartment buildings in slum areas to provide decent housing for the poor, primarily Negroes. And FHA's record in assisting Negro Americans acquire housing is a poor one. Even as Mr. Brownstein spoke, his department had a confidential survey of Negro occupancy of housing built with federally insured mortgages. In late 1962 President Kennedy had fulfilled a campaign promise and signed an executive order barring discrimination in housing built with federally insured mortgages. Supposedly this meant that the FHA no longer would be able to finance "white only" suburbs. If the FHA insured the mortgages, then the suburban area had to sell to Negro and white on an open-occupancy basis. Five years later, however, the results of FHA's response to that order were dismal. Since the executive order had been issued, the FHA had insured mortgages on 410,574 houses. Less than 10 percent, only 35,000, had gone to nonwhites. The nonwhites included American Indians, Orientals, and Spanish-Americans as well as Negroes. Actually, Negroes had acquired only 14,000 of the FHA-insured homes in the five-year period. There is no dispute that more Negroes wanted to buy homes and were financially capable of doing so—if they could have broken through the racial prejudice of the builders and the local FHA offices.

Those statistics were reeled off to the FHA officers from the local communities by Philip J. Maloney, a deputy assistant secretary of the agency. "You have been measured and found wanting," he bluntly told the FHA insuring officers. He called on them to give their "loyalty and zeal" for the cause of housing members of a minority and eradicating the slums. "If you can't give this much to your positions of leadership in the department," he said, "I suggest that, in good conscience, you should step aside for men who can provide leadership in these areas."

Such honest and direct language from men in Washington is one of the more heartening developments in the nation's capital. How much it will accomplish is a matter of conjecture. In April 1968 President Johnson appointed a group of prominent business leaders to become the board of a "think tank" to develop new approaches to solving the problems of the cities. It was remarked that the Department of Housing and Urban Development (the FHA's parent agency) had been established in the mid-1960s to do just that. But officials there answered that even if they came up with all of the best ideas in the world, they could never persuade the bureaucracy they commanded to carry them out.

But there are other actions in the field of housing, in addition to sparking up the bureaucrats, that could be taken. There is, for example, a substantial drawback with all publicly supported housing. If the tenant's income rises above a certain level, he no longer is eligible to stay in the housing. If his income goes above six thousand dollars, or whatever figure is the local measure for a family of four, he is forced to find housing in a regular commercial building. The best probability is that he would not be able to find a decent place to live, even though his income has risen somewhat. This restriction works to discourage one from improving his income status.

The U.S. Gypsum Company became involved with an experimental project in the East Harlem section of Manhattan. The section has been called the worse slum in the city. The company's intent was to develop new uses for its products in the rehabilitation of substandard dwellings. It bought several old buildings. Working with the tenants, it developed a rehabilitation plan for the buildings. The tenants were moved, with U.S. Gypsum's assistance, while the rehabilitation work was going on, then returned to the renovated apartments. Committees of tenants were formed to look after maintaining the buildings, to become active in self-help projects. A real community program is beginning. And several of the families living in the apartments are experiencing increases in income. Since the work was done with mortgages insured by FHA, those families face, or so company officials fear, the prospect of giving up their renovated apartments. It is a discouraging experience for U.S. Gypsum. The company is concerned that tenants will be reluctant to support rehabilitation. Accepting federal aid seems to mean that eventually you will have to move to another slum.

The law should be changed to permit a little more freedom for persons with rising incomes in publicly supported housing. Not only is it unfair to force people such as those who participated in the U.S. Gypsum project to accept eviction as their reward, but also a neighborhood is a better one with residents of varying incomes. The higher income people tend to act as a pull upward on those with lower incomes. A third reason the law should be changed is the growing realization that a good many people who go from slums to publicly supported housing are going to experience income increases. Whether they would have if they had remained in the slums is not known. The fact is, once they move into a better home, there is a good chance their incomes will go up. The increase in the incomes is not enough to buy a house in the suburbs, or even to rent an apartment in a middle-class area of the city, but often it is enough to make the family ineligible for public housing. If publicly supported housing is not to be only a brief stopover for families between one slum dwelling and another, then the law must be liberalized.

How rapidly incomes rise for people who move from slums to decent housing was dramatically illustrated by a project in Washington, D.C., in the mid-1960s. The National Capital Housing Authority leased fifty large-family dwellings, renovated them and made them available to families in need of decent housing at rents below the going rates. "The tenants were selected chiefly on the basis of severe need," according to an independent evaluation made of the program. The fifty homes all were located "in neighborhoods which ranked among the District's worst in such indexes as bad housing, overcrowded conditions, unemployment, and low income and educational level of residents," according to the evaluation. Although the new homes were far superior to what the families had known, the evaluation seemed to be saying, they still were not located in middle-class America. Even so, the income statistics are impressive.

"About three-fourths of the families experienced an increase in net incomes during the demonstration period; and in almost half, the rise amounted to more than $1,000," according to the evaluation which was made by the Washington Center for Metropolitan Studies. It added: "Such impressive increases are not typical of District of Columbia public housing residents in general." The evaluation suggested several reasons for the increase. One was that the families understood they were involved in an experimental project and responded by making a little more effort in all phases of their lives. A second is that while the families were chosen on the basis of great need, they also were chosen with an eye toward the program's success; the National Capital Housing Authority selected families it hoped would not disappoint it. But a third reason, which all parties to the program agreed on, was the stimulus to the breadwinner in the family from living, perhaps for the first time, in a decent home. He may be able to work a little better knowing his children will not be bitten by rats.

Whatever the reason, this increase in income among residents in publicly supported housing is a recognized fact of life. That should be the intention of public housing, as it should be the intention of all publicly supported welfare programs, to assist a family raise its income. The law should be changed to encourage that intention, not discourage it. That change would not cost a cent.

Professor Galbraith, in his speech before the City Club of New York, argued that private-industry involvement in housing construction would be ineffective because, among other reasons, city development needs comprehensive planning which can only be done by a public body. But there is no reason why a public body cannot plan and control the development of a city and then encourage private enterprise to do the job. If the public body is tough enough in the laws it enacts and in the manner it enforces them, it should be able to guide private industry.

Michael Harrington, whose *The Other America* so stirred the American conscience, has said much the same thing as Professor Galbraith. "America," wrote Mr. Harrington in a magazine article, "whether it likes it or not, cannot sell its social conscience to the highest corporate bidder. It must build new institutions of democratic planning which can make the uneconomic, commercially wasteful, and humane decisions about education and urban living which this society so desperately needs."

To illustrate the dangers of not doing so, Mr. Harrington drew a parallel with the dangers of the military-industrial complex when a lobby presses "for strategies which are determined, not by any objective analysis of the needs of the nation, but by its own stake in the decision." He cites as a classic case the debate during the Kennedy Administration over whether to build the B-70 bomber. It was a classic case, but not in quite the way Mr. Harrington believes. The military-industrial complex failed. The B-70 was not built. And that was not an isolated example.

A better case involves the F-105 fighter bomber. Most old hands at the Pentagon concede that marked the high-water mark of the pressure exerted by the military-industrial complex. In 1962 the Defense Department announced its intention to phase out production of the airplane. Immediately a major campaign was launched to keep the plane's producer, the Republic Aviation Corporation of Long Island, not only in business but in the business of making the F-105. The White House received fifty thousand letters, most of them from working men, good Democrats and all voters. The letters demanded that the Democratic Administration reverse the Pentagon's decision to phase out the F-105. Businessmen and union leaders went to the White House, to the Pentagon, to the secret offices of the Democratic Party in Washington. All forty-three members of New York State's Congressional delegation, led by Representative Emanuel Celler, Democrat of Brooklyn, one of the most distinguished of the House members, joined in the plea. Representative Celler even led a Congressional delegation to the White House.

But when it was all over, the decision to phase out the F-105 stayed. The military-industrial complex had been defeated. Tough leadership had won out. And that kind of leadership can win in the cities.

To bypass this chance for cooperation between government and private industry and to rely, instead, solely on public funds—to rely on an approach that has failed in the past—is to bet the nation's future on a slow horse.

Actually, there are strong indications that private industry is ready to move into this field. As it should be, private industry is interested in making a profit. It should be able to. The U.S. Gypsum Company estimated the market in rehabilitating housing at $50 billion. Its East Harlem project, in addition to experimenting with new products that can be used in slum rehabilitation, also was trying to demonstrate whether an entrepreneur can make a decent profit with rehabilitated houses. The company's indications are that it can be done. One U.S. Gypsum official said the project was demonstrating "that a builder can go in there and earn 10 per cent on his cost." Added the official: "That's a pretty good profit." A really enterprising builder, the company official continued, could probably earn double that because he can do two projects a year and earn a 10 percent return on his money on each of them. U.S. Gypsum reports it has been approached by some one hundred companies interested in joining the home-rehabilitation industry.

There is no reason why government cannot offer incentives to private industry to give industry's search for those profits in housing and other industries a push. The best way appears to be though the tax system. Again the advantages of offering tax concessions is that it frees the industry involved from being dependent on the attitude of Congress in a particular year. And it also eliminates the need for an expensive and time-consuming bureaucracy. Such a tax-break program would not eliminate the need for some government-built housing, but it would assume most of the burden of providing low-cost housing.

The technique of using income-tax concessions to produce desired social ends is not new. Most of the present tax system is so structured. That a citizen purchase a home and assume all the solid attributes of the home owner, as opposed to his remaining a renter, is considered socially desirable. As a result, the tax system encourages home ownership. The owner's mortgage interest and his real-estate taxes are deductible on his income-tax return. The renter also pays interest and taxes as part of his rent, but they are not deductible for him. The deductions allowed for gifts to charities, hospitals, churches and educational institutions have the effect of encouraging donations by individuals to those institutions. The tax system so influences such donations that every institution, when making an appeal for funds, always points out the tax advantages in the giving.

The depreciation allowance given to business is supposed to be in recognition of the fact that business equipment eventually wears out. But actually depreciation schedules are based, instead, on the policy of constantly encouraging industry to modernize. So the depreciation allowance arbitrarily assumes that a machine will last only one third or perhaps one fourth the time it actually can be used. The hope is that with such a generous depreciation allowance industry will constantly modernize by buying new equipment.

Not everyone agrees that the concept of tax concessions should be broadened. One of the more significant opponents is Representative Wilbur D. Mills, Democrat of Arkansas. As chairman of the House Ways and Means Committee, which writes tax laws, he has a commanding voice in determining the shape of the tax code. He has denounced such concessions as a "hidden" form of spending. (He is, of course, absolutely correct. Such concessions are a means of spending money without having to go through the Budget Bureau review, the Congressional appropriations process and then the federal bureaucracy.)

"Most of the benefit of these credits," said the Congressman, "goes to business firms or individuals who would have undertaken the desired expenditures even if no credit were available. For these taxpayers, the credit provides a windfall."

Perhaps. Perhaps the concessions provide something else also. Perhaps they provide a needed incentive that otherwise would be lacking. Perhaps also they give a direction to the economy, pointing up priorities. Perhaps they suggest to industry where profits in the next decade or beyond may lie.

Why not, for example, grant tax concessions to industries that install antipollutant devices? Government funds could pay for the needed research to develop such devices, then a tax break would encourage individual industries to install them. In 1965 *Fortune* magazine, in an article titled "We Can Afford Clean Air," reported that polluted air was causing property damage in the amount of $11 billion a year as well as lowering property values and creating a severe health hazard. The article estimated that such pollution could be reduced by about two thirds with an annual expenditure of $3 billion.

"With an awakened public," the article continued, "there would be no need to employ subsidies and other economic gimmicks to hasten industry's cleanup." Since the article appeared there has been a great deal of discussion about polluted air and its dangers and some response by industry, but the air enveloping the United States continues to grow dirtier and dirtier. A tax concession is an "economic gimmick," but the business community has enjoyed such gimmicks for decades. There is no reason to refrain from using them at a time when they could create some public good.

In addition to cleaning up the polluted air enveloping America, such a tax gimmick also would spark development of a new industry—an industry engaged in the fighting of pollution. The job potential would be enormous. Scientists and engineers would be needed to develop and manufacture the necessary antipollutant equipment. Salesmen would be needed to sell it to industry. Skilled mechanics would be needed to maintain it. The federal government would be entering the private economy to fill a demonstrated need in a manner consistent with the American tradition and—most importantly—in a manner that will bolster the free-enterprise system. By the use of tax concessions, rather than by the use of direct handouts as with the SST, the government would be throwing the field open. Any company can join in the competition. No single company will be given a head start.

Whether a turn toward a creative society employs the devices suggested here, others like them, others different from them, some perhaps not even yet considered, depends not on a single individual or even on a group of individuals creating a new "gimmick." Rather, such a turn must begin with society's switching its emphasis in a new direction.

Two

The question before the House of Representatives the afternoon of Thursday, July 20, 1967, was whether it should consider a proposal to make $20 million a year available to local communities for three years to assist them to rid their slum areas of rats. The funds would be "seed" money; local communities would have to put up funds of their own before receiving any of the federal assistance. The discussion began with Representative Spark M. Matsunaga, Democrat of Hawaii, explaining to the House members:

> Last year, in seven cities alone in the United States there were approximately one thousand reported cases of rat bite. There is reason to believe the actual statistics are much higher because many persons are reluctant to report rat-bite incidents, and many units of local and state government do not require such reports. Only two days ago, it was reported by the news media that an eight-month-old boy was bitten to death by rats right here in our nation's capital. . . . In addition to the disease-carrying threat which these pesky animals pose, they, in fact, cause enormous damage to both food and property. It has been estimated that there are at least ninety million rats in the United States and that each causes an average of ten dollars damage per year. This means a national loss of $900 million to the rats every year, unless we do something about it.

The proposal, however, was decisively defeated. The vote was

207 against it and only 176 in its favor. What kind of arguments were used against it?

Representative James A. Haley, Democrat of Florida:

> I wonder sometime if some of our distinguished committees that bring before us a monstrosity such as this would just take into consideration the fact that we have a lot of cat lovers in the nation, and why not just buy some cats and turn them loose on the rats and thereby we could take care of this situation.

Representative Delbert L. Latta, Republican of Ohio:

> In view of the fiscal situation facing this country today, this is the one program we can do without. This Congress has already raised the debt ceiling during this session in order to be able to meet its financial responsibilities. . . . It seems to me that here is a request for $20 million for 1968 and $20 million for 1969 that we can refuse.

Representative Joel T. Broyhill, Republican of Virginia:

> I think the most profound statement the gentleman [Representative Latta] made is the fact that it [the bill] does set up a new bureau and sets up possibly a commissioner on rats or an administrator of rats and a bunch of new bureaucrats on rats. There is no question but that there will be a great demand for a lot of rat patronage. I think by the time we get through taking care of all of the bureaucrats in this new rat bureau along with the waste and empire building, none of the $40 million will be left to take care of the two and one-half percent of the rats who were supposed to be covered in the bill. . . . I think the "rat smart thing" for us to do is to vote down this rat bill "rat now."

Those comments were typical—unfortunately typical—of the discussion on the floor of the House of Representatives that day. Two days earlier, on Tuesday, July 18, the House had before it an appropriation of $142 million for the supersonic transport. That money was for only one year's expenditures, meaning the amount for the SST was seven times what would be asked two days later for one year's work against rats. The SST appropriation flew through the House. Neither Representative Haley of Florida nor Representative Latta of Ohio nor Representative Broyhill of Virginia—all of whom would be so upset by the rat-control bill two days later—spoke against the SST expenditure.

A Republican speaking in favor of the SST was Representative Gerald R. Ford of Michigan, the Republican leader in the House. "The appropriation for the SST," he announced to the House, "is needed." Two days later when the rat-control bill was before the House, Representative Ford was not even on the floor of the House. He was recorded as being against the rat-control bill, however. (In 1968, when the criticism of the SST financing had become even stronger, Representative Ford did have a change of heart. He announced that he was not against the program but that he would investigate whether private industry could pick up more of the costs. This brings him toward agreement with the position taken years earlier by Senator William Proxmire and Senator Robert Kennedy.)

There are several things about those two bills, coming coincidentally close together in the House, that are all too standard in Congressional actions. Federal assistance to business usually wins easy approval, as the SST did this time and as it has done on almost every occasion when it has been before Congress. Federal assistance to help poor persons, however, frequently has trouble, as did the rat-control bill. In that one instance the House outsmarted itself. Its attitude appeared so callous that an adverse reaction was created. At one time in the debate, for example, when a member tried to defend the rat-control bill, Representative H. R. Gross, Republican of Iowa, hooted him down with "The gentleman can make that speech if he wants to on his own time." (Representative Gross considers himself a great advocate of economy. He did not speak against the SST appropriation, but the same day he did move to cut money allotted for state and community highway safety from $20 million to $10 million.) The reaction to the House action on rat control from newspapers, local civil-rights groups, state and local politicians was so great that the House a few weeks later sheepishly approved the rat-control bill in a slightly altered version.

The disturbing element is not only that business benefits and poor people do not but that people and industries which do not need public funds, or who do not need public funds in the amount offered, are kindly treated by Congress. The guarantee comes to those who do not need it. The assistance to those in need comes not at all or only grudgingly.

Rat control must be a community problem. The individual homeowner can do all in his power to rid his home of rats, but he accomplishes nothing unless the entire community joins in the effort. Perhaps the federal government should claim this is a local problem and not assist cities in such efforts, although this kind of assistance has been offered to farm areas for years (even rat-control money is available to rural areas). But certainly if Congress is going to hand money to industries that can raise the funds privately, as the government did with the SST, it should not be so reluctant to assist individuals and communities that cannot.

But Congress has been handing out funds to industries and middle-class Americans too long to change easily. Charles L. Schultze, when he was director of the Budget Bureau, made a speech before the Union League Club of New York in the fall of 1966. Some excerpts portray how Congress continually shifts funds away from those in need to those who can afford to care for themselves. He said:

> There has existed since 1950 a so-called "impacted area" school assistance program. Under this program the federal government makes payments to school districts based on the number of children whose parents work on federal property. The object of the program is presumably to help offset the burden from federal installations which take land off the local property tax base. The cost of the program now exceeds $400 million per year. But the formula for assistance is inequitable. Payments under the program have little relation to actual need. And in many cases it is difficult to describe a federal installation as a "burden," judging by the decibels of clamor from local communities to get a federal installation or to protest its closing.
>
> The 1967 budget proposed to revise the formula, tighten it up, and thereby save some $233 million in budget costs. An additional reason behind this proposed reduction is the fact that the new elementary and secondary education program enacted in 1965 will substantially increase federal assistance to education and channel it to areas of greatest need. Indeed, counties which would lose $233 million under the cut in the impacted area program will receive, in the aggregate, more than double that amount under the new program. Some wealthy counties, such as Montgomery [in Maryland] and Arlington [in Virginia]—which are to Washington, D.C.,

what Westchester and Nassau are to New York City—will lose. But most will gain.

In short, this proposal did what budgets are supposed to do, indicate priorities. Payments to school districts—many of them wealthy —are being curtailed so that greater provision can be made for educational assistance where it is needed. Yet the outcry has been tremendous. Communities which vie for location of federal installations, which protest loudly at their closure, have been quick to claim that federal installations impose terrible burdens which must be fully compensated.

Several months ago the House of Representatives rejected this reduction and voted to appropriate the full amount for this impacted area program. The Senate Appropriations Committee followed suit last week.

In another case we proposed a reduction in the school lunch program. That reduction would have reduced the general federal subsidy to school lunches—which subsidizes your children and mine—by one cent per day, equal to about two percent of the cost of a lunch. At the same time, additional funds were proposed to get hot lunches to lower-income children who really needed them. Here again, the choice we made was to reduce expenditures where the program was simply subsidizing the well-to-do, and concentrate assistance on those children for whom the program represented a real benefit.

The Agriculture appropriation bill enacted last month rejected this reduction.

A similar proposal was made to reduce the federal special milk program. Twelve years ago dairy surpluses were filling government warehouses. Rather than let the surpluses rot, a program was enacted providing federal subsidized milk for schools. This was extra milk at recess and in the afternoon, since the regular school lunch program already provided milk at lunch time. Today the surpluses are gone. There are shortages of dairy products, and prices have mounted. The President proposed, therefore, to reduce the special milk program, eliminating the general across-the-board subsidy and concentrating assistance for children in those low-income areas who might not otherwise get milk at all.

Again the Agriculture appropriations bill restored the program to its full amount and, for good measure, added a bit to it.

Mr. Schultze is too knowledgeable a Washingtonian to believe his comments could have shocked anyone. The priority of self-interest has long taken precedence over that of national need. And that is why the guaranteed society is coming. Each self-interest demands more and more for itself. Each self-interest thinks only of its immediate need, never bothering to question where the avenue of the guaranteed society will take it. And the Congressional system is geared to support this kind of self-interest. A Congressman from a constituency in which many airplane manufacturing companies are located naturally seeks to join a Congressional committee with jurisdiction over aviation. If he gets re-elected enough times, the seniority system eventually will make him chairman of that committee and the most important man in Congress as far as aviation is concerned. The aviation industries in his constituency know how that game is played and so they will always support his re-election. One obvious example is Senator Magnuson of Washington, whose constituency includes the major Boeing plants and whose position as chairman of the Senate Commerce Committee gives him a strong voice in aviation. Another example is the Lockheed aircraft company, which traditionally locates large installations in the state of Georgia. The senior Senator from that state is Richard B. Russell, chairman of the Armed Services Committee and the Armed Services appropriations subcommittee. In that dual position he has much to say about how many Lockheed airplanes the Pentagon buys a year. Until a few years ago the chairman of the House Armed Services Committee was Carl Vinson, also a Georgian. The circle becomes a vicious one. The Congressman must continue to support his home-town industry in Washington when it appeals for government contracts or relief from what it considers onerous government pressures. If he does not, he will not have that industry's support when he runs for re-election. And so the reward for self-interest grows and grows until it outstrips any reasonable assistance and becomes, instead, a guarantee.

Does this mean that a guaranteed society is the inevitable end product of a representative government?

When John F. Kennedy was a member of the United States Senate he wrote that "in Washington we are 'United States Senators' and members of the Senate of the United States as well as Senators from Massachusetts and Texas. Our oath of office is administered by the Vice President, not by the Governors of our respective states; and we come to Washington, to paraphrase Edmund Burke, not as hostile ambassadors or special pleaders for our state or section, in opposition to advocates and agents of other areas, but as members of the deliberative assembly of one nation with one interest."

In reality, as President Kennedy knew, members do come to Congress as "special pleaders" and so act in most cases. On occasion, however, each member of Congress must realize that a national good transcends the local interst he represents. Some members do this. In 1966, before the SST subcontractors were announced, Senator Robert Kennedy voted against the airplane. After the subcontractors were listed and it was learned that a considerable amount of the SST money would go to industries located on Long Island, which Senator Kennedy represents, he had another opportunity to vote on the SST. He still voted against it. This second time, in fact, he joined with Senator Proxmire of Wisconsin in leading the Senate fight against the airplane.*

Other members of Congress have voted against their constituencies in the past. Some have been defeated at the polls for it; some have been handsomely re-elected because of it. It is a problem for each individual member of Congress: Which direction does he wish America to go? Each member of Congress himself must determine if he wishes to contribute to bringing a guaranteed society to America or if he wishes to support a creative, free-enterprise society. And it is a problem for each individual voter: What kind of Congressman does he want?

While it may be understandable when a member of Congress tends to support a selfish interest of his constituency, as opposed to the national interest, it also should be understandable that the President support and declare the national interest.

"It is only the President," said former President Harry S Truman in best summing up the President's role, "who is responsible to all the people. He alone has no sectional, no occupational, no economic ties. If anyone is to speak for the people, it has to be the President."

*Senator Kennedy said that his opposition was based on a matter of priorities and that the United States could not afford to fight a war in Vietnam, a war against poverty at home and build the SST. He pointed out that the Vietnamese war did not exist when President Kennedy first proposed the SST.

As Mr. Schultze's speech in the fall of 1966 suggests, President Johnson has at times attempted to assert that national interest. At other times, however, he has not. In 1965 President Johnson's designated head of the Federal Aviation Agency, General William F. McKee, was having trouble winning Senate approval. General McKee, retired from the Air Force, was considered a brilliant administrator, but his appointment had run up against the law that the head of the FAA be a civilian. Special legislation was required to permit the general to hold the post and to receive both his salary as head of the FAA and his retirement income from the Air Force.

President Johnson pressed hard and ultimately successfully for that special legislation because, as he explained it, he considered General McKee "the best man in the country to carry through the supersonic transport program." At the time, the United States government—theoretically at least—had not made a final commitment to the SST. Cost studies were still going on. Potential contractors were still drawing up their submissions. Federal officials still claimed then that the final decision could go against the SST if it proved economically unfeasible. The reservation had been part of President Kennedy's original announcement back in 1963.

And then President Johnson insisted on a man to head the FAA who would "carry through" the program. Mr. Johnson's personal support for the SST program had been well known; he had recommended, when he was Vice President, to President Kennedy that the government embark on such a program. His selection of General McKee to head the FAA and to push through the SST program, however, gave that personal support the official imprint of the White House. The SST would fly. Any lingering hope that the federal government would retain any objectivity toward the SST ended at that point. The agencies involved, the aircraft manufacturers, the airlines, all knew the government intended that an American SST should fly. The cost of the national effort would be incidental, as it has since proven to be in the minds of the SST supporters within the federal government.

And the cork was out of the bottle. The Administration had surrendered its role as the judge of such projects. It was responding, to use Harry Truman's choice of words, to sectional, occupational and economic ties. It no longer was responding to the national interest. It was not surprising, then, that other such ties—the merchant marine, the oil interests seeking the shale in the Colorado mountains, and the other pressure groups—felt free to make their push and succeeded. To turn away from the guaranteed society, the Presidency more than any other institution must once again, also in Harry Truman's words, learn "to speak for the people."

The movement toward a guaranteed society has had help from the news media. Any large news-gathering organization has reporters with "beats" such as aviation, the merchant marine, the Interior Department and the like. Eventually these newsmen begin to take on the coloration of the beats they cover. Whatever one's reactions to the subsidies for the SST or to the merchant marine, however one responds to the "giveaway" of the oil shale and of the patents, whatever one thinks of the guaranteed annual income, one would find very little in the way of objective reporting in newspapers about these programs. The few stories that appear, instead, tend to reflect the attitudes of the agencies covered by the newsmen.

The agencies' views of the subjects are repeated in print over and over again until they take on the certainty of fact. In its issue of December 8, 1967, for example, *Time* magazine wrote an "Essay" about where to cut the federal budget and where not to cut the federal budget. *Time* supported the SST expenditures, saying they should not be cut from the budget because:

> Aircraft make up the nation's second biggest export, after food, and the U.S. has sold $2.4 billion worth of commercial jets to foreign buyers. The SST market will be much richer—estimates run to $40 billion over 20 years.

Whether the SST market will be much richer, as *Time* claimed, is not a fact; it is a highly dubious assertion made by the FAA and the friends of the SST. It has been challenged by responsible studies made at the Pentagon, by students of aviation and by professors of aeronautical engineering at major universities. One would not know this from reading the *Time* essay.

There are, of course, other pressures working on the newsmen in addition to their own prejudices. Newspapers by practice offer surface treatments of serious subjects. The typical news story is that someone did something yesterday and that a second person may react to it tomorrow. In recent years there has been a trend toward interpretative reporting, offering a deeper look at the negative as well as the plus side of an issue. So far, however, this has been confined largely to issues of foreign policy. Occasionally a newspaper will take a searching look at a domestic subsidy program, such as the Washington *Post* has done with the SST. But these occasions are rare exceptions. Speaking of some of the moral problems facing the United States in the late 1960s, James Reston of *The New York Times* commented that ". . . the need to get at causes instead of the newsworthy effects of these problems is great." The comment is equally applicable to the economic problems facing the nation.

Another pressure working on newsmen can be called the "big story" syndrome. Reporters trip over each other when a Bobby Baker, Adam Clayton Powell or Thomas Dodd case pops up, each reporter searching for that one extra detail, that one colorful incident the opposition reporter has missed and which will earn a "good job" note from the editor or bureau chief. The public probably could not care less about such incidental information, but newspaper people consider it significant.

Still another pressure working on newsmen is the matter of time. A newsman in Washington, for example, may cover three or four Congressional hearings in one morning. "Cover" is an inappropriate word. He stops by the hearing room, picks up copies of the prepared statements, skims through them quickly, and then writes about four or five paragraphs. He misses the question-and-answer period, the commentary of the members of the Congress and usually the real meaning of the prepared statements. If he wishes to examine one story in depth, he runs up against the general practice of newspapers—to spread the reporter's time thinly in an effort to have a little reporting about everything that happens. And the newspaper ends with little reporting in depth about anything that happens.

Another problem with the news media is that sometimes it becomes as much a pleader for the special interests as does any narrow-based member of Congress. When the Kennedy Administration determined to phase out production of the F-105 military airplane which was built on Long Island, it was the local newspapers there that led the battle to have the decision reversed. The issue, as the newspapers presented it, was not the military worthiness of the F-105 but the government's obligation to shore up Long Island's economy—to guarantee a number of jobs. No matter what their personal thoughts, the members of the House of Representatives from Long Island, the Senators from New York, the industries affected, all had to join in with this plea for the coming of the guaranteed society when the cry was sounded so vigorously by the news media. That F-105 fight—which failed to win a reversal—was considered at the Pentagon to be the roughest fight it has ever experienced in the arena of special interest. But it was not the only such fight. The Long Island newspapers are not the only ones to argue for the coming of the guaranteed society, coming at least for their constituents.

The tragedy of the press's failure is that the news media must be the watchdog on the government. That is its role. It is only the press that can fulfill that role. Two hundred million citizens cannot query their elected and appointed officials; the press must do it for them. The press must read the documents, ask the questions, interpret the answers, and then inform the public. When the press shirks that role, as it too often has done, then the public is not informed.

And generally an informed public makes intelligent choices and supports wise decisions by its elected leaders. The great strength of the American people always has been that they rise to meet their obligations—once those obligations are articulated. That rising up to do the required job never is unanimous; America is too diversified a continent for that. But always that rising up is sufficient to accomplish what must be done. The response of the people to George Washington in the time of the Revolutionary War was a fragile response, true, but an adequate one. The American people responded to Abraham Lincoln's call for a union preserved, as they later responded to Franklin D. Roosevelt's demand to preserve the American economic system by making it a more equitable one. And more recently the American people responded to John Kennedy's plea, in June of 1963, for equality before the law for all Americans.

Mr. Reston summed it up, saying: "There is today no agreement about what kind of society we want in the future or what the relationship of that society should be to the rest of the world. And as things are now going we will not be well advised to leave these two fundamentals to the politicians."

As the United States moves through the late 1960s and the early 1970s, it is time again for enough good men both to lead and to respond.

The crucial question is how to handle economic abundance. Even the vast expenditures of the Vietnamese war could not cloud that question. Late in 1967 when the Johnson Administration was pressing for a 10 percent surtax on regular income-tax bills to meet a deficit soaring toward $30 billion, there was mounting evidence that the situation already was reversing itself. *Fortune* magazine, for example, asserted that by early 1969 the budget would be moving into balance even without the passage of the Johnson Administration's surtax proposal. And if the Vietnamese war ends, most responsible economists were predicting substantial surpluses—in the tens of billions of dollars—by the mid-1970s.

Even if these predictions do not prove true—although generally economic predictions are understated rather than overstated—money still can be raised to pay for the job of building an educated, a creative society. If an income-tax surcharge can be proposed to pay for America's foreign problems, why can it not be enacted to pay for solving America's domestic problems? Even a total surcharge of 20 percent, 10 percent for the costs of the Vietnamese war and 10 percent for the costs of improving American life, would bring the federal tax bite only to a point where it was prior to the tax cut of 1964. Or if a travel tax can be proposed to right America's balance of payments, why cannot a sales tax be enacted to right America's imbalance of peoples?

But the proposition must be made. The need must be articulated. The package must be sold to the public. That is the challenge facing political and other American leaders in the coming years.

Their problem is not money. The money is there. For the first time the question is not the old one of where the money will be raised. The "new economics" of the 1960s, demonstrating, as it has done, that an economy can be expanded, answers that question. Shortly after the United States entered its eightieth month of economic boom—an unprecedented development—Mr. Reston wrote, "We are not only being led into temptation but kicked into it."

The new question is, instead, how that money will be spent.

Will the government guarantee profits to industry without industry taking risks? Will the government guarantee income to individuals capable of labor who choose not to work?

Or will the United States choose to use its riches to encourage opportunity, to call on each individual to develop himself to the fullest of his abilities? Will the United States choose a society where, if every endeavor is not successful, every endeavor is at least a cause of pride?

If the guaranteed society comes, it will be a society of takers. In the past America has been a society of doers.

What will it be in its future?

ACKNOWLEDGMENTS
and SOURCES

I am indebted to a number of government officials who, over many years, took the time to discuss with me the matters reported in this book and to guide me through the intricacies of government finance and federal subsidies. Several federal officials either have read sections of this book and given me their comments or have discussed with me in great detail the areas covered in this book. I am appreciative of that assistance.

I wish to express my appreciation to Peter V. Ritner of The Macmillan Company. His assistance was of immeasurable help to me in the writing of this book.

Sources listed below are those which are not identified in the text. All references to the *Congressional Record—CR* in the notes below—are to the daily edition unless otherwise specified. All citations of Congressional hearings should be preceded by "United States Congress." All government publications were printed by the Government Printing Office in Washington. The number preceding the note identifies the page in the text to which the note refers.

SST: THE BILLION-DOLLAR TICKET

1–2. President Kennedy's SST announcement was printed in *The New York Times*, June 6, 1963, p. 1.

2. Wiesner's comments, *United States Commercial Supersonic Aircraft Development Program*, Hearings before the Aviation Subcommittee of the Committee on Commerce, U.S. Senate, 88th Congress, 1st Session, Oct. 1963, p. 209.

3. Proxmire's comments, CR, Aug. 9, 1966, p. 17863.

5. Fowler's comments, text of his speech before the Kentucky Chamber of Commerce, Brown Hotel, Louisville, Ky., Apr. 10, 1967, pp. 11 and 7.

6. CAB statement, reprinted in *Subsidy and Subsidy-Effect Programs of the U.S. Government*, Materials Prepared for the Joint Economic Committee, 89th Congress, 1st Session, 1965, p. 56.

9. General Eisenhower's comments, *Mandate for Change*, 1963, p. 501.

10. Ackley's comments, text of his speech before New England Conference on the Opportunities and Problems of Defense Conversion, Boston, Sept. 21, 1964, p. 9.

12. Monroney-Halaby dialogue, 1963 hearings previously cited, p. 133.

12. Boyd's comments, 1963 hearings, p. 47.

13. Wilson comment, CR, Dec. 13, 1963, p. 23391.

13. Wydler statement, text of his weekly newsletter of Apr. 30, 1964.

14. Serling estimate, Washington *Post*, May 20, 1966, p. D8.

14. Boeing estimate, *The New York Times*, Jan. 1, 1967, p. 1.

14. *Newsday* editorial, Jan. 5, 1967, p. 35.

15. Meeds comment, CR, July 18, 1967, p. H8823.

15. Van Deerlin comments, CR, July 18, 1967, p. H8848.

15. Adams comment, CR, July 18, 1967, p. H8822.

16. Tipton comments, text of his speech before the Aero Club of Washington, D.C., March 28, 1967.

17. Hart question, 1963 hearings previously cited, p. 144.

18. Monroney comment, 1963 hearings, p. 2.

20. General Eisenhower's comments, reprinted in *Waging Peace*, 1965, p. 616.
22. McNamara comment, text of his statement before the Senate Armed Services Committee, Feb. 1, 1968, p. 140.
24. Monroney comment, 1963 hearings, p. 2.
25. Hart comment, 1963 hearings, p. 154.
28. Proxmire comments, CR, May 31, 1967, p. 7514.
29. "development costs . . ." comment, text of a talk before the American Economics Association, San Francisco, Dec. 28, 1966, on "Government-Industry Development of a Commercial Supersonic Transport," by Stephen Enke, former Deputy Assistant Secretary of Defense for economics.
30. Magnuson comment, CR, Aug. 29, 1966, p. 20200.
30–31. Boeing comment, text of speech by John O. Yeasting before the Aero Club of Washington, D.C., Apr. 28, 1964.
31. "In the budget . . ." comment, statement by Rep. Joseph L. Evans, Dem., Tenn., CR, May 10, 1966, p. 9744.
32. "seriously underequipped . . ." and *Time* magazine statement, *Time*, March 31, 1967, pp. 52-63.
32. Saltonstall comment, CR, Aug. 9, 1967, p. 17874.
33. Black-Osborne quote, from their report, p. 8.
33. Magnuson comments, CR, Aug. 29, 1966, p. 20198.
34. Halaby comments, 1963 hearings previously cited, pp. 82 and 100.
34–35. Boyd comments, 1963 hearings, pp. 44 and 48.
35. Tipton comment, his March 28, 1967, speech previously cited.
36–37. Tipton comment, his March 28, 1967, speech.
37. Black-Osborne quote, from their report, p. 7.
38. "The market for . . ." statement, House Report 484, 90th Congress, 1st Session, p. 17.
39. Ronan comments, quoted in *The New York Times*, Apr. 24, 1967, p. 8.
40. Hohenemser comments, his article "The Supersonic Transport," *Scientist and Citizen*, April 1966, p. 10.
41. Enke comment, his Dec. 28, 1966, speech previously cited.
41–42. Adams comments, his speech before Aero Club of Washington, D.C., quoted in *The New York Times*, March 5, 1967, p. 88.
42. *New York Times* headline, issue of Feb. 2, 1967.
42. "the government will . . ." and subsequent quotes, House Report 484, 90th Congress, 1st Session, pp. 16-19.
44. Boland comments, CR, July 18, 1967, p. H8818.
47. Morison quote, from his *The Oxford History of the American People*, 1965, p. 110.
49. Fitts Ryan comment, CR, Oct. 17, 1967, p. H13480.

MERCHANT MARINE: THE SUBSIDIZED SAILOR

51–52. Baldwin comments, text of his speech before the 60th convention of the Propellor Club, Oct. 5, 1966, Washington.

52. Curran comment, *The New York Times*, Jan. 26, 1967.

52. "far below the . . ." quote, *The New York Times*, Jan. 26, 1967.

52. Hood comments, "Putting the Maritime Problem in Clear Perspective," a paper presented by Mr. Hood, Apr. 7, 1967, before the 18th annual Institute on Foreign Transportation and Port Operations, sponsored by Tulane University, Graduate School of Business Administration.

53. Johnson comment, text of his remarks before the Subcommittee on Merchant Marine of the Committee on Merchant Marine and Fisheries, House of Representatives, March 22, 1966, p. 5.

55–56. Black committee quotes, printed in Nicholas Johnson, "Senator Black and the American Merchant Marine," UCLA *Law Review*, Jan. 1967, pp. 411-412.

59. Maritime Administration statement, "Merchant Shipping Support in the Viet Nam Crisis," issued March 2, 1966.

60–61. Garmatz letter, printed in *The New York Times*, Nov. 19, 1965, p. 66.

61. Baldwin comment, his Oct. 5, 1966, speech previously cited.

61–62. Starr comments, text of his speech to Hawaiian Economic Association, Oct. 28, 1965.

62. Baldwin comments, his Oct. 5, 1966, speech.

63–65. McNamara comments, text of his statement before a joint session of the Senate Armed Services Committee and the Senate Subcommittee on Department of Defense Appropriations, Jan. 23, 1967, pp. 113-115.

65. Gulick statement, quoted in *Congressional Quarterly*, Oct. 14, 1966, p. 2496.

67. President Johnson statement, printed in *The New York Times*, March 3, 1966, p. 20.

69–70. Brown comments, CR, Aug. 24, 1966, pp. 19524 and 19525.

70–71. Holifield, Albert comments, CR, Aug. 29, 1966, pp. 20053-20054.

74. Humphrey comments, quoted in *The New York Times*, Nov. 19, 1965, p. 66.

75. Ashley statement, CR, Aug. 30, 1966, p. 20369.

78. Joint Economic Committee statement, "Discriminatory Ocean Freight Rates and the Balance of Payments," Aug. 1966, p. 15.

84. Johnson comments, Leonard Baker, "Modernizing the Maritime," *The New Leader*, Feb. 28, 1966, p. 14.

85. Curran, Rooney comments, *New Leader* article cited above, p. 16.
87. Boyd comment, quoted in *The New York Times*, May 2, 1967, p. 32.
87. Johnson comment, from his "Senator Black" article previously cited, p. 427.
88. Land comment, quoted in *Congressional Quarterly*, Oct. 14, 1966, p. 2496.
88. Hood comment, text of the President's Report, Shipbuilders Council of America, Apr. 14, 1965, p. 5.

OIL SHALE: GUSHING DOLLARS

90. Hart statement, *Competitive Aspects of Oil Shale Development*, Hearings Before the Subcommittee on Antitrust and Monopoly of the Committee on the Judiciary, U.S. Senate, 90th Congress, 1st Session, 1967, p. 1.
90. Udall comment, text of Udall news conference, Feb. 17, 1965.
91. "Competition here is . . ." quote, 1967 hearings previously cited, p. 3.
96. Bureau of Mines prediction, J. Wade Watkins and Harry R. Johnson, *Oil Shale: Its Status and Problems*, 1966, p. 1.
97–98. Galbraith-Cohen comments, "Interim Report of the Oil Shale Advisory Board to the Secretary of the Interior," Feb. 1965, p. 23.
98. Stoddard comments, text of his letter to Hart, Apr. 28, 1967.
99. Udall comments, text of Udall statement before Senate Interior Committee, Feb. 21, 1967, p. 4.
99. "About forty thousand . . ." quote, Watkins and Johnson paper previously cited, p. 4.
99–100. Udall comments, his Feb. 21, 1967, statement previously cited, p. 4.
100. Weinberg comments, 1967 hearings previously cited, pp. 379 and 380 of subcommittee transcript.
100. Mesch-Hart dialogue, 1967 hearings, p. 378 of subcommittee transcript.
100. Hart-Weinberg dialogue, 1967 hearings, p. 392 of subcommittee transcript.
102. Proxmire speech, quoted in the Washington *Post*, June 6, 1964, p. C15.
102. Childs comment, "Interim Report" previously cited, pp. 14-15.
102. Galbraith comment, "Interim Report," p. 11 footnote.
107. "The general opinion . . ." quote, text of Fisher-Udall news conference, Feb. 17, 1965.

109–110. "Let us concede . . ." quote, Udall's Feb. 21, 1967, statement previously cited, pp. 10-11.

110. "I am keenly aware . . ." text of Udall statement before Senate Antitrust Subcommittee, Apr. 21, 1967, pp. 3-4.

111. Galbraith-Cohen comment, "Interim Report," p. 21.

112. "At our first . . ." statement, 1967 hearings, p. 44 of subcommittee transcript.

112. "there is the . . ." statement, "Interim Report," p. 16.

112. Nelson question, transcript of hearings before the Senate Committee on Interior and Insular Affairs, May 12, 1965, pp. 36-37.

113. Galbraith-Cohen comment, "Interim Report," p. 21.

113. Mead comment, his paper on "The Use of Competitive Markets in Federal Oil Shale Lease Policy" presented before the Antitrust Subcommittee on May 2, 1967, pp. 23-24.

114. Mead statement, his paper cited above, p. 2.

114–115. Galbraith comment, 1967 hearings, p. 47 of the subcommittee transcript.

115. Hart comment, text of his statement, Apr. 18, 1967, p. 4.

115–116. "Certainly all must . . ." quote, "Interim Report," p. 14.

116. "In the recent . . ." quote, CR (bound volume), V. 103, Part 3, March 1, 1957, p. 2891.

116. Douglas, Carroll comments, Leonard Baker, "Oil Interests Drill Deeply in Power Politics," Newsday, Dec. 14, 1963, p. 42.

117. Arnall comment, Leonard Baker, "Oil Bonanza—For Whom?" The Progressive, Aug. 1965, p. 17.

118. Proxmire comment, his 1964 speech previously cited.

119. "basic policy decision . . ." quote, reported in Newsday, Dec. 10, 1963, p. 2 by this author.

119. "I have had . . ." comment, text of Udall news conference, Feb. 17, 1965.

121. Galbraith-Cohen comment, "Interim Report," p. 27.

122. Aspinall comments, text of his speech before the annual meeting of the Rocky Mountain Oil and Gas Association, Brown Palace Hotel, Denver, Colo., Sept. 30, 1965.

123. Galbraith comment, "Interim Report," p. 20.

124. Galbraith on Teapot Dome, "Interim Report," p. 22 and 1967 hearings, p. 19 of subcommittee transcript.

124. Hansen charge, 1967 hearings, p. 26 of subcommittee transcript.

PATENTS: GOLDEN GRANTS

126. Guthrie quotes, his letter to Rudolph Hormuth, specialist in services for mentally retarded children, Division of Health Services, Department of Health, Education and Welfare, dated Dec. 4, 1963, reprinted in CR, May 17, 1965, p. 10345.

128–129. Oettinger comments, her memorandum to Herschel Clesner, Inventions Coordinator, Office of the Surgeon General, Public Health Service, dated Nov. 5, 1963, reprinted in CR, May 17, 1965, pp. 10344-10345.

129. "Such time and ..." statement, Clesner to Geoffrey Edsall, M.D., Superintendent, Institute of Laboratories, Commonwealth of Massachusetts, dated Nov. 27, 1963, reprinted in CR, May 17, 1965, p. 10345.

129–130. MacCready comments, MacCready to Clesner, Dec. 13, 1963, reprinted in CR, May 17, 1965, p. 10345.

130. "four follow-up ..." quote, Clesner memorandum, Oct. 9, 1964, reprinted in CR, May 17, 1965, pp. 10346-10347.

133. Banta quote, Patent Policies, Hearings Before the Select Committee on Small Business, 86th Congress, 1st Session, p. 358.

133. Long quote, CR, June 25, 1965, p. 14294.

136. "The contractor refused ..." quote, Comptroller General of the United States, Review of the Procurement of 5-Fluordeoxyuridine, Aug. 1960, p. 10.

136. Burdick-Smith dialogue, Government Patent Policy, Hearings Before the Subcommittee on Patents of the Committee on the Judiciary, U.S. Senate, Part 1, 89th Congress, 1st Session, pp. 232-233.

137. Ribicoff quote, CR, June 25, 1965, p. 14289.

139–140. Thompson Ramo definitions, Comptroller General of the United States, Initial Report on Review of Administrative Management of the Ballistic Missile Program of the Department of the Air Force, May 1960, p. 47.

140–141. GAO comments, Administrative Management cited above, pp. 44 and 45.

141. "A complete rape ..." quote, CR, Feb. 1, 1965, p. 1669.

142. GAO comment, Comptroller General of the United States, Inventions Not Disclosed ... with Lockheed Missiles & Space Company, Nov. 1964, no page number.

142. "Apparently each Air ..." quote, Comptroller General of the United States, Patent Royalty Costs Improperly Charged ... with Lockheed Aircraft Corporation, June 1965, p. 8.

142. "We also found ..." quote, Comptroller General of the United States, Inventions Not Disclosed ... with Certain Divisions of Thompson Ramo Wooldridge, Inc., Nov. 1964, p. 6.

143. Long statement, Government Patent Policy previously cited, Part 1, p. 337.

144. Long quotes, CR, June 25, 1965, p. 14291.

146–147. McClellan statement, CR, June 28, 1965, p. 14405.

147. Yarborough quotes, CR, June 28, 1965, p. 14400.

147–148. Yarborough statement, *CR*, June 28, 1965, p. 14407.

149. E. M. Kennedy comments, Committee on the Judiciary, U.S. Senate, *Federal Inventions Act of 1966*, Report 1461, 89th Congress, 2nd Session, Aug. 1966, p. 32.

150. "The nature of . . ." statement, *Federal Inventions* cited above, p. 29.

150. Long quotes, the Washington *Post*, May 26, 1966, p. G3.

152. "Our feeling has . . ." quote, *Government Patent Policy* previously cited, Part 2, p. 409.

153. Miller quote, CR, Jan. 28, 1965, p. 1497.

GAI: MINTED MOONLIGHT

156. Townsend quote, Arthur M. Schlesinger, Jr., *The Politics of Upheaval*, 1960, p. 31.

157. Churchill quote, Leonard Baker, "What's All This about a Guaranteed Annual Income?" *The Kiwanis Magazine*, June 1966, p. 18.

157–158. "Conquest of poverty . . ." quote, *Economic Report of the President*, Jan. 1964, p. 77.

158. "Increasing concern about . . ." statement, *Economic Report of the President*, Jan. 1966, p. 115.

158. Advisory Council statement, *Having the Power, We Have the Duty*, June 1966, pp. xii-xiii.

159. President Johnson statement, *The New York Times*, Jan. 27, 1967, p. 15.

159. "Despite the prospective . . ." statement, *Economic Report of the President*, Feb. 1968, p. 147.

162. FDR quote, Arthur M. Schlesinger, Jr., *The Crisis of the Old Order*, 1957, p. 392.

164. R. F. Kennedy statement, text of his speech before Day Care Council of New York, May 8, 1967, p. 3.

165. R. F. Kennedy statement, his May 8, 1967, speech cited above, p. 3.

166. Cohen statement, reprinted in *Morgan Guaranty Survey*, Aug. 1965, p. 11.

166. Ball statement, *Private Pension Plans*, Hearings Before the Subcommittee on Fiscal Policy, Joint Economic Committee, 89th Congress, 2nd Session, Part 2, p. 386.

167–168. "I work as . . ." quotation, *Private Pension Plans*, Part 2, p. 347.

168. Solenberger statement, *Private Pension Plans*, Part 1, p. 128.

171–172. Friedman quotes, reprinted in *The National Observer*, Dec. 19, 1966, p. 10.

172. Shriver statement, from text of *Face the Nation* broadcast, July 24, 1966, pp. 14-15.
177. Theobald statements, Robert Theobald (ed.), *The Guaranteed Income*, 1966, pp. 227-228.
178. Wickenden statement, "Social Welfare Law: The Concept of Risk and Entitlement," *University of Detroit Law Journal*, V. 43, 1966, p. 535.
179. White statement, Theodore H. White, *The Making of the President 1964*, 1965, p. ix.
179–180. Moynihan quotes, "The Case For a Family Allowance," excerpts of Congressional testimony reprinted in *The New York Times Magazine*, Feb. 5, 1967, p. 13.
180–181. Ad Hoc Committee quotes, printed in *The New York Times*, March 23, 1964, p. 1.
182. Theobald statement, *Guaranteed Income* cited above, p. 90.
183. Wyman quote, "Public Welfare in New York State," Report, May 15, 1967, p. 2.
184. Ackley quote, transcript of interview with Mr. Ackley, published in the Washington *Post*, Jan. 10, 1965, p. L2.
185. "At the present . . ." quote, *Guaranteed Income*, p. 95.
189. Wyman quotes, "Public Welfare," p. 4.
190–191. "Providing the poor . . ." quote, Sar A. Levitan, *Programs in Aid of the Poor*, 1965, p. 47.
191. Humphrey statement, from an interview with Robert B. Semple, Jr., Aug. 20, 1967, p. E3.
195. Malcolm X quote, *The Autobiography of Malcolm X*, 1965, p. 37.
199. Wyman quote, "Public Welfare," p. 2.
200. Rustin quotes, made before the Religious Action Center of the American Hebrew Congregations, quoted in *The New York Times*, Dec. 5, 1966, p. 35.
201. Ford quotes, text of his speech Nov. 17, 1967.
207. Keyserling statement, "Employment and the New Economics," *The Annals of the American Academy of Political Science*, Sept. 1967, p. 103.
211. Rustin statement, "A Way Out of the Exploding Ghetto," *The New York Times Magazine*, Aug. 13, 1967, p. 16.
212. Ribicoff quote, "Family Allowance" cited above, p. 68.
213. "If man is . . ." quote, reprinted in the Washington *Post*, Feb. 13, 1966, p. K1.

TOWARD A CREATIVE SOCIETY

217. "a long time . . ." quote, Norbert Muhlen, *The Incredible Krupps*, 1959, p. 66.

219. MacGregor comment, CR, July 18, 1967, p. 8821.
219–220. Moore comment, reprinted in "Papers and Proceedings of the 79th Annual Meeting of the American Economic Association," *American Economic Review*, May 1967, pp. 103-105.
224. "I must now . . ." quote, *The New York Times*, May 2, 1967, p. 32.
224–225. Shannon quote, *The New York Times*, Sept. 18, 1967, p. 42.
228. Wirtz comment, *Private Pension Plans*, Hearings Before the Subcommittee on Fiscal Policy, Joint Economic Committee, 89th Congress, 2nd Session, Part 2, 1966, p. 359.
229. Surrey statement, *Private Pension Plans*, Part 2, pp. 414-415.
233. *Times* editorial, Sept. 25, 1967, p. 42.
234–235. Ford statement, text of his speech before the National Urban League, Nov. 17, 1967.
236–237. Brownstein quotes, text of his speech, Oct. 23, 1967.
237–238. Maloney quotes, reprinted in *The New York Times*, Nov. 21, 1967, p. 30.
241. "America, whether it . . ." quote, Michael Harrington, "The Social-Industrial Complex," *Harper's*, Nov. 1967, pp. 55-60.
243. Mills quotes, *The New York Times*, Dec. 16, 1967, p. 1.
245–246. All rat-bite quotes are from CR, July 20, 1967, pp. H9114-H9116.
252. "the best man . . ." quote, reprinted in *The New York Times*, June 29, 1965, p. 69.
254, 256. Reston quotes, *The New York Times*, Oct. 29, 1967.

INDEX

Freeman, Orville L., 225
Friedman, Milton, 171–172, 177

Galbraith, John Kenneth, 96–98,
    102–103, 111–115, 121, 123,
    124, 224, 240, 241
  on Robert Kennedy's housing legis-
    lation, 233–234
Garmatz, Edward A., 60–61, 73, 123
General Accounting Office (GAO),
    135
  established, 134
  patent investigations, 139–142
General Electric Company, 14, 42, 47
General Motors Company, 4
Geological Survey agency, 92–93
Grant, Murray, 187–188
Gross, H. R., 247
Guaranteed annual income, 155–214
  background of, 156–157
  income tax system and, 172–173
  support of, 171–172, 177, 212–213
  welfare programs and
    education, 192–198, 214
    family allowance system pro-
      posal, 179–180
    job training, 201–210, 214
Guaranteed Income, The (ed. Theo-
    bald), 177
Gulick, James W., 65
Guthrie, Robert, 126, 128–132, 137
  invention report of, 130

Haggerty, Patrick E., 172
Halaby, Najeeb E., 12, 34
Haley, James A., 246
Hall, Paul, 70–71, 75
Hansbury, Lorraine, 194–195
Hansen, Clifford P., 124
Harding, Warren G., 116
Harrington, Michael, 185, 241
Hart, Philip A., 17, 25, 98, 100, 114,
    115, 116, 150
  on oil-shale industry, 90, 91
Heiskell, Andrew, 201
Herter, Christian A., Jr., 201
Hoffa, James R., 72
Hohenemser, Kurt H., 40
Holifield, Chet, 70
Homestead Act of 1862, 7, 160–161,
    162
Hood, Edwin M., 52, 75–76, 88
Hoover, Herbert, 94, 99

Housing industry, 45
  creative society and, 233–244
Hughes, Langston, 195
Humble Oil and Refining Company,
    95
Humphrey, Hubert H., 74, 191, 208

Ickes, Harold L., 117
Income tax system
  guaranteed annual income and,
    172–173
  pension plans and, 230
  for social ends, 242–244
Indians (American), 165
Industrial Revolution, 161, 189
Industry
  automobile, 9, 80, 168–169, 182,
    229, 231
  aviation, 6–7, 250
    Supersonic Transport program
      (SST), 1–49, 54, 66, 68, 75,
      90, 151, 217, 252, 253
  housing, 45, 233–244
  merchant-marine, 51–88
  mining, 10, 13, 80
  motel, 186–187
  oil-shale, 89–124, 151, 217
  railroad, 5–6, 12, 13, 220–221
  See also names of corporations
Internal Revenue Service, 102, 228
International Brotherhood of Boiler-
    makers, Iron Ship Builders,
    Blacksmiths, Forgers and
    Helpers, 74
Interstate highway system, 9
Inventions
  federal funds and, 138
  report filing, 130

Job Corps, 203–204
Job-training programs, 201–210, 214
  Congressional opposition to, 204–
    205
Johnson, Lyndon B., 12, 19, 41, 42,
    43, 67, 73–74, 85, 108, 118,
    119, 146, 167, 201–202, 204–
    205, 209, 224, 233, 252
  1967 economic report, 158–159
  oil-shale dispute, 119–120
Johnson, Nicholas, 53, 81, 83–85,
    87, 222, 223
Johnson, R. Tenney, 152
Juvenile delinquency, 189